THE YEAR OF THREE KINGS

1483

THE YEAR
OF THREE KINGS

1483

There has been a prediction,
by I know not what prophet, yet
circulating on the lips of all the crowd,
that three kings in three months
should possess England.

Dominic Mancini. 1483.

Giles St Aubyn

COLLINS
8 Grafton Street, London W1
1983

William Collins Sons & Co. Ltd
London · Glasgow · Sydney · Auckland
Toronto · Johannesburg

British Library Cataloguing in Publication Data

St. Aubyn, Giles
The year of three kings 1483.
1. Richard III. *King of England*
I. Title
942.04'6'0924   DA260

First published 1983

© Giles St. Aubyn, 1983
ISBN 0 00 216889 8

Family trees drawn by Les Robinson
Photoset in Linotron Bembo by
Rowland Phototypesetting Ltd,
Bury St Edmunds, Suffolk.

**Printed and bound in Great Britain by
Robert Hartnoll Ltd. Bodmin, Cornwall**

*This book is dedicated to
the memory of my father,
who inspired the affection
and respect of all who knew
him.*

CONTENTS

	Dramatis Personae	17
1	'This Sun of York' *1422–1483*	37
2	*Richard's Early Historians*	64
3	'The Young Prince' *1 April–28 April 1483*	74
4	'The Mighty Dukes' *29 April–4 May, 1483*	91
5	'Kings' Games' *5 May–13 June, 1483*	108
6	'This Palpable Device' *14 June–22 June, 1483*	132
7	'A World of Cares' *23 June–6 July, 1483*	149
8	'Young Edward Lives' *7 July–25 December, 1483*	171
9	'A Scum of Bretons' *1484–1485*	197
10	'The Throne Majestical'	218
11	*History and Myth*	239
	Source references	254
	Select Bibliography	269
	Index	276

ILLUSTRATIONS

between pages

Portrait of Edward IV in the Royal Collection 48–49
By Gracious permission of H. M. The Queen

A seventeenth century print of a sermon from
St Paul's Cross
By courtesy of the Society of Antiquaries of London

Lord Rivers presenting Edward IV with his book.
Edward V is the boy on the right of the picture, and
Richard III is the ermined figure standing on Rivers' left
*His Grace the Archbishop of Canterbury and the Trustees of
Lambeth Palace Library*

Portrait of Elizabeth Woodville from the stained glass
window (c 1482) in the north transept of Canterbury
Cathedral
The Dean and Chapter of Canterbury Cathedral

Sir Thomas More, after Holbein
National Portrait Gallery, London

The Royal Oak under which Edward IV reputedly met
his future Queen
Photograph by the Author

St Mary the Virgin, Grafton, where Edward IV married
Elizabeth Woodville
Kenneth Plummer

From left to right, these painted wooden panels from 96–97
St George's Chapel, Windsor, portray Henry VII, the
uncrowned Edward V, Edward IV and Henry VI
By permission of the Dean and Canons of Windsor

Stained glass portrait of Edward V at Little Malvern
Priory
Rev. J. E. T. Cox, Little Malvern Priory

Middleham Castle
By permission of the Controller of H. M. Stationery Office

	between pages
Sheriff Hutton Castle *Geoffrey Wheeler*	96–97
A contemporary portrait of Richard III, which once belonged to the Paston family *By courtesy of the Society of Antiquaries, London*	128–129
The Princes in the Tower, as portrayed by Millais in 1878 *By kind permission of Royal Holloway College*	
Lithograph, 1842, by Thomas Shotter Boys, of the interior of Guildhall *Guildhall Library, City of London*	160–161
Richard's handwritten postscript about Buckinghams's rebellion in a letter of 12 October 1483 to the Lord Chancellor, Bishop Russell *By permission of the Controller of H. M. Stationery Office*	
Hastings' castle at Kirby Muxloe *Christina Gascoigne*	
Pietro Torrigiano's bronze sculpture of Henry VII and Elizabeth of York in Westminster Abbey *By courtesy of the Dean and Chapter of Westminister Abbey*	
Portrait of Richard III in the Royal Collection *By Gracious permission of H. M. The Queen*	192–193
Northward view of Market Bosworth from Ambien Hill *Saxton Barton*	

GENEALOGIES AND MAP

Descendants of Edward III	14–15
The Duke of York's claim to the Throne	40
Neville–York marriages	42
Queen Elizabeth Woodville's relations	51
The Houses of Stafford and Bourchier	92
The Tudor claim to the Throne	188
The Battle of Bosworth	210

PREFACE

This book tells the story of Richard III's seizure of the Throne from his nephew Edward V in 1483. Chapter I consists of a review of English history from the accession of Henry VI in 1422 to the death of Edward IV in 1483. Chapter II surveys the primary sources on which the narrative principally depends. The next six Chapters describe the events of the year of three Kings. Chapter IX takes the story down to Richard III's death at the Battle of Bosworth, Chapter X analyses the purpose and nature of his usurpation, and Chapter XI traces his posthumous fate in the writings of historians. Source references to quotations in the text are listed below on page 254 to page 268.

I gratefully acknowledge the permission of the Oxford University Press to quote copyright material from Armstrong's *The Usurpation of Richard III* 1969 and Hanham's *Richard III and his Early Historians* 1975. I am indebted to the Richard III Society for permission to use extracts from *British Library Harleian Manuscript 433* Volumes i and ii, edited by Horrox and Hammond; the Yale University Press for allowing me to cite copyright material from Sylvester's edition of More's *History of Richard III*; and Alan Sutton for letting me print passages from Kincaid's edition of Sir George Buck's *The History of King Richard III*. Finally, I am most grateful to Professor Charles Wood for permission to quote his articles both published and unpublished.

I have been exceedingly fortunate in the generous help I have received whenever I have sought it. It would be difficult to speak too highly of the tireless assistance of Mrs P. W. Hammond, Honorary Librarian of the Barton Library of the Richard III Society. I am most grateful to Mr John Howarth who devoted a Sunday morning to showing me Sheriff Hutton Castle and St Helen's Church. I am also indebted to Anne Mansbridge of Eyre Methuen for sending me a proof copy of Professor Ross' *Richard III*. I am deeply aware of the benefit I have derived from the constructive criticism of an early draft of *The Year of Three Kings* I submitted to three friends: Richard Ollard, the book's editor, José Garciá-Ordónez, and Patrick Savage.

From the work's first conception, the gloom of authorship has been lightened by the cheerful efficiency and faultless typing of Chris Ayland. I am also most grateful to Mrs Sheila Collins for preparing the final, revised draft.

HARTLAND'S QUAY,   GILES ST AUBYN
TANGIER LANE,   1982
ETON.

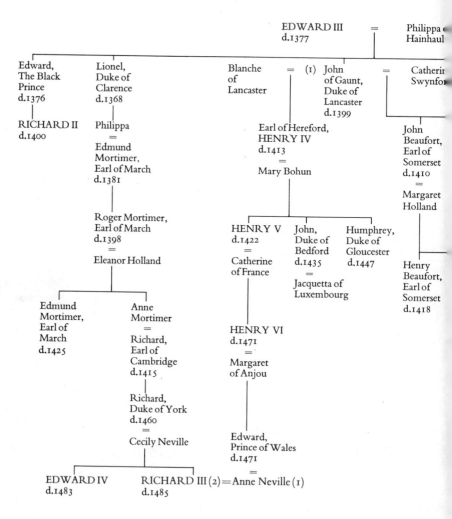

EDWARD III
d.1377
= Philippa
Hainhaul

Edward,
The Black
Prince
d.1376

RICHARD II
d.1400

Lionel,
Duke of
Clarence
d.1368

Philippa
=
Edmund
Mortimer,
Earl of March
d.1381

Roger Mortimer,
Earl of March
d.1398
=
Eleanor Holland

Edmund
Mortimer,
Earl of
March
d.1425

Anne
Mortimer
=
Richard,
Earl of
Cambridge
d.1415

Richard,
Duke of York
d.1460
=
Cecily Neville

Blanche
of
Lancaster
= (1) John
of Gaunt,
Duke of
Lancaster
d.1399
= Catherin
Swynfor

Earl of Hereford,
HENRY IV
d.1413
=
Mary Bohun

HENRY V
d.1422
=
Catherine
of France

HENRY VI
d.1471
=
Margaret
of Anjou

Edward,
Prince of Wales
d.1471
=

John,
Duke of
Bedford
d.1435
=
Jacquetta of
Luxembourg

Humphrey,
Duke of
Gloucester
d.1447

John
Beaufort,
Earl of
Somerset
d.1410
=
Margaret
Holland

Henry
Beaufort,
Earl of
Somerset
d.1418

EDWARD IV
d.1483

RICHARD III (2) = Anne Neville (1)
d.1485

DESCENDANTS OF EDWARD III

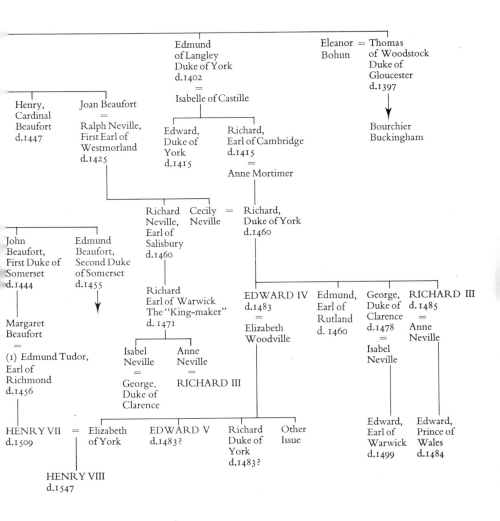

Edmund
of Langley
Duke of York
d.1402
=
Isabelle of Castille

Eleanor = Thomas
Bohun   of Woodstock
           Duke of
           Gloucester
           d.1397

Henry,
Cardinal
Beaufort
d.1447

Joan Beaufort
=
Ralph Neville,
First Earl of
Westmorland
d.1425

Edward,
Duke of
York
d.1415

Richard,
Earl of Cambridge
d.1415
=
Anne Mortimer

Bourchier
Buckingham

Richard
Neville,
Earl of
Salisbury
d.1460

Cecily = Richard,
Neville   Duke of York
             d.1460

John
Beaufort,
First Duke of
Somerset
d.1444

Edmund
Beaufort,
Second Duke
of Somerset
d.1455

Margaret
Beaufort
=
(1) Edmund Tudor,
Earl of
Richmond
d.1456

Richard
Earl of Warwick
The "King-maker"
d. 1471

Isabel
Neville
=
George,
Duke of
Clarence

Anne
Neville
=
RICHARD III

EDWARD IV
d.1483
=
Elizabeth
Woodville

Edmund,
Earl of
Rutland
d. 1460

George,
Duke of
Clarence
d.1478
=
Isabel
Neville

RICHARD III
d.1485
=
Anne
Neville

HENRY VII
d.1509

= Elizabeth
  of York

EDWARD V
d.1483?

Richard
Duke of
York
d.1483?

Other
Issue

Edward,
Earl of
Warwick
d.1499

Edward,
Prince of
Wales
d.1484

HENRY VIII
d.1547

DRAMATIS PERSONAE

The first eight entries in this list of Dramatis Personae deal with the Kings of England from 1327 to 1509. If read consecutively, they provide a thumb-nail sketch of English history in the late Middle Ages. Subsequent entries are listed in alphabetical order. Further information may be found by consulting the index, or by pursuing cross-references below. Uncertain dates are indicated by question marks. The dates given for kings are those of their lives not reigns.

EDWARD III. 1312–1377.

Edward's reign began in 1327 when his mother, Queen Isabella, deposed his father, Edward II. His spectacular victories at Crecy (1346) and Poitiers (1356) began the Hundred Years War (1338–1453) with France. Many of the problems of fifteenth century kings arose from rivalries between Edward's five sons and their descendants. His eldest son, the Black Prince, died in 1376, so he was succeeded by his grandson, Richard II.

RICHARD II. 1367–1400.

Richard was only ten when he succeeded Edward III. He soon proved an impetuous, self-willed youth, with a fondness for governing with the help of upstart favourites. This so antagonized the traditional ruling class that they plotted the execution of the King's closest advisers. In 1397 Richard took his revenge, beheading some of his rivals, imprisoning, and probably murdering, his Uncle, Thomas, Duke of Gloucester, and banishing his cousin Henry, Earl of Hereford, John of Gaunt's heir (see Lancaster. John, Duke of). When Gaunt died in 1399 Richard seized his estates and embarked on a War with Ireland. Henry returned from banishment soon afterwards to claim his rightful inheritance. So enthusiastic was his welcome that he deposed the King and proclaimed himself Henry IV. In 1400 Richard died in prison at Pontefract, probably murdered on his usurper's orders.

HENRY IV. 1367–1413.

Henry was the eldest son of John of Gaunt. At the age of fifteen he married Mary Bohun, co-heiress of the last Earl of Hereford: a title he later acquired. In 1399 he seized the Throne from his cousin, Richard II. His subsequent reign was troubled, and several rebellions challenged his right to the Crown. Indeed, the dubious title of the Lancastrians dogged his grandson, Henry VI, and contributed to the downfall of his dynasty (see Mortimer, Anne).

HENRY V. 1387–1422.

In 1415, Henry, the eldest son of Henry IV, revived the claim of Edward III to France, and waged war on Charles VI. He concluded a series of famous victories, of which Agincourt (1415) is best known, by signing the Peace of Troyes (1420). It was agreed in this treaty that Charles would acknowledge Henry as his heir, and that Henry would marry the French King's daughter, Catherine of Valois. Understandably, the Dauphin, later Charles VII, refused to accept the arrangement. In 1422 Henry returned to France to assert his rights but soon after died of a fever.

HENRY VI. 1421–1471.

Henry VI succeeded his father, Henry V, when he was only nine months old. Shortly afterwards, he succeeded Charles VI, (his maternal grandfather), as King of France. His long minority witnessed a series of feuds between his uncles. Between 1435 and 1453 Henry fought a losing war in France, until only Calais remained in English hands. In 1445, during a truce in the war, Henry married Margaret of Anjou, Charles VII's niece. Their only son, Prince Edward of Lancaster, was born eight years later. Unfortunately, the King was out of his mind at the time. For the remainder of his reign he was little more than a puppet in the hands of his masterful Queen. A disastrous result of Henry VI's feebleness was a protracted power-struggle: the so-called 'Wars of the Roses'. The War began in 1455 with an encounter at St Albans between Richard, Duke of York, and the King's retinue. The engagement ended in Henry VI's capture and a period of Yorkist dominance. In 1460, the King was persuaded to acknowledge the Duke of York as his heir. The Queen, enraged by the dispossession of her son, collected an army in the north of England. In December 1460 the Duke of York attacked this force at Wakefield and perished during the fighting. In March 1461, his son, the Earl of March, was proclaimed Edward IV. Before the month was out the new king totally destroyed the Lancastrian army at Towton. After evading capture for some years, Henry VI was taken prisoner in 1465 and lodged in the Tower. He was briefly restored by Warwick 'the Kingmaker' in 1470, but was recaptured after the Earl's defeat at Barnet. His cause was finally lost on May 4th 1471 when Queen Margaret's army was scattered at Tewkesbury and Prince Edward of Lancaster was killed. Some time during the night of May 21st Henry VI died in the Tower: possibly from grief, but more probably murdered on Edward IV's orders. His reign was calamitous, but he is still gratefully remembered by his foundations of Eton and King's.

EDWARD IV. 1442–1483.

Edward was the eldest son of Richard, Duke of York, and Cecily Neville. Two months after the Duke's death at Wakefield, a 'Great Council', largely consisting of Edward's Neville relations, proclaimed him King. (3 March 1461). On 29 March, he made good his claim to the Throne by destroying Henry VI's army at the battle of Towton. In 1464 Edward IV married Elizabeth Woodville. In 1469, Warwick 'the Kingmaker', who had become disenchanted with the independent policies pursued by his erstwhile protégé, resorted to open rebellion. He was helped by the King's brother, George, Duke of Clarence, who had recently married his daughter, Isabel Neville. In March 1470 Clarence and Warwick were proclaimed traitors and fled to the French Court, where they signed the treaty of Angers with Margaret of Anjou. In September, they invaded England, and Edward IV, narrowly evading capture, took ship to Flanders. Early in 1471, with the help of his brother-in-law, Charles the Bold, (see Burgundy, Duke of) Edward landed at Ravenspur and marched south towards London. Shortly after, Clarence was persuaded to desert Warwick and support Edward's restoration. On Easter day, 1471, Warwick was killed attempting to escape from the battle-field of Barnet. That very morning Queen Margaret landed at Weymouth. Three weeks later her army was defeated at Tewkesbury, and her son, Prince Edward, was killed. On the night of 21 May, within hours of Edward's triumphant return to London, Henry VI died in the Tower. For the remainder of his reign Edward IV ruled unchallenged: except by Clarence, who was executed as a traitor in 1478. In 1475 Edward led an expedition to France, but allowed himself to be bought off by Louis XI. His only subsequent military adventure was his invasion of Scotland in 1482 (see James III). Towards the end of his reign, Edward IV exploited the laws of inheritance to promote the interests of his family, (see Exeter, Anne, Duchess of; Norfolk, John Duke of) thus leaving his son prey to a clique of aggrieved nobles.

EDWARD V. 1470–1483?.

Edward was born in Sanctuary at Westminster on 2 November, 1470. He was the eldest son of Edward IV and Elizabeth Woodville. In 1471 he was created Prince of Wales. Between 1473 and 1483 he resided at Ludlow Castle under the governorship of his uncle, Anthony, Lord Rivers. Soon after his father's death on April 9th 1483, he was seized by his Uncle, Richard, Duke of Gloucester, (see Richard III) who claimed to be his Protector. On 22 June the Duke had his nephew denounced as a bastard. A fortnight later he was himself crowned King. Edward V and his younger brother (see York, Richard, Duke of) disappeared in the Tower of London between June and September 1483.

RICHARD III. 1452–1485.

Richard was the son of Richard, Duke of York, and Cecily Neville. Soon after his brother became Edward IV, Richard was created Duke of Gloucester (1461). Much of his youth was spent in the household of Warwick 'the Kingmaker'. Unlike his brother, Clarence, Richard served Edward IV loyally, sharing his exile in 1470 and helping to recover his Kingdom at Barnet and Tewkesbury. In 1472, Richard married his first cousin, Anne Neville. A year later their only child was born (see Edward, Earl of Salisbury). In 1482 Richard was given command of the invasion of Scotland. (See James III). When Edward IV died, Richard vociferously proclaimed his loyalty to Edward V. Nevertheless, shortly before the young King's coronation, he set him aside and had himself crowned. Soon ugly rumours began circulating that he had murdered his nephews: Edward V and Richard, Duke of York. In October 1483 Richard III crushed Buckingham's rebellion, but when Henry, Earl of Richmond, (see Henry VII) invaded England in 1485, Richard perished at Bosworth.

HENRY VII. 1457–1509.

Henry was the son of Edmund Tudor, Earl of Richmond, and Margaret Beaufort, a great granddaughter of John of Gaunt. After the death of Henry VI in 1471, he became the principal Lancastrian claimant to the throne. In October 1483, he attempted to invade England, but was obliged to return to Brittany after the failure of

Buckingham's rebellion. In 1485, having defeated Richard at Bosworth, Henry was crowned King. The following year, he married Elizabeth of York, thereby uniting the rival dynasties engaged in the Wars of the Roses.

★   ★   ★

ANJOU.   See Margaret of, Queen.

ANNE, of York.   See Exeter, Anne, Duchess of.

ANNE. Queen.   See Neville, Anne.

BEAUFORT.   See Somerset. Dukes of.

BEAUFORT.   Lady Margaret.   1443–1509.

Margaret was the heiress of John Beaufort, first Duke of Somerset. She married her first husband, Edmund Tudor, when she was fifteen. Edmund died in 1456 just before the birth of his son, Henry (see Henry VII). Margaret's second husband was Henry Stafford, a younger son of the first Duke of Buckingham. Soon after Stafford's death in 1481, she married Thomas, Lord Stanley, later Earl of Derby. Lady Margaret was exceedingly rich, remarkably learned, and a pious patron of Oxford and Cambridge.

BEDFORD.   Jacquetta, Duchess of.   1416?–1472.

Jacquetta of Luxembourg was the daughter of the Count de St Pol. In 1433 she married John, Duke of Bedford, Henry IV's third son. Soon after his death in 1435 she married Sir Richard Woodville. In 1464 her daughter, Elizabeth Woodville, married Edward IV.

BEDFORD.   Jasper, Duke of.   See Pembroke. Jasper, Earl of.

BEDFORD.   John, Duke of.   1389–1435.

John was the third son of Henry IV. In 1422 his brother, Henry V, appointed him Regent of France. When Joan of Arc fell into his hands in 1431 he had her burnt as a witch. In 1433 he married Jacquetta of Luxembourg.

BOHUN.   Eleanor and Mary.   See Gloucester, Thomas, Duke of;   Henry IV.

21

BOURCHIER. Thomas, Archbishop of Canterbury. 1404?–1486.

Thomas was the son of William Bourchier, Count of Eu. His mother was Lady Anne Plantagenet, daughter of Thomas, Duke of Gloucester. In 1454 he was appointed Archbishop of Canterbury, and in 1473 he was made a Cardinal. As Archbishop, he crowned Edward IV, Richard III and Henry VII.

BUCKINGHAM. Humphrey, First Duke of. 1402–1460.

Humphrey Stafford was the son of Edmund, Earl of Stafford, and Anne Plantagenet, widow of William Bourchier. (See Bourchier, Thomas.) Humphrey was created Duke of Buckingham in 1442 for services in France. He married Lady Margaret Beaufort, a daughter of the second Duke of Somerset. (Not to be confused with her first cousin, the daughter of the first Duke of Somerset, also called Lady Margaret Beaufort.) Buckingham perished in the battle of Northampton fighting for Henry VI.

BUCKINGHAM. Henry, Second Duke of. 1453?–1483.

Henry Stafford succeeded to the dukedom in 1460 after his grandfather's death during the battle of Northampton. In 1466, Duke Henry, at that time Edward IV's ward, was married to the King's sister-in-law, Catherine Woodville. In 1483 Buckingham assisted Richard, Duke of Gloucester seize the Throne, but later rebelled against him. The rising proved abortive and Buckingham was executed.

BURGUNDY. Charles 'the Bold', Duke of. 1433–1477.

Charles, Count of Charolais, married Edward IV's sister, Margaret (see Burgundy, Margaret, Duchess of) in 1468. In 1471 he helped Edward IV recover his Throne. Charles was killed in the battle of Nancy and was succeeded by his daughter Mary. (See Burgundy, Mary, Duchess of.)

BURGUNDY. Margaret, Duchess of. 1446–1503.

Margaret was a daughter of Richard, Duke of York. In 1468, her brother, Edward IV, negotiated her marriage to Charles, Duke of Burgundy.

BURGUNDY. Mary, Duchess of. 1457–1482.

Mary succeeded her father Charles, Duke of Burgundy, in 1477. Abortive attempts were made to marry her to George, Duke of

Clarence. In the end, she married Archduke Maximilian, later Emperor of Austria, thereby saving Burgundy from the grasp of Louis XI.

BUTLER. Lady Eleanor. 1435?–1466.

Lady Eleanor was the daughter of John Talbot, first Earl of Shrewsbury. In 1450? she married Sir Thomas Butler, who died some ten years later. After Edward IV's death, it was alleged that he had been pre-contracted to wed Lady Eleanor at the time of his marriage to Elizabeth Woodville.

CAMBRIDGE. Richard, Earl of. 1375–1415

Richard's father was Edmund, Duke of York, Edward III's fourth son. Richard married Anne Mortimer, daughter of Roger Mortimer, fourth Earl of March. He was beheaded by Henry V in 1415 for plotting to make his brother-in-law, Edmund Mortimer, King of England (see Mortimer, Anne for Edmund's claim to the Throne). Shortly after Richard's execution, his elder brother, Edward, Duke of York, was killed at Agincourt. Consequently, Richard's infant son inherited the dukedom. (See York, Richard, Duke of.)

CHARLES 'the Bold'. See Burgundy, Duke of.

CHARLES VI of France. 1368–1422.

Charles VI, King of France, spent much of his reign (1380–1422) trying to preserve his kingdom from the Dukes of Burgundy and Henry V. His problems were not assisted by serious bouts of insanity. On his death, the infant Henry VI was proclaimed King of France, as agreed in the Treaty of Troyes (1420). Charles VI's daughter, Catherine, was Henry VI's mother.

CHARLES VII of France. 1403–1461.

When Charles VII succeeded his father, Charles VI, in 1422, he had to make good his claim to the Throne against that of Henry VI. In 1429, with the help of Joan of Arc, he was crowned King at Rheims. By the end of his reign, France recovered virtually all she had lost earlier in the Hundred Years War.

CLARENCE.   George, Duke of.   1449–1478.

George was the third son of Richard, Duke of York. Soon after his brother, Edward, became king in 1461, George was made Duke of Clarence. In 1469 he married Isabel Neville, against Edward IV's orders, and then helped his father-in-law, (see Warwick, Richard, Earl of) to depose the king. In 1471 Clarence was finally persuaded to abandon Warwick and restore his brother. After Isabel died in 1476, Clarence sought the hand of Mary of Burgundy, once more against the King's wishes. Two years later, Parliament convicted him of treason, and he was supposedly drowned in a butt of Malmsey. Throughout his career he showed himself to be vain, fractious, perfidious and grasping.

CLARENCE.   Isabel, Duchess of.   See Neville, Isabel.

CLARENCE.   Lionel, Duke of.   1338–1368.

Lionel was the second surviving son of Edward III. His daughter, Philippa, married Edmund Mortimer, third Earl of March. She bequeathed her father's claim to the Throne to her Mortimer heirs (see Mortimer, Anne).

DORSET.   Thomas, First Marquis of.   1451–1501.

Thomas Grey was Elizabeth Woodville's elder son by her marriage to Sir John Grey. In 1466 Thomas married Anne Holland, the Duchess of Exeter's daughter (see Exeter, Anne, Duchess of). After Anne died without issue, Thomas married Cecily Bonville, by whom he had a son, another Thomas Grey. In 1475 he was created Marquis of Dorset. When Edward IV died in 1483, Dorset was in possession of the Tower of London and the treasure therein. Not only did he reject Gloucester's claim to act as Protector to Edward V, but after the Duke became Richard III joined Buckingham's rebellion against him. When the rising failed, Dorset joined the Earl of Richmond's exiled court in Brittany (see Henry VII). Dorset's son, Thomas Grey, (1447–1550) was betrothed to Anne St Leger.

EDWARD of Lancaster.   Prince of Wales.   1453–1471.

Edward was the son of Henry VI and Margaret of Anjou. In 1454 he was created Prince of Wales. Six years later the King disinherited him by the Act of Accord. After Edward IV became King in 1461, Prince Edward spent most of his life in exile with his mother. In 1470 he was betrothed to Anne Neville. On 4 May, 1471, he was killed at

Tewkesbury. (He is buried in the choir of Tewkesbury Abbey with a Yorkist sun smiling down on him!)

EDWARD of York. Earl of Salisbury. Prince of Wales. 1473–1484.

Edward was the only child of Richard, Duke of Gloucester, and Anne Neville. He was born and brought up at Middleham Castle. Edward's Uncle, Edward IV, created him Earl of Salisbury in 1478. When Richard III became king, he made his son Prince of Wales. The Prince died, aged eleven, after a long illness.

ELIZABETH of York. Queen of Henry VII. 1466–1503.

Elizabeth was the oldest child of Edward IV and Elizabeth Wood-ville. In 1483 she was betrothed to Henry Tudor, Earl of Richmond. There were rumours in the spring of 1485, after the death of Queen Anne, that Richard III intended to marry her. She married Henry VII in 1486 and was crowned the following year.

EXETER. Anne of York. Duchess of. 1439–1476.

Anne, the eldest child of Richard, Duke of York, was the sister of Edward IV and Richard III. In the last years of the reign of Henry VI she married Henry Holland, Duke of Exeter. The Duke remained loyal to the Lancastrians and continued to fight the Yorkists. Consequently, when Edward IV became King, the Holland estates were forfeited to the Duchess. In 1472 Anne divorced the Duke and married her lover, Sir Thomas St Leger. Their daughter, Anne St Leger, became heir to the Holland estates on her mother's death, and was betrothed in infancy to Dorset's son, Thomas Grey. In January 1483 an Act of Parliament was passed confirming that Anne was the sole heiress of the Holland inheritance: thereby depriving Ralph, Lord Neville, of his legal rights. In October 1483 Sir Thomas St Leger supported Buckingham's rebellion and was eventually captured. Richard III remained deaf to pleas for clemency and insisted upon his brother-in-law's execution.

EXETER. Henry, Duke of. –1475. See Exeter, Anne, Duchess of.

FAUCONBERG. See Neville, Thomas, bastard of.

GAUNT. John of. See Lancaster, John, Duke of.

GLOUCESTER. Duchess of. See Neville, Anne, Queen.

GLOUCESTER.   Humphrey, Duke of.   1390–1447.

Humphrey was the youngest son of Henry IV and Mary Bohun. In 1414 he was created Duke of Gloucester by his brother, Henry V. In 1422, after his infant nephew became king (see Henry VI), the Duke claimed the right to govern as Regent. After heated debate, Parliament grudgingly agreed to concede him the title 'Protector' with carefully limited power. Duke Humphrey died in captivity under mysterious circumstances. He was known as the 'good Duke' because of his patronage of learning.

GLOUCESTER.   Thomas Duke of.   1355–1397.

Thomas of Woodstock was the fifth and youngest son of Edward III. Through his marriage to Eleanor Bohun he was the progenitor of the Stafford (Dukes of Buckingham) and Bourchier families. Eleanor's sister, Mary Bohun, married Thomas' nephew (see Henry IV). In 1385, Thomas was created Duke of Gloucester by Richard II. In 1397 the Duke was reputedly killed on the King's orders.

GLOUCESTER.   Richard, Duke of.   See Richard III.

GREY.   Sir John.   1432–1461.   See Woodville, Elizabeth.

GREY.   Richard.   1453?–1483.

Richard was the younger son of Elizabeth Woodville and Sir John Grey. As a young man he acquired an unsavoury reputation as a profligate companion of Edward IV. On 30 April, 1483 he was arrested by Richard, Duke of Gloucester, in the presence of his half-brother, Edward V. Some weeks later he was executed with his Uncle, Anthony, Earl Rivers, at Pontefract castle.

GREY.   Thomas.   See Dorset, First Marquis of.

HOLLAND.   See Exeter, Duchess of.

HOWARD.   John.   See Norfolk, Duke of.

JACQUETTA of Luxembourg.   See Bedford, Duchess of.

JAMES III of Scotland.   1452–1488.

James succeeded his father, James II, as King of Scotland in 1460. In 1482, James' brother, the Duke of Albany, claimed the Throne, alleging that James was a bastard. Edward IV, having decided to help

Albany, gave the Duke of Gloucester command of the Scottish expedition. Although Gloucester captured Edinburgh, with barely a scuffle, he failed to exploit his advantage. The English army withdrew and Albany sought refuge at the court of Louis XI.

LANCASTER. Edward, Prince of Wales. See Edward, of Lancaster.

LANCASTER. John of Gaunt, Duke of. 1340–1399.

John was the third surviving son of Edward III. As a result of his marriage to Blanche of Lancaster in 1359 he became the most powerful magnate in England. His eldest son by this marriage (see Henry IV) deposed Richard II in 1399 and proclaimed himself King. Later in life, Gaunt had a second family, the Beauforts, (see Somerset, Dukes of) by his mistress, Catherine Swynford. By an Act of 1397 this liaison was retrospectively legalised, but in 1407 Henry IV added a rider debarring his father's Beaufort descendants from succeeding to the Throne. The legality of this disqualification was later disputed because Parliament never sanctioned it. Gaunt's great granddaughter, Margaret Beaufort, was the mother of Henry VII.

LOUIS XI of France. 1423–1483.

Louis succeeded his father, Charles VII of France, in 1461. During his reign he enforced the royal authority throughout his kingdom, despite the ravages of the Hundred Years War. In 1475 he persuaded Edward IV to withdraw his invading force by means of lavish bribes. Louis was cruel, perfidious, greedy, and exceptionally successful.

MARCH. Edward, Earl of. See Edward IV.

MARGARET of York. See Burgundy, Duchess of.

MARGARET of Anjou, Queen of Henry VI. 1430–1482.

Margaret was the daughter of René, Duke of Anjou, and niece of Charles VII. In 1445 she married Henry VI as part of a truce designed to end the Hundred Years War (1338–1453) between England and France. She was a 'manly woman' who dominated her feckless husband. Her vehement preference for a favoured clique of nobles, and her remorseless vendetta with Richard, Duke of York, was a principal cause of the Wars of the Roses (1455–1485). When Henry VI disinherited their son (see Edward, of Lancaster) by the Act of Accord (1460), Margaret raised an army in the north of England, defeated and killed the Duke of York at Wakefield, and marched on

27

London to regain control of the King. Three months later (March 1461) Edward IV decisively defeated her army at Towton, and obliged her to seek refuge in France. In 1470, Margaret signed the Treaty of Angers with Warwick and Clarence, by which she consented to her son's marriage to Anne Neville, and accepted plans to restore Henry VI. Her hopes, however, were dashed in May 1471 with the deaths of her husband and son, and the defeat of her army at Tewkesbury.

MORTIMER. Anne. 1388–

Anne's grandmother was Philippa, daughter of Lionel, Duke of Clarence. Her father was Roger Mortimer, fourth Earl of March. Anne married Richard, Earl of Cambridge, who was executed in 1415 for plotting to depose Henry V in favour of her brother, Edmund, fifth Earl of March. By the Act of Accord (1460) her son (see York. Richard, Duke of) was acknowledged as Henry VI's heir. It was arguable that he should always have been king seeing that he was descended from Edward III's *second* son, Lionel, Duke of Clarence; whereas Henry IV, Henry V, and Henry VI, were descended from Edward III's *third* son, John, Duke of Lancaster. The Lancastrians appealed to the Salic Law (debarring inheritance through the female line) to refute the argument from primogeniture.

NEVILLE. Anne. Queen. 1456–1485.

Anne was Richard, Earl of Warwick's younger daughter. In 1470 she was betrothed (and possibly married) to Prince Edward of Lancaster, who was killed at the battle of Tewkesbury (1471). In 1472 she married Richard, Duke of Gloucester, (see Richard III) and in 1473 bore him a son, Edward, Earl of Salisbury. She was crowned on July 6th 1483.

NEVILLE. Catherine. See Norfolk, Dowager Duchess of.

NEVILLE. Cecily. See York. Cecily, Duchess of.

NEVILLE. George, Archbishop of York. –1476.

George was the youngest brother of Richard, Earl of Warwick, 'the Kingmaker'. In 1456 he became Bishop of Exeter, and in 1461 helped his brother make Edward IV king. Four years later, he was appointed Archbishop of York. In 1470 he played a prominent part in Warwick's restoration of Henry VI. After Edward IV recovered his crown, the Archbishop spent three years in prison.

NEVILLE. Isabel. 1451–1476.

Isabel was the elder daughter of Richard, Earl of Warwick. In 1469 she married her first cousin, George, Duke of Clarence, despite Edward IV's prohibition. She had two children, both of whom were later beheaded: Edward, Earl of Warwick (1475–1499), and Margaret, Countess of Salisbury (1473–1541).

NEVILLE. Ralph, Lord. –1484.

Ralph was a grandson of his namesake, Ralph Neville, first Earl of Westmorland. His mother was Anne Holland, sister of Henry, Duke of Exeter. Ralph's expectations to the Holland estates were dashed by Edward IV (see Exeter. Anne, Duchess of). In 1483 he supported Richard III's usurpation.

NEVILLE. Ralph. See Westmorland, Ralph, Earl of.

NEVILLE. Richard. See Salisbury, Richard, Earl of.

NEVILLE. Richard. See Warwick, Richard, Earl of.

NEVILLE. Thomas. 'Bastard of Fauconberg'. –1471.

Thomas was the bastard son of William, Lord Fauconberg, Earl of Kent (son of Ralph, Earl of Westmorland). In 1471 Thomas was given command of the Channel Fleet by Warwick. While Edward IV was engaged in his Tewkesbury campaign, Thomas sailed up the Thames on behalf of Henry VI, and was only repulsed at London Bridge after a hard fight. The episode is said to have convinced Edward IV of his need to dispose of his rival.

NORFOLK. Catherine Neville. Dowager Duchess of. 1397?–1484.

Catherine was a daughter of Ralph, First Earl of Westmorland. She married John Mowbray, second Duke of Norfolk, when she was sixteen. The Duke died in 1432 leaving his widow a jointure on his estates. In 1465, when Catherine was approaching seventy, she married her fourth husband: the Queen's brother, John Woodville, a youth of twenty.

NORFOLK. John Howard, First Duke of. 1430?–1485.

John was the son of Sir Robert Howard, head of an ancient East Anglian family. His mother was Margaret Mowbray, daughter and heiress of Thomas Mowbray, first Duke of Norfolk of the Mowbray

line. Throughout his career John was unfailingly loyal to the Yorkists. In 1482 he accompanied Richard, Duke of Gloucester, on his
expedition to Scotland. Towards the end of his reign Edward IV
deprived John Howard of his rights to the Mowbray estates. In 1476,
John Mowbray, fourth Duke of Norfolk, died, leaving his daughter,
Anne Mowbray, his heir. Soon after, Edward IV married Anne to
his five year old son, Richard, Duke of York. Unfortunately, she
died in 1481. Under ordinary circumstances John Howard would
have inherited most of her estates, but in January 1483 the King
passed an Act of Parliament making the Duke of York her heir. On
Edward IV's death, Howard was one of Gloucester's principal
agents in deposing Edward V. The moment Richard III was proclaimed king, he gave Howard the Mowbray estates and the title of
Duke of Norfolk. In 1485 Norfolk died fighting for Richard at
Bosworth. He remained to the end, rough, violent and unscrupulous
in achieving his purposes.

NORFOLK. Second Duke. See Surrey, Thomas, Earl of.

NORTHUMBERLAND. Henry Percy, Fourth Earl of. 1446–1489.

Henry's Father, the third Earl, died fighting for Henry VI at Towton
(1471). Henry, however, supported the Yorkists, and helped
Richard III to usurp. In June 1483 he commanded the northern army
which helped to overawe London. In 1485 he joined Richard at
Bosworth but never engaged his force. The history of the Percies in
the fifteenth century was one of remorseless treachery.

OXFORD. John de Vere. Thirteenth Earl of. 1443–1513.

John was the son of the twelfth Earl and Margaret Howard. Despite
marrying Margaret Neville, Warwick 'the Kingmaker's' sister, he
remained a zealous Lancastrian all his life. As late as 1473 he
temporarily seized St Michael's Mount from its Yorkist garrison. In
1485 he commanded the van of the Tudor army at Bosworth.

PEMBROKE. Jasper, Earl of. 1431–1495.

Jasper was the younger son of Owen Tudor and Catherine of Valois.
In 1453 he was created Earl of Pembroke by Henry VI. When
Edward IV became king he fled abroad, but returned in 1470 to
support Henry VI. After the Lancastrian defeat at Tewkesbury in
1471, he took refuge in Brittany, taking his nephew, the Earl of
Richmond (see Henry VII) with him. In 1485 Henry VII made him

Duke of Bedford. Later that year, Jasper married Catherine Woodville, the Dowager Duchess of Buckingham.

PERCY.   Henry.   See Northumberland, Fourth Earl of.

PRINCE OF WALES.   See Edward V;   Edward, Prince of Lancaster;
Edward, Earl of Salisbury.

RICHARD   Prince.   See York.   Richard, Duke of.   1473–1483?.

RICHMOND.   Countess of.   See Beaufort, Lady Margaret.

RICHMOND.   Edmund, Earl of.   –1456.

Edmund was the elder son of Owen Tudor and Catherine of Valois,
the widow of Henry V. He married Lady Margaret Beaufort, but
died before the birth of his son, Henry Tudor (see Henry VII).

RICHMOND.   Henry, Earl of.   See Henry VII.

RIVERS.   Richard Woodville.   First Earl of.   –1469.

Richard was the son of Sir Richard Woodville, the Duke of Bedford's Chamberlain. Shortly after the Duke's death in 1435, young
Richard married his widow (see Bedford, Jacquetta. Duchess of). In
1448 Henry VI made him a peer, and two years later a Knight of the
Garter. Rivers fought for Henry at Towton (1461), but then recognized that the Lancastrian cause was lost and transferred his allegiance to Edward IV. In 1464 his daughter, Elizabeth, married the
King. In 1469 Rivers was executed on Warwick's orders after the
battle of Edgecote.

RIVERS.   Anthony Woodville.   Second Earl of.   1442?–1483.

Anthony was the eldest son of Jacquetta, Duchess of Bedford and her
second husband, Richard, first Earl Rivers. In 1460 Anthony married Elizabeth, Lady Scales, a well endowed heiress. Having fought
for Henry VI at Towton, he transferred his allegiance to Edward IV.
After his sister, Elizabeth, became Queen, he rose rapidly in royal
favour. In 1470 he accompanied the King into exile, and was
wounded the following year at the battle of Barnet. In 1473 Edward
IV appointed him Governor of the Prince of Wales' household at
Ludlow Castle. In April 1483 Rivers escorted Edward V on his
journey to London to be crowned, but was taken prisoner by
Richard, Duke of Gloucester, at Northampton. He was executed at

Pontefract Castle on 25 June. Rivers was cultivated, chivalrous, and devout.

RUTLAND. Edmund, Earl of. 1443–1460.

Edmund was the second son of Richard, Duke of York, and Cecily Neville. He was killed with his father at the Battle of Wakefield at the age of seventeen.

SALISBURY. Edward, Earl of. See Edward, Earl of Salisbury.

SALISBURY. Richard, Earl of. 1400–1460.

Richard was the son of Ralph Neville, first Earl of Westmorland, and Joan Beaufort, John of Gaunt's daughter by his marriage to Catherine Swynford. He supported his brother-in-law, Richard, Duke of York, in 1460, and was executed after the Battle of Wakefield. His son was Warwick 'The Kingmaker'.

ST LEGER. Anne. 1473?–. See Exeter. Anne, Duchess of.

ST LEGER. Sir Thomas. –1483. See Exeter, Anne, Duchess of.

SOMERSET. John, First Duke of. 1404–1444.

John's father was John Beaufort, the eldest son of John of Gaunt and Catherine Swynford. John's daughter, Lady Margaret Beaufort, was the mother of Henry VII. In 1443 John was made Duke of Somerset and given command of the English army in Normandy.

SOMERSET. Edmund, Second Duke of. 1406?–1455.

Edmund, brother of John, First Duke of Somerset, married Eleanor Beauchamp. He was a great favourite of Margaret of Anjou, and fought hard to deprive Richard, Duke of York, of his rightful role in government. He lost this struggle when he was killed in the battle of St Albans.

SOMERSET. Henry, Third Duke of. 1436–1464.

Henry was the son of the Second Duke of Somerset. He inherited his family's feud with the Yorks and Nevilles, and was executed in 1464 for supporting Henry VI.

SOMERSET. Edmund. Fourth Duke of. 1438?–1471.

Edmund was the younger brother of the third Duke. In 1471 he commanded the Lancastrian army at Tewkesbury. After the battle, he sought sanctuary in the Abbey but was dragged out and executed. He was the last of the male Beaufort line. Once it became known that Henry VI was dead, Lancastrian hopes focused on Margaret Beaufort and her son (see Henry VII).

SURREY. Thomas, Earl of. Second Duke of Norfolk. 1443–1524.

Thomas was the son of John Howard, first Duke of Norfolk. In 1483 Richard III made him Earl of Surrey and a Knight of the Garter. He fought valiantly for Richard at Bosworth, and spent the early years of the new reign in the Tower. After his release, he served Henry VII and Henry VIII with conspicuous loyalty. In 1513 he won the battle of Flodden and was restored to the forfeited dukedom of Norfolk.

TUDOR. See Henry VII; Pembroke, Jasper Tudor, Earl of; Richmond, Edmund Tudor, Earl of.

TUDOR. Owen. 1400–1461.

Owen was the son of Theodore Tudor, a brewer of Beaumaris. He accompanied Henry V to France in 1415 and distinguished himself at Agincourt. In 1428 he secretly married Henry's widow, Catherine of Valois. He was captured by Edward, Earl of March, (see Edward IV) at the battle of Mortimer's Cross, and beheaded at Hereford. His elder son, Edmund, Earl of Richmond, was Henry VII's father. His younger son, Jasper, Earl of Pembroke, was later made Duke of Bedford.

WARWICK. Edward, Earl of. 1475–1499.

Edward was the son of George, Duke of Clarence, and Isabel Neville. After Clarence's death in 1478, Edward's aunt, Anne, Duchess of Gloucester, took him into her household. Richard III appears to have made Warwick his heir on the death of his son (see Edward, Earl of Salisbury) in 1484. During the reign of Henry VII Warwick was kept in the Tower. In 1487 he was impersonated by Lambert Simnel, and twelve years later was executed on what appears to have been a trumped-up charge.

WARWICK. Richard, Earl of. 'The Kingmaker'. 1428–1471.

Richard Neville was the son of Richard, Earl of Salisbury, and Joan Beaufort, John of Gaunt's daughter. Edward IV and Richard III were his first cousins. In 1449 he was created Earl of Warwick, as his wife, Anne Beauchamp, was the only surviving child of the previous holder of the title. Warwick had two daughters: Isabel and Anne. Isabel married George, Duke of Clarence in 1469, and Anne married Richard, Duke of Gloucester, in 1472. Warwick played a leading part in deposing Henry VI and crowning Edward IV. But eventually he fell out with his protégé, and with the help of his son-in-law, Clarence, rebelled against Edward IV (1469) and restored Henry VI (1470). Edward IV, however, managed to reconquer his kingdom and Warwick was killed at the Battle of Barnet. No more 'overmighty subject' ever exploited his own interests at greater cost to his country.

WESTMORLAND. Ralph, Earl of. 1365–1425.

Ralph Neville was a member of the Court Party in the reign of Richard II. In 1397 he was created Earl of Westmorland. Two years later he supported Hereford's (see Henry IV) rebellion against the King. Westmorland married twice. His first wife was Margaret, daughter of the second Earl of Stafford. His second wife was Joan Beaufort, John of Gaunt's daughter by Catherine Swynford. Ralph was survived by most of his twenty-three children. He was the grandfather of Edward IV and Richard III by his second marriage.

WOODVILLE. Anthony. See Rivers, Anthony, Second Earl of.

WOODVILLE. Catherine. 1442?–1512?.

Catherine was the daughter of Richard, Earl Rivers, and Jacquetta, Dowager Duchess of Bedford. Her sister was Queen Elizabeth. In 1466 Catherine married Edward IV's ward, the second Duke of Buckingham, who showed a patrician disdain for his wife's family. In 1485 she married Henry VII's uncle, Jasper, Duke of Bedford.

WOODVILLE. Elizabeth. Queen of Edward IV. 1437?–1492.

Elizabeth was the daughter of Richard, Earl Rivers, and Jacquetta, Dowager Duchess of Bedford. In 1452 she married Sir John Grey who was killed at the second battle of St Albans (1461). Twelve years later she was secretly married to Edward IV. It was unprecedented for a King to marry a subject, and it was not a popular match. The favours which Edward bestowed on his wife's relations provoked envious resentment. Many of the problems of Edward IV and Edward V may be traced to the Woodville marriage. During Warwick's rebellion, Elizabeth took sanctuary at Westminster in 1470 where she gave birth to a son (see Edward V) on 2 November. When Richard, Duke of Gloucester, seized Edward V at Stony Stratford in

April 1483, Queen Elizabeth sought refuge at Westminster for a second time. Later the same year, she encouraged the betrothal of her daughter, Elizabeth, to the Earl of Richmond (see Henry VII).

WOODVILLE. John. 1445?–1469.

John was the second son of Richard, Earl Rivers, and Jacquetta, Dowager Duchess of Bedford. In 1465 he married the Dowager Duchess of Norfolk. He was then twenty and she was approaching seventy. John was captured after the battle of Edgecote and beheaded on Warwick's orders.

WOODVILLE. Lionel. Bishop of Salisbury. 1453?–1484.

Lionel was a younger brother of Elizabeth Woodville. He was appointed Archdeacon of Oxford at the age of nineteen, and later became Bishop of Salisbury. In October, 1483, he supported Buckingham's rebellion. After its failure, he joined Richmond's (see Henry VII) Court in Brittany.

WOODVILLE. Sir Richard. See Rivers, First Earl of.

YORK. Cecily, Duchess of. 1415–1495.

Cecily Neville was the daughter of Ralph Neville, First Earl of Westmorland, and Joan Beaufort, John of Gaunt's daughter. In 1415 Cecily's father was given wardship of Richard, Duke of York. Richard and Cecily were brought up together and in due course the Earl arranged their marriage. Two of their sons became kings: Edward IV and Richard III. Cecily was exquisitely beautiful ('The Rose of Raby') as were most of her children. She was also proud, ambitious, loyal, affectionate, and pious.

YORK. Edmund, Duke of. 1341–1402.

Edmund 'of Langley' was the fourth son of Edward III, and father of Edward, Duke of York, –1415, and Richard, Earl of Cambridge, –1415.

YORK. Edward, Duke of. 1373–1415.

Edward was the son of Edmund, Duke of York. He was killed at the battle of Agincourt in 1415. As he died without issue, the dukedom descended to Richard, Duke of York, the son of his younger brother, Richard, Earl of Cambridge.

YORK. Elizabeth. See Elizabeth, of York, Queen of Henry VII.

YORK.   Richard, Duke of.   1411–1460.

Richard was the son of Richard, Earl of Cambridge, and Anne Mortimer (see Mortimer, Anne, for Richard's claim to the Throne). He was brought up as the ward of Ralph, Earl Westmorland. The estates he inherited from his parents made him one of the most powerful men in the kingdom. In 1438 he married Westmorland's daughter, Cecily Neville, and became the father of two kings, (Edward IV and Richard III) and a Queen (Henry VII's wife, Elizabeth of York). In 1454 Richard was made Protector during Henry VI's breakdown. Between 1455, when he began the Wars of the Roses (1455–1485) by seizing the King at the first battle of St Albans, and 1460, when he was killed during the battle of Wakefield, the Duke of York was involved in a protracted struggle for control of royal government. The Duke's principal opponents were Queen Margaret of Anjou and succeeding dukes of Somerset, and his chief allies were his wife's Neville relations, particularly Warwick 'The Kingmaker'. The Queen contrived to make life so dangerous for York that he was obliged to claim the Throne as a means of self-preservation. By the Act of Accord (1460), Richard forced Henry VI to acknowledge him as his heir. This arrangement was totally unacceptable to the Queen, who clung ferociously to her son's rights, and collected an army in the north of England to free Henry VI from Yorkist control. Richard was killed at Wakefield in an attempt to destroy this force.

YORK.   Prince Richard, Duke of.   1473–1483?.

Richard was the younger son of Edward IV and Elizabeth Woodville. In 1478 he married Anne Mowbray, the heiress of the fourth and last Mowbray Duke of Norfolk. Anne died in November 1481. In February, 1483, Edward made Richard heir to Anne's estates by an act of Parliament, thereby disinheriting John Howard. Queen Elizabeth took Richard into Sanctuary with her in April 1483, but reluctantly handed him over to the Duke of Gloucester on 16 June, who sent him to join his brother, Edward V, in the Tower. The boys gradually disappeared from sight and were thought to have been murdered by their Uncle, Richard III. Between 1491 and 1497, a youth, claiming to be the Duke of York, challenged Henry VII's right to the Throne, but turned out to be an imposter named Perkin Warbeck. Perkin was executed in 1499 with Edward, Earl of Warwick. Some people believe that Perkin was forced to confess under torture, and was, as he first claimed, Prince Richard of York.

CHAPTER ONE

'This Sun of York'
1422–1483

Now is the winter of our discontent
Made glorious summer by this sun of
York.

Shakespeare *Richard III* I.1.

There is no better example of the natural perversity of English-men than their treatment of Henry VI. Not satisfied with deposing him twice over they sought to have him canonized. Few things enhance a man's reputation more than his wanton murder. It may seem a meagre reward for a lifetime of probity to be battered to death in the Tower, but such was the fate of this saintly simpleton. At least his martyrdom dimmed the memory of the fiascos of his reign.

Government in the fifteenth century was centred on the Sovereign, so whether a kingdom flourished or declined depended on its ruler. The qualities demanded of crowned heads were so exacting that they often eluded hereditary lotteries. Henry V, however, was richly endowed with the necessary attributes of his office: a commanding presence, a shrewd judgment, a resolute nature, and martial ardour. His sudden death from dysentery while campaigning in France in 1422, when he was still young enough to have known nothing of failure, left him a legendary reputation by which his son was judged and found wanting.

No man could be less like his father than Henry VI. Even his virtues were such as to disqualify him from wearing the Crown. Henry possessed in good measure the instincts of the cloister but lacked the heroic qualities of the battlefield. The Tudors ingeniously struggled to justify his shortcomings in the hope of securing his canonization. But the myth of the holy innocent would have astonished Henry's contemporaries, who had no illusions about his regal defects. A Dutchman living at Ely suggested that a sheep would be more appropriate than a ship on coins of the realm. The Abbot of St Albans, writing from personal knowledge, dismissed Henry as his 'Mother's stupid offspring' who was too 'half-witted' to manage affairs of state. The ruthless world of intrigue presided over by Louis XI, the Borgias, and Vlad the Impaler, was no place for innocents abroad. In such company it is hardly surprising that Henry was powerless to prevent the dissolution of the French Empire his father had bequeathed him.

Henry VI was born at Windsor Castle on December 6th 1421 and became king before he was nine months old. In October 1422, he succeeded his grandfather, Charles VI, as King of France, as laid down in the Treaty of Troyes. Henry V in his will appointed his brother, the Duke of Bedford, Regent of France, and his younger brother, Humphrey, Duke of Gloucester, Regent of England. Heedless, however, of Gloucester's protests, Parliament and the Council revoked many of the powers bestowed on him, and affirmed the principle that nobody on his own was entitled to wield the royal authority on behalf of a minor. Such power, they insisted, could only properly be exercised by Parliament or the Council. In order to emphasise the restricted status they were prepared to concede him, they appointed Gloucester 'Protector': an office which lapsed the moment his nephew was crowned in November 1429.

In 1445, in an effort to make peace with Charles VII, who was proving alarmingly successful in advancing his claim to the French Throne, Henry married Margaret of Anjou. She showed from the first that she possessed a 'stomach and courage more like to a man than a woman'. Her domineering meddling aroused widespread antagonism. The civil wars and violent deaths which ended the reigns of Edward II, Henry VI, and Charles I, were partly provoked by the zeal of their foreign wives for interfering in politics.

Henry conspicuously failed in the foremost tasks of a

38

sovereign: to maintain law and order at home and his kingdom's interests abroad. The disorders of his reign were partly the consequence of the partisan fashion in which he exercised patronage. By showering favours on a privileged clique he generated the faction it was his duty to discourage. Disaster abroad was a further cause of despair. By the summer of 1450 the English had been driven out of Normandy, and the 'The King's son had lost all his father won'.

In 1453, Henry VI suffered a mental breakdown from which he never entirely recovered. The stupor which rendered him helpless for the next eighteen months may have begun when he heard of the Battle of Castillon, a defeat so disastrous that it ended the Hundred Years War with France. His malady was probably inherited from his grandfather, Charles VI, a notorious madman. Throughout his illness, Henry was so listless and unresponsive that he could not look after himself. In October 1453, eight years after her marriage, Queen Margaret gave birth to Prince Edward. It was hoped that the sight of his son might arouse the King from his torpor, but he showed not a flicker of interest. Some people alleged that the Duke of Somerset was the child's father, while others believed that Henry had clung to celibacy with the fervour of Edward the Confessor. If this was indeed so, news of the Queen's pregnancy may have caused his collapse. When at last he began to show some concern for his son, he is said to have attributed paternity to the Holy Ghost.

During the King's illness, Richard, Duke of York was made Protector of the realm, with precisely the powers bestowed on Humphrey, Duke of Gloucester in 1422. Richard himself was of royal descent on both sides of his family. Indeed, he was later to argue that his claim to the Throne was better than Henry VI's. Richard's mother, Anne Mortimer, was a great grand-daughter of Lionel, Duke of Clarence, Edward III's second son; whereas Henry VI was a great grandson of John of Gaunt, Duke of Lancaster, Edward's third son. According to the law of primogeniture, which requires inheritance to descend through the senior branch of a family, Richard should have been king. The Lancastrians, however, appealed to the

THE DUKE OF YORK'S CLAIM TO THE THRONE

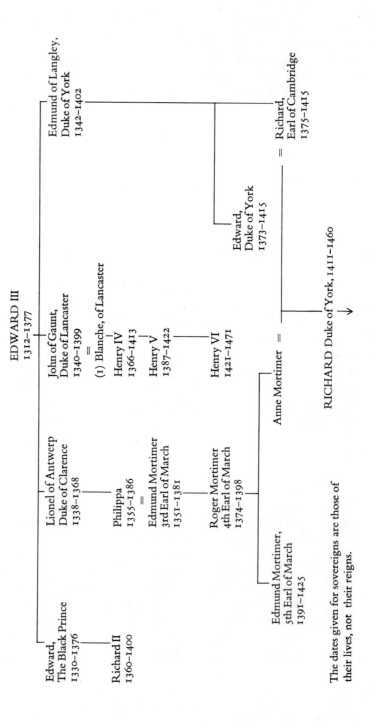

EDWARD III
1312–1377

Edward,
The Black Prince
1330–1376

Richard II
1360–1400

Lionel of Antwerp
Duke of Clarence
1338–1368

Philippa
1355–1386
=
Edmund Mortimer
3rd Earl of March
1351–1381

Roger Mortimer
4th Earl of March
1374–1398

Edmund Mortimer,
5th Earl of March
1391–1425

Anne Mortimer =

RICHARD Duke of York, 1411–1460

John of Gaunt,
Duke of Lancaster
1340–1399
=
(1) Blanche, of Lancaster

Henry IV
1366–1413

Henry V
1387–1422

Henry VI
1421–1471

Edmund of Langley,
Duke of York
1342–1402

Edward,
Duke of York
1373–1415

= Richard,
Earl of Cambridge
1375–1415

The dates given for sovereigns are those of
their lives, not their reigns.

Salic law to justify their claim, although it only prevailed in parts of Europe. This law asserted that no woman could reign in her own right, or pass on a title to the Throne through her side of the family. In fact, the Lancastrians applied this principle to suit the needs of the moment, disregarding the clear precedent of the reign of Queen Matilda, and the fact that Henry VI's claim to the French Crown derived from Queen Isabel, Edward III's mother. The reigns of Queen Mary, Queen Elizabeth I, Queen Anne, Queen Victoria and Queen Elizabeth II, do not suggest that the Salic Law carries much weight in England.

On his father's side of his family, Richard, Duke of York was descended from John of Gaunt's younger brother, Edmund, Duke of York. Edmund's eldest son, Edward, succeeded in 1402, but died, without issue, thirteen years later at Agincourt. Edmund's second son, Richard, Earl of Cambridge, married Anne Mortimer. Only a few weeks before his brother fell in battle, he was beheaded for conspiring to depose Henry V in favour of Edmund Mortimer, Anne's brother. Consequently, in the autumn of 1415, his four-year-old son became Duke of York. The boy was brought up at Raby Castle in the household of Ralph Neville, first Earl of Westmorland, and in 1438 married his childhood companion, Westmorland's youngest daughter, Cecily Neville, 'the Rose of Raby'. She was devout, studious, and devoted to her husband, but like many Nevilles haughty and ambitious. Not only did she pass on her singular beauty to most of her children, but also a title to the Throne from her grandfather, John of Gaunt. Duke Richard was already the greatest landowner in England after Henry VI, and his Neville marriage made him so powerful that two of his sons later became Kings: Edward IV and Richard III. It is doubtful, however, that the House of York could ever have supplanted the Lancastrians, without the help of Cecily's brother, Richard, Earl of Salisbury, and his son, Richard, Earl of Warwick.

The brief Protectorate of the Duke of York came to an end in February 1455, by which time Henry has sufficiently recovered to restore the rule of his faction. Its foremost member,

NEVILLE – YORK MARRIAGES

John of Gaunt,
Duke of Lancaster
1340–1399
= (3) Catherine Swynford
d.1403

Joan Beaufort
=

(2) Ralph Neville,
First Earl of Westmorland
d.1425

Richard,
Earl of Salisbury
d. 1460
=
Alice, dt. of
Earl of Shrewsbury + Salisbury

William
d.1463
} Thomas,
Bastard of
Fauconberg

Robert,
Bishop of Durham
d.1457

Catherine
(1) John,
Duke of Norfolk
(4) John Woodville

Anne
=
Humphrey Stafford,
First Duke of
Buckingham
d. 1460

Cecily
d.1495
=
Richard,
Duke of York
1411–1460

Richard,
Earl of Warwick
"King-Maker"
d.1471
=
Anne, dt. of
Earl of Warwick

John,
Earl of Northumberland
(Montagu. 1470)
d.1471

George,
Archbishop of
York. d.1476

EDWARD IV
1442–1483

Edmund,
Earl of Rutland
1443–1460

George,
Duke of Clarence
1449–1478
=
Isabel Neville
1451–1476

RICHARD III
1452–1485
=
Anne Neville
1456–1485

Isabel
1451–1476
=
George,
Duke of Clarence
1449–1478

Anne
1456–1485
=
RICHARD III
1452–1485

Edmund Beaufort, second Duke of Somerset, persuaded the King to exclude the Duke of York from any share in government. When York learned of this decision he immediately rode to the Court at St Albans to demand his rightful place on the Council. Negotiations broke down, and the skirmish which followed is generally referred to as the 'Battle of St Albans'. Despite its military insignificance it was of great political moment. During such fighting as there was in this opening campaign of the Wars of the Roses, a number of Henry's principal councillors were killed, including Somerset. Ancient antagonisms became ferocious blood feuds: the Queen openly associating herself with the defeated clique.

From 1455, until Henry VI's deposition in 1461, contending factions struggled for mastery of his policy. On Lady Day, 1458, he made a dramatic gesture to end growing strife, somehow persuading the survivors of St Albans to join a procession to St Paul's for a service of reconciliation. Salisbury, and Somerset's heir, the third Duke, led the way, followed by York and Queen Margaret holding hands. The King wore his crown as proof that the 'Loveday' opened a new era. In fact, this characteristic display of futile benevolence changed nothing and solved nothing.

The Queen was in no way deterred by such innocent charades from destroying the power of York and his Neville associates. So successful was she in crippling their influence, that the Duke felt obliged in October 1459 to summon his forces to Ludlow Castle, intending once more to confront the King. Most of York's army, however, deserted him when they heard that a royal force was approaching Ludford Bridge, which crosses the river Teme on the southern approach to the town. The Duke escaped to Ireland, while Salisbury, Warwick, and Edward, Earl of March, York's eldest son, took refuge in Calais. The 'Parliament of Devils', which met after the rout at Ludford, took a dangerous revenge on the rebels by ordering the wholesale confisaction of their property, despite the fact that no King could afford to violate the rights of his most powerful subjects without risking his overthrow. Such

43

vindictive measures confronted York with the stark choice of accepting defeat or resorting to arms.

In June 1460, the Yorkist Earls published a manifesto from Calais in which they announced their intention of rescuing Henry VI from his evil advisers. In July, Warwick and March met the Royal army at Northampton in a torrential downpour. They spent the morning in fruitless negotiation and the afternoon in defeating the King's forces. Two of his closest councillors, the Duke of Buckingham and the Earl of Shrewsbury, were slaughtered after the battle. The Queen and Prince of Wales escaped, but Henry was captured, and resignedly started to dance to his new masters' tunes. The acts of the 'Parliament of Devils' were repealed, the King's former advisers were proscribed, and the rebels richly rewarded. But the greatest triumph of all for the Duke of York was the 'Act of Accord', which acknowledged him to be next in line to the Throne. The Queen, however, refused to see her son disinherited and resolved to defend his claim. On 30 December 1460, she won the Battle of Wakefield, in which the Duke and his son, Rutland, were killed, and Salisbury was captured and executed. The rebels' heads, festooned with paper crowns, were sent to York to grin down from Micklegate on the Minster. Duke Richard lost his life and shattered his cause in an impetuous sortie from the safety of Sandal Castle.

Early in the New Year, the Queen's army marched towards London. Some of her troops had been lent by James III of Scotland in exchange for the border town of Berwick. This 'whirlwind from the North' laid waste the country in its path 'over a space of thirty miles in breadth'. Rumours of atrocities were exaggerated but festered for many years to come in the mythology of the South. The Lancastrian soldiery were accused of slaughtering priests who endeavoured to save their churches from plunder or profanity.

On 17 February, 1461, Shrove Tuesday, the Earl of Warwick met the Queen's forces at St Albans. The King sat laughing and singing under a tree while a battle raged around him to decide who should govern his kingdom. Warwick, who seldom fought an engagement he did not lose, was taken by surprise and driven from the field, leaving Henry in the hands of his masterful consort. Up to the Second Battle of St Albans, contending factions had struggled for control of his person, but now the Yorkists' best chance of survival depended on deposing him.

The Lancastrians failed to follow up their victory by capturing London. It was said they withdrew northwards for fear their troops would sack the city, but more probably they were paying the penalty of recapturing the King: the need to seek his advice. Certainly their sudden display of fecklessness bears the imprint of his spiritless strategy. Fortunately for the rebels, Edward Earl of March, the son of York, won a decisive victory over Jasper Tudor, Earl of Pembroke, a loyal Welsh supporter of Henry VI. The two armies met on 2 February 1461, at Mortimer's Cross, near Wigmore in Herefordshire. Although Jasper suffered a devastating defeat, he managed to flee abroad, but his father, Owen Tudor, was captured, and beheaded at Haverfordwest without a trial.

Prince Edward next joined Warwick at Chipping Norton and marched on London. On 27 February he was met on the outskirts of the city by a deputation from the Provost and Fellows of Eton, fearful for the safety of Henry VI's foundation. The Prince, who was young enough to be a pupil of their College, gave them a written promise of protection. The document, which may be seen in the Library at Eton, was better preserved than the promises it contained. 'Be it known,' it declares, 'that we Edward, by the grace of God of England, France, and Ireland, true and just heir, Duke of York, Earl of the March and Ulster, have by these our letters taken and received the Provost and fellowship of the College of Eton into our defence and safeguard.'

The Yorkists now finally decided that having lost their royal prisoner at St Albans they must make Edward King. Indeed, they could see no other way to end Lancastrian misgovernment and save themselves from perishing as traitors. Accordingly, on Sunday, 1 March, Warwick stage-managed a ceremony at St John's Fields, in which his brother, George Neville, Bishop of Exeter, listed the ways 'in which King Henry VI had offended against the realm' and forfeited the allegiance of his subjects. He explained that the King – in reality the Queen – by waging war against the late Duke of York had broken the Act of Accord. He then 'demanded of the people whether the said Harry was worthy to reign still and the people cried "Nay!"' Finally, he pointed out that Prince Edward was lawfully heir to the Throne as acknowledged by Henry himself. The crowd dutifully shouted its acclaim and a deputation was sent to tell the Duke 'that the people had chosen him King.' Two days later, a number of Yorkist peers, including Thomas Bourchier, Archbishop of Canterbury, Warwick, and George Neville, held a meeting at Baynard's Castle where they agreed to proclaim Edward King. Next day, Wednesday, 4 March, Bishop Neville preached a sermon from Paul's Cross in which he repeated the arguments he had used at St John's Fields. Later that morning, Edward IV formally inaugurated his reign by taking his seat on the marble throne of King's Bench in Westminster Hall, attired in royal robes with the Cap of Estate on his head.

Impressive as such ceremonies were, the most conclusive justification of Edward's title was 'trial by battle'. As one of his later proclamations declared: there is no 'more evident proof or declaration of truth, right and God's will' than military victory. On 29 March, 1461, Palm Sunday, the two Kings met during a snowstorm at Towton, twelve miles south-west of York. The engagement which followed was bloody and decisive. The divine verdict plainly favoured King Edward. Although the Lancastrian Royal Family contrived to escape to Scotland, Henry's army suffered fearful casualties, and most survivors made their peace with the victor.

Few people in the Middle Ages believed that governments owed their sanction to the people. It was generally assumed that a King's right to govern derived direct from God. Men obeyed governments partly because the penalties of the law made it unwise to do otherwise, and partly because to defy the decrees of God's lieutenants on earth was to thwart the divine will. Disobedience was not merely a crime but a sin, risking eternal damnation. Only the strongest conceivable pro-

vocation could justify rebellion. Even then it was arguable
that

> Not all the water in the rough rude sea
> Can wash the balm from an anointed King.

Henry VI was deposed because some of his most powerful subjects could no longer endure his misgovernment. The remorseless attempts of the Court party to
obliterate their rivals drove their opponents to attack the
King's Ministers, and eventually the King. After years of
faction and chaos, it seemed that the best way to restore law
and order was to crown Prince Edward. Anarchy once
savoured tends to lose its enchantment. Most Englishmen in
the declining years of Lancastrian rule echoed Margaret Paston's prayer that God should 'set a good rule in this country
in haste' to prevent lawlessness, 'robbery and manslaughter.'
While the task of maintaining order was assigned to those
who most flagrantly abused it, there could be little hope of
redress. By 1461, Henry VI had demonstrated his total in-
ability to exercise royal authority and thereby forfeited the
loyalty of his long suffering people.

The youth who seized the crown in March 1461 was the
most handsome prince in Christendom. When his coffin was
opened in 1789 his skeleton was found to measure six feet three
and a half inches, and a lock of his golden hair found its way to
the Ashmolean at Oxford. Edward's father was short and
dark, so he presumably inherited his looks from his maternal
grandfather Ralph Neville, or his great grandfather Edmund,
Duke of York, who, like all Edward III's sons, was a giant.
Unlike Henry VI, the young prince looked every inch a King,
and never missed a chance to adorn or exhibit his person.
Unfortunately, he soon lost his figure by over-eating and
drinking. Nor was his appetite for women any more inhibited.
His subjects, however, forgave his 'vanities, debauchery,
extravagance and sensual enjoyments' and loved him despite
his faults. He never forgot a face, and his genial familiarity put
people at their ease. In times of prosperity, he was indolent,
pleasure-loving and over-trusting; but once roused by

47

adversity, he proved swift, vigorous and decisive. No other King of England, apart from Henry V, rivalled his military genius. As a boy he had been brought up a pious Christian by his mother, and although possessing a generous 'share of the frailties inherent to the lot of mankind', remained devoutly religious, and 'a most loving encourager of wise and learned men and of the clergy.'

In June 1463 Margaret of Anjou, and her son Prince Edward, settled at St Michael in Barrois in the Meuse Valley. Her exiled Court included John Morton, later to become Cardinal Archbishop of Canterbury, and Sir John Fortescue a former Lord Chief Justice. In the following year, effective Lancastrian resistance was destroyed by Warwick's brother, John Neville, at Hedgeley Moor and Hexham. Finally, in 1465 the fugitive Henry VI was captured, and paraded on horseback through the streets of London with his feet bound to his stirrups. For the next few years he remained a prisoner in the Tower, where he was allowed a priest to say Mass daily, and wine from the royal cellars. For some months after their defeat at Towton, the Lancastrians hoped for help from France, but in 1463 Louis XI recognized the new dynasty, preferring to ally with the established Yorkist government than commit himself to a lost cause.

No King since the Norman Conquest had married a commoner, so the news that Edward IV had taken Elizabeth Woodville for his wife created consternation. Indeed, the mésalliance proved disastrous to his dynasty. In the next century, the matrimonial misadventures of his grandson Henry VIII showed once more how rash it could be for a sovereign to marry a subject. Nevertheless, it was a gross distortion of truth to describe the new Queen as of 'mean calling' and 'humble origin'. In fact, her mother, Jacquetta, claimed descent from Charlemagne through her father the Count of St Pol, and was the widow of Henry V's brother, the Duke of Bedford. Richard Woodville her second husband, was less exalted, but was, nevertheless, a Knight of the Garter, a Privy Counsellor, and a peer. Inevitably, Elizabeth was criticized for her Lancastrian connections. Her father, and her brother

Portrait of Edward IV in the Royal Collection.

A seventeenth century print of a sermon from St Paul's Cross.

This boke late translated here in sight
By Antony Erle   that vertuup knyght
Please it to accepte to youre noble grace

Above left: Lord Rivers presenting Edward IV with his book. Edward V is the boy on the right of the picture, and Richard III is the ermined figure standing on Rivers' left.

Above right: Portrait of Elizabeth Woodville from the stained glass window (c.1482) in the north transept of Canterbury Cathedral.

Left: Sir Thomas More, after Holbein.

The Royal Oak under which Edward IV reputedly met his future Queen.

St. Mary the Virgin, Grafton, where Edward IV married Elizabeth Woodville.

Anthony, fought against Edward IV at Towton; and her first husband, Sir John Grey, heir to Lord Ferrers of Groby, died fighting for Henry VI while commanding the last furious cavalry assault at the Second Battle of St Albans.

The Woodvilles had lived at Grafton in Northamptonshire since the eleventh century, and it seems probable that Elizabeth returned there after Sir John was killed. Edward is known to have stayed at Stony Stratford, a few miles south of Grafton, on two occasions in 1461: on his way from Mortimer's Cross to London, and on his return from the Battle of Towton. Tradition has it that the young widow waylaid him out hunting and implored him not to deprive her two boys of their father's estates. The oak tree under which she supposedly stood when she first met the King survives to the present day. Her austere beauty, demure smile, and beguiling wit, instantly won his heart. Nor did he long to possess her the less when she refused to become his mistress. Indeed, 'where he was a little before heated with the dart of Cupid, he was now set all on a hot burning fire'. It was even rumoured that he tried to seduce her by force but that she resolved 'to die rather than live unchastely'. A couple of years after they were married, an Italian writer, Antonio Cornazzano, wrote a poem in which Edward reproaches Elizabeth for 'withholding her tribute of love'. She replies by seizing a dagger and warning him:

> If my honour is taken from me,
> I will pierce my body to the ground with this knife.

So besotted was the King that he fell back on a most desperate resort: marriage. In so doing, he defied the protests of his family, the warnings of his Counsellors, and the dictates of expediency.

Most people could see little to recommend the Queen, apart from her graceful appearance, and she was commonly regarded as an avaricious upstart. Certainly her devotion to the interests of her family was such as to encourage that construction. But she did not merit all the obloquy which envy heaped upon her. By patronizing the arts she played a valuable role in civilizing the Court. One of the first books, if not the earliest, which Caxton printed in England was translated from the French by her brother, Anthony. A picture in the Library at Lambeth Palace shows him presenting a copy of 'The Dictes and Sayings of the Philosophers' to Edward IV in the presence of two future Kings: Edward V and Richard III.

Edward's mother is alleged to have made strenuous efforts to persuade him to change his mind, protesting that it would be to his 'honour, profit, and surety also, to marry in a noble progeny out of his realm', and arguing that 'it was not princely to marry his own subject for a little wanton dotage on her person'. She even objected to the fact that Dame Elizabeth Grey was a widow. But the King, it is said, insisted on his right to be guided by his heart, and claimed that as God has inclined 'the parties to love together', it was preferable to bow to His will than to seek 'any temporal advantage'. Nor could he believe that his fellow-countrymen would hold it against him 'that he disdained not to marry with one of his own land'. Finally, the fact that the lady was a widow with two lusty sons suggested that the union would prove fruitful: an argument whose cogency was later confirmed by ten royal children.

Edward was secretly married at Grafton on 1 May 1464. He spent the previous night at Stony Stratford but rose so early next morning that nobody saw him leave. The ceremony was probably conducted by Thomas Leson, the incumbent of St Mary the Virgin, the church adjoining the Manor. An act of 1484, designed to justify the deposition of Edward V, alleged that the service took place 'privily and secretly without edition of banns, in a private chamber, a profane place, and not openly in the face of the Church.' The wedding was solemnized in the presence of 'the spouse, the spousesse, the Duchess of Bedford, the priest, and two gentlemen and a young man whc helped the priest to sing.' No other King of England was ever married with so little ceremony. On his return to Stony Stratford, Edward told his anxious courtiers that he had been out hunting. Some days later, he paid his parents-in-law an official visit at Grafton, and Elizabeth was smuggled into his apartments after the household retired for the night.

QUEEN ELIZABETH WOODVILLE'S RELATIONS

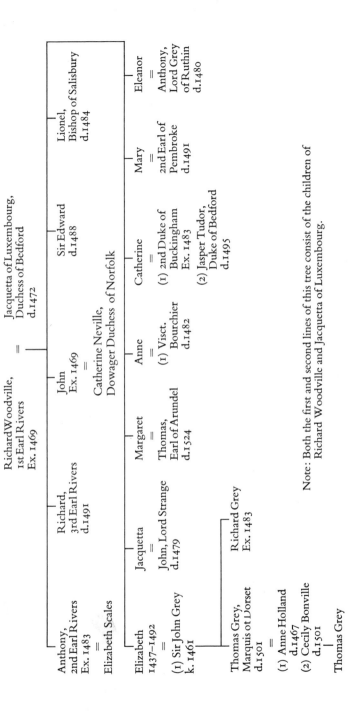

Note: Both the first and second lines of this tree consist of the children of Richard Woodville and Jacquetta of Luxembourg.

Edward was eventually compelled to confess his secret, at a Council held at Reading in September 1464, in order to prevent Warwick committing him to a matrimonial alliance with France. When the King was asked whether he would agree to marry Louis XI's sister-in-law, Princess Bona of Savoy, he replied 'in right merry guise that he would take to wife Dame Elizabeth Grey', only to be told 'that she was not his match, however good and fair she might be.' Many of the chief men of the kingdom were 'treuly chafyd' to learn of Edward's 'dishonourable' marriage to which he had been 'led by blind affection and not by rule of reason'. Warwick especially resented being made to look foolish, and deplored the waning of his influence over his cousin.

Elizabeth Woodville had five brothers and six sisters. Her eldest brother Anthony, who succeeded his father as Earl Rivers in 1469, was the most attractive member of an unloved family. In some respects he was grasping, ambitious and worldly, but he was also an accomplished courtier, a chivalrous knight, and a pious scholar. In 1460 he married an heiress, Elizabeth Scales, who brought him considerable estates, including Sandringham. After Henry VI's defeat at Towton he abandoned the Lancastrian cause and transferred his allegiance to Edward IV. His brother, Sir Edward Woodville, acquired an unsavoury reputation as a dissolute companion of the King, but appears to have exercised no influence other than encouraging debauchery. Lionel Woodville was more deserving and better rewarded. In 1472, at the age of nineteen, he was made Archdeacon of Oxford, in 1479 Chancellor of Oxford, and in 1482 Bishop of Salisbury.

The Queen was understandably eager to promote the careers of her sons as well as her brothers and sisters. In 1475 her eldest boy, Thomas Grey, was made Marquis of Dorset, and the following year a Knight of the Garter. 'The Marquis', as he was familiarly known, was one of the principal 'promoters and companions' of the King's vices, along with his Uncle, Sir Edward, and his brother, Richard Grey. Indeed, the Queen only contrived to retain her influence over her husband by tolerating his promiscuity, perceiving that he was less interested in the capture of his quarry than the exhilaration of the chase.

Elizabeth used her influence to arrange seven splendid marriages for her family. Her sister, Catherine, married the second Duke of Buckingham; her brother, John, the Dowager Duchess of Norfolk; and her son, Thomas Grey, the Duke of Exeter's daughter, Anne Holland. Four of her sisters married Earls or their heirs. Margaret married Thomas, Earl of Arundel; Anne married William Viscount Bourchier, nephew of Thomas Bourchier, Archbishop of Canterbury, a great grandson of Edward III; Eleanor married Anthony, Lord Grey of Ruthin, the Earl of Kent's son; while Mary became the wife of William Herbert, second Earl of Pembroke. Within a couple of years of her own marriage the Queen's kin had become a powerful political alliance.

The Duke of Buckingham, as the King's Ward, had his bride chosen for him, and never concealed his patrician disdain for his wife's family. Warwick was also deeply incensed by the Queen's match-making, which deprived his daughters of eligible husbands outside the Royal Family. Between 1464 and 1470, every available male heir to an earldom married one of the Queen's sisters, as did the Duke of Buckingham, the most splendid catch of all. Nor did Warwick care for John Woodville's marriage to his Aunt Catherine, the Dowager Duchess of Norfolk. She had already buried three husbands and was some forty-five years older than the bridegroom.

Two consequences of Edward's marriage have often been exaggerated: the hostility it aroused, and the extent of his generosity to his wife's family. Nothing showed more clearly that many nobles accepted the Queen's relations than their readiness to marry them. It is true that her father and brother Anthony were handsomely endowed, but none of the Woodvilles were as lavishly patronized as were Warwick, Hastings or Herbert. Naturally, they benefited from royal favour and equally naturally were envied, but the Queen's court was not extravagant nor was the cost of her family's marriages excessive. Edward's relations, however, never accepted the Woodvilles. His mother did her best to discourage the match, and his brother, the Duke of Clarence, publicly denounced the Queen's 'obscure family'. Under these circumstances, it was hardly surprising that she in turn 'highly maligned the King's kindred', the more so as 'women commonly, not of malice, but of nature, hate them whom their husbands love'.

The unpopularity of the Woodvilles was largely their own fault, for they were greedy, overbearing and acrimonious. Nor was it unreasonable to hold them responsible for encouraging Edward's lascivious tastes. When Warwick in 1469 denounced the King's policy, he was at pains to ascribe it to the Queen's relations, accusing them of encouraging Edward to exclude 'the great lords of his blood' from his inner Council, and of offering him seditious, deceitful and covetous advice to serve their own ends. Looking back on the disasters which befell the Yorkist dynasty, the Tudor historian Hall saw clear signs of God's punishment of Edward's impetuous love-match. At first, he wrote, the marriage appeared 'very pleasant to the king' and even 'more joyous to the Queen and profitable to her blood', but those who marked 'the sequel of this story' could not but perceive 'what murder, what misery, and what trouble ensued by reason of this marriage', in consequence of which Warwick and Clarence were slain, Edward's sons 'were deprived of their lives', and 'the Queen's blood was confounded and utterly destroyed'.

Between 1469 and 1471 Edward IV lost and recovered his Throne. The rebellion which temporarily forced him into exile was led by Warwick, who was driven to despair by his declining influence over his protégé, the growing power of the Woodvilles, and the marriage in 1468 of the King's sister, Margaret, to Charles the Bold, Duke of Burgundy. Since 1463, Warwick had advocated an alliance with Louis XI, partly in the hope of extending Neville influence to Europe. But Edward preferred to continue the traditional Burgundian alliance, in order to safeguard Calais, the Straits of Dover, and the wool trade. Warwick won powerful support from George, Duke of Clarence, a handsome extravagant, fickle youth of nineteen, who only too often 'forgot the brother of a King is but a subject'. In July 1469 the Duke married Warwick's eldest daughter, Isabel, in defiance of Edward's orders, and a fortnight later he and Warwick defeated a royal army at Edgecote, near Banbury. The Queen's father, her brother John, and the King's friend Lord Pembroke, were captured and beheaded. Three days later the King himself fell into rebel hands. After some months as Warwick's prisoner, he was reluctantly released, it having become clear that nobody would obey proclamations until he was set free.

In March 1470, Edward denounced Clarence and Warwick as guilty of high treason, and the two men fled to the French Court. Some weeks later, with the help of Louis XI, they signed a treaty at Angers with Margaret of Anjou, in which it was agreed that Prince Edward of Lancaster would marry Warwick's younger daughter, Anne Neville, and that the Earl would invade England, restore Henry VI, and join France in a war against Burgundy. In fulfilment of these commitments, the rebels landed at Dartmouth in September, and the King, finding himself deserted and betrayed, set sail for the Low Countries. So precipitate was his flight that he was obliged to pay the ship's captain by giving him his gown.

Edward was accompanied into exile by his youngest brother Richard, who had been born at Fotheringhay Castle on 2 October 1452, eighteen years to the day before they embarked at King's Lynn. Richard spent most of his childhood with his mother, whose pious precepts were more often heard on his lips than proclaimed in his life. After his father's death at Wakefield, he and his brother George were given asylum by Philip, Duke of Burgundy, Charles the Bold's father, but returned to England when Edward became king. In June 1461 Richard was made Duke of Gloucester. Soon afterwards, he served his apprenticeship in the martial arts in Warwick's Household at Middleham in Yorkshire, but remained loyal to the King when the Earl rebelled in 1469.

Richard was short, slight and dark like his father, in striking contrast to his brothers, all of whom inherited the fair hair, gigantic stature and handsome features of their Plantagenet and Neville ancestors. But there is little reason to believe that he was born a 'Crouchback'. No writer who is known to have set eyes on him – with one possible exception – describes him as being deformed, nor does his prowess at Bosworth suggest infirmity. The legendary hunchback of Tudor polemics appears to owe less to accurate observation than the prevailing belief that warped minds inhabited twisted bodies.

Richard has sometimes been praised a shade too fervently for his loyalty to the King, as if to behave better than Clarence was proof of impeccable principles. He could hardly have been insensible to the fact that it paid handsomely to put Edward in his debt, nor was he so rash as to incur the penalties of treason. Moreover, there is nothing particularly virtuous in avoiding the palpable drawbacks of being hung, drawn, and quartered. As for his devotion to his brother, within three months of his death, he had proclaimed him a bastard, denounced him for bigamy, and dispossessed his sons.

Among others who accompanied the King into exile were Lord Rivers and William, Lord Hastings. William came from a family of prosperous landowners in Yorkshire and the Midlands, who had served the House of York for four generations. He began his career in Duke Richard's household and joined Edward soon after Mortimer's Cross. From then onwards, he became his trusted companion in triumph and disaster. Following the victory of Towton, in which he played a prominent part, William became a peer, Knight of the Garter, and Lord Chamberlain. He was furthermore richly rewarded by grants of forfeited Lancastrian estates in Leicestershire and elsewhere. In 1462 he made a powerful marriage to the King's first cousin, Catherine Neville. Unfortunately, a bitter hostility developed between the Woodvilles and Lord Hastings, 'against whom the Queen specially grudged for the great favour the king bore him, and also for that she thought him secretly familiar with the king in wanton company.' So long as Edward lived, he was able to control this feud, but when he died it sealed the fate of his sons.

In November 1470, Warwick summoned a Parliament, which authorized him to act as regent for Henry VI, and proclaimed Edward and Richard guilty of treason. The following February, the Lancastrian government declared war on Burgundy, as agreed in the Treaty of Angers, thus encouraging Charles the Bold to help restore the Yorkists. Edward set sail from Flushing on 11 March, landed at Ravenspur like Henry IV before him, and was joined by three thousand retainers of Lord Hastings as he marched south. Clarence, who had been under fierce family pressure to abandon Warwick, and had come to realize how dim his prospects must be while Henry remained on the Throne, was reconciled to his brother. Just before Edward reached London, Archbishop Neville tried to rally support by parading Henry through the streets. The pathetic spectacle of this shabby half-wit being led by the hand through his capital prompted the city to open its gates to his rival.

One of the first things Edward did on returning to London was visit the Queen, who on the night he took ship from King's Lynn had taken sanctuary at Westminster with her daughters: Elizabeth, Mary and Cecily. There, on All Souls' Day, 2 November 1470, she gave birth to Prince Edward. Soon after seeing his son for the first time, the King heard that Warwick was marching on London. At dawn, on a foggy Easter Day, 14 April 1471, the two cousins fought a furious and confused battle north of Barnet. Eventually the King was victorious, and Warwick was killed while attempting to escape. That very morning, Queen Margaret and her son landed at Weymouth where the Duke of Somerset joined them. Edward, appreciating the need to prevent her joining her supporters in Wales and Cheshire, intercepted her at Tewkesbury and annihilated her army on the outskirts of the town. Her son was killed, she herself was captured at Malvern Priory, and Somerset, who had taken refuge in Tewkesbury Abbey, was dragged out and executed. On 21 May Edward entered his capital in triumph after a swift and brilliant campaign. During his absence in the west, London was attacked by the 'Bastard of Fauconberg', a natural son of his uncle William Neville, who sailed up the Thames, burned thirteen houses on London Bridge, and was only driven off with the greatest difficulty.

On the night of 21 May, or early the next morning, King Henry died in the Tower of what a Yorkist Chronicle described as 'pure displeasure and melancholy'. It is, of course, just conceivable that he succumbed to the shock of the news that his son was dead, his wife a captive, and his cause lost. But Edward had such powerful reasons for wishing his rival dispatched that his timely demise was bound to arouse suspicion. There is no evidence whatever for the Tudor legend that the Duke of Gloucester slaughtered Prince Edward in cold blood and subsequently murdered his father. Contemporary accounts agree that Henry's son died fighting on the battlefield, and nobody other than Edward IV would have ordered the death of a King. Richard's supposed guilt rests solely on unconfirmed rumour.

The chief threat to Edward in the second part of his reign came from the bitter disputes dividing his family, one of the most damaging of which arose over Richard's proposal to marry Anne Neville, whom he had known since his boyhood days in her father's Household. She had previously been betrothed to Edward of Lancaster, Prince of Wales, under the agreement signed in the summer of 1470 between Warwick and Queen Margaret. When the Prince was killed at Tewkesbury, Anne was put into the safe-keeping of her sister, Isabel. The moment Clarence discovered that Richard intended to marry her, he was consumed with resentment at the prospect of having to share the Neville estates, 'which he wished to come to himself alone in right of his wife'. In an effort to break up the match, he concealed Anne 'in the habit of a kitchen maid' in an obscure part of London. Richard, however, contrived to find her, and had her removed to the Sanctuary of St Martin-le-Grand. The violent dissensions aroused by these proceedings forced Edward to intervene. In the end, some time after Easter 1472, Richard and Anne married, and later an Act of Parliament divided Warwick's estates between his two daughters. There are good reasons for believing that Richard, unlike the King, chose his wife on the customary principles guiding royal marriages. The substantial advantages of the alliance for both partners implies it was no mere love match.

Nor can the voracious zeal with which the Duke defended his interests be reconciled with romantic fancies.

In December 1476 the Duchess of Clarence died leaving two children in the care of her younger sister. Her son Edward, who was given her father's title Earl of Warwick, spent much of his later life in the Tower where Henry VII imprisoned him. In 1499 the wretched youth was beheaded on a trumped up charge, but his real offence was possessing a better claim to the throne than the king who occupied it. Isabel's daughter, Margaret, married Sir Richard Pole, and suffered the fate of her brother in 1541, partly because of her Yorkist blood, and partly because her son, Cardinal Reginald Pole, denounced the Reformation.

Soon after Charles the Bold was killed in battle in 1477, his widow, Margaret, began negotiating a marriage between her brother George and her step-daughter Mary, the new ruler of Burgundy. But Edward IV, recognizing that the Duke's 'contemplated exaltation' would make him more fractious than ever, 'threw all possible impediments in the way'. Clarence was so incensed that he refused to come to Court. The King's patience was finally exhausted when the Duke seized one of Isabel's servants, accused her of poisoning her late mistress, and browbeat a jury into hanging her for murder. These grotesque proceedings suggest a disturbed balance of mind.

In January 1478, Edward published a Bill of Attainder accusing Clarence of conspiring 'new treasons', such as intending 'to exalt himself and his heirs to the regality and crown of England', and falsely alleging 'that the King our Sovereign Lord was a bastard and not begotten to reign upon us.' Throughout the proceedings against Clarence nobody uttered a word against him apart from the King, and 'not one individual made answer except the Duke'. Edward won the verdict, and sentence of death was pronounced by the Duke of Buckingham. It was believed, as far afield as Naples, that Clarence met his end by being plunged headfirst into a butt of Malmsey. So persistent are reports of this improbable method of execution that they could even be true. It is more likely, however, that the Duke was given poison in a glass of Malmsey wine. Alternatively, the story may have arisen because his remains were kept in Malmsey on the journey to Tewkesbury Abbey, where he and Isabel are buried, just as after Trafalgar Nelson's corpse was preserved in a barrel of brandy.

It was commonly believed that the Queen encouraged her husband to prosecute Clarence because she thought he intended to dispossess her sons. Richard was also held responsible for bringing about his death. There is no evidence whatever to sustain this charge, but it is difficult to believe that Edward would have proceeded with the attainder had Richard strenuously opposed it. Nevertheless, it was Clarence himself who drove the King to fratricide, by his insatiable avarice, obsessive jealousy, and untroubled conviction that renegade traitors were somehow uniquely deserving. Indeed, few men have ever more richly merited the penalty of treason.

After his restoration in 1471, Edward pursued a peaceful foreign policy, apart from brief campaigns against France and Scotland. Ever since Edward III claimed the throne of France in 1338, through his mother Queen Isabella, and started the Hundred Years War to enforce his rights, it became the ambition of most English Kings to be crowned at Notre Dame or Rheims. In the summer of 1475, Edward set sail for Calais, dreaming no doubt of Agincourt and Crecy. It is possible, however, that the expedition was a bluff, designed to extract concessions from the enemy. Suddenly, after a few weeks desultory fighting in which his allies broke all their promises of help, Edward sued for peace. In August, he met Louis XI on a bridge at Picquigny, which crossed the Somme three miles south of Amiens. Elaborate precautions were taken against treachery, and discussions took place through a hole in a specially built screen. In return for a seven year truce, the French King agreed to pay Edward an annual pension of fifty thousand crowns, and to offer the Dauphin's hand to Princess Elizabeth of York. The Duke of Gloucester made no secret of his belief that the treaty was ignominious.

In 1482 Mary of Burgundy died from injuries received after

falling from a horse, and, soon afterwards, Louis signed an agreement whereby his son was betrothed to her daughter. This flagrant breach of the marriage clause of the settlement reached at Picquigny, naturally infuriated King Edward, who deeply resented the ill-treatment of his daughter, 'Madame la Dauphine'. Preparations were begun for another war with France, but nothing came of them as both Kings died in the course of 1483.

The Scottish campaign of 1482 was provoked by border raids, and James III's refusal to keep a promise to marry his eldest son to Edward's daughter Cecily. When James' younger brother, the Duke of Albany, claimed the throne of Scotland, on the ground that the King was illegitimate, Edward agreed to support him, and put Gloucester in command of an expeditionary force of some twenty thousand men. In July, Berwick opened its gates to the English army, but the Castle refused to capitulate. Only after a protracted siege did its garrison surrender to Lord Stanley. Meanwhile, Richard captured Edinburgh almost without a skirmish. He owed his good fortune to the rebel Earl of Angus, who took the opportunity of the English invasion to seize James, hang his ministers, and reduce Scotland to anarchy. In the end, Richard withdrew with nothing to show for his enormously expensive campaign apart from Berwick, which subsequently cost so much to defend that it was hard to decide 'whether to call it "gain" or "loss"'

Gloucester's military achievements have often been exaggerated. His reputation depends upon Barnet, Tewkesbury and the Scottish campaign. Barnet was fought in a fog, and was so confused there was little scope for generalship. Moreover, it is by no means certain that Richard was even present. At Tewkesbury, he is said to have employed an ingenious ruse to lure Somerset to destruction, and to have played an energetic part in pursuing the shattered remnants of the Queen's army. But the Lancastrians might well have won the day had not Lord Wenlock refused to engage his forces. There can be no doubt that Somerset blamed him for defeat as he dashed out his brains with a battle axe to show his displeasure. The Scottish campaign of 1482 met hardly any resistance, except at

Berwick, which yielded to Lord Stanley. Moreover, Richard's impulsive withdrawal threw away such advantage as he had won for no adequate return. Parliament might speak of the 'noble gests, acts and services' of the Duke of Gloucester, but the King remained deaf to their grovelling rhetoric, and expressed himself 'vexed' at the 'frivolous outlay of so much money'.

Edward IV had been made King in 1461 to put an end to years of Lancastrian misgovernment. He soon justified his supporters' choice by restoring the rule of law and reviving the Crown's finances. Nevertheless, towards the end of his reign, he deeply antagonised several powerful subjects by threatening their inheritance. Such dubious proceedings gave their incensed victims a common interest in the destruction of his family.

Nobody suffered more from the King's predatory policy than Lord Howard. John Howard's mother was Margaret Mowbray, daughter of Thomas Mowbray, first Duke of Norfolk. John fought for Edward at Towton, Barnet and Tewkesbury, commanded a squadron of ships in the war against Scotland, and was one of his most trusted Privy Counsellors. Under the Yorkists, the Howards became all powerful in East Anglia. John was a tough, ill-tempered, violent man, whose lawless behaviour landed him in prison. In 1476 John Mowbray, the fourth Duke of Norfolk, died. Two years later his daughter and heiress, Anne Mowbray, was married to Edward IV's younger son, Richard Duke of York. The bride was six years old and the groom four. As a wedding present the Prince was given the title Duke of Norfolk. Unhappily, Anne followed her father to the grave in 1481, and in the last months of his reign the King persuaded Parliament to settle her inheritance on his son. This shabby transaction deprived Lord Howard of his Common law rights as heir to the Mowbray estates. His best hope of reviving his claim was over the Prince's dead body.

Ralph, Lord Neville, who was heir to his uncle Henry Holland, Duke of Exeter, was another casualty of the King's family settlements. The Duke, who married the King's sister,

Anne, left no surviving children. In 1472, three years before he died, his wife divorced him, and married her lover, Sir Thomas St Leger. Anne St Leger, the daughter of this union, was later appointed sole heiress to the Holland estates, by means of an Act of Parliament, and betrothed to Thomas Grey, Dorset's heir by his second marriage to Cecily Bonville.

The second Earl of Pembroke was also given good cause to complain of the way he was treated by the King. His father, William Herbert, had been one of Edward's closest friends and most loyal supporters, but that did not save him from being forced to change his title to Huntingdon and to surrender his Welsh estates for others elsewhere. The intention of these exchanges was to enhance the authority of the Prince of Wales in governing his Principality, but the cogent arguments for so doing were lost on the injured party.

The sons of Edward IV were too young to have enemies of their own and their father was much to blame for making so many for them. The dissident nobles, who later supported Richard, had nearly all suffered from Edward's rapacious assaults, and were quick to seize the chance to redress their wrongs. Their discontent only needed kindling to set the kingdom on fire. More injudicious still, was the King's use of Parliament to disinherit Lord Neville and Lord Howard. By exploiting the law to perpetrate injustice, he showed how the rights of his sons might be set aside, and Richard, faithful as ever, followed in his footsteps.

CHAPTER TWO

Richard's Early Historians

Imitating the bees which laboriously gather
their honey from every flower, I collected with
discretion material proper for a true history.

Polydore Vergil

The task of an historian is much like that of a restorer who carefully scrapes away layers of over-painting to reveal the original picture hidden beneath. The nearer he gets to the canvas the closer he comes to truth. Throughout the Tudor period, successive strata of legend gradually came to obscure the genuine portrait of Richard. Consequently, most of his best likenesses were sketched during his lifetime. Unfortunately, our knowledge of Richard's reign suffers from two defects: the partiality of most prominent witnesses, and provoking gaps in the evidence. Prudent as Richard was to keep his own counsel, his discretion deprives us of vital information. No coherent account of the Usurpation is therefore possible without resort to inference and surmise.

The earliest known account of Richard's Usurpation was written by an Italian visitor to England, Dominic Mancini, who resided in London throughout the period covered by his History. Mancini finished his narrative on 1 December 1483, having left England some time in July, soon after Richard was crowned. For over four centuries his manuscript lay fallow in the hands of private collectors before being presented to the Bibliothèque Municipale at Lille. In 1936 it was published by a young English scholar, Charles Armstrong. Mancini's account was designed as a private report for his patron, Angelo

Cato, Archbishop of Vienne, and a trusted physician and Councillor to Louis XI.

It is probable that Mancini was unable to speak English and hence was restricted to obtaining information from fellow Italians in London. He also appears to have consulted John Argentine, an Italian-speaking Englishman, who was Edward V's physician. Sometimes Mancini wrote with the authority of an eye-witness, as, for example, when he tells us 'I have seen many men burst into tears' at the thought of the fate of the Princes in the Tower.

The defects of Mancini's History, *The Usurpation of Richard III*, are principally those of omission. His account seldom looks beyond London, although this matters less than may seem as so many events took place within sound of Bow Bells. His knowledge of English geography was inclined to be hazy and his understanding of the British Constitution preserved its mysteries intact. Throughout the whole of his History he only supplies one date, and that he gets two days wrong.

Mancini's shortcomings are greatly outweighed by the merits of his work. Few Englishmen have found it possible to contemplate Richard dispassionately. Hence the importance of a writer who remains a detached spectator of the strange scenes he describes. One has only to read Mancini to see how acute are his critical powers and how deep his respect for Truth. His repeated use of such phrases as 'according to common report', 'the story runs', 'men say', shows his desire to distinguish rumour from fact. His History, moreover, is notably free from omens, set speeches, and moralizing, so beloved of Renaissance scholars.

The Usurpation provides a valuable yardstick for measuring the worth of later writers. By remaining unknown for so long it retains an unique independence, and stands alone as the only account of Richard's bid for power which was written before its eventual outcome was known. Above all, Mancini proves that Richard was widely regarded by his subjects as acting like a tyrant. Beginning with Sir George Buck in the seventeenth century, attempts have been made to dismiss hostile criticism of Richard as figments of Tudor malice. But the time-bomb ticking away in the Municipal Archives at Lille has blown this defence sky high.

The most reliable contemporary account of the reign of Richard III is that of the Croyland Chronicle. The Abbey of Croyland, founded in 716, stood in the midst of the Lincoln-shire Fens. Amongst its treasures was an History of England, beginning in the middle of the seventh century. The manu-script, which was almost certainly spurious, was attributed to Abbot Ingulph, who died in 1109. It was kept up to date during the Yorkist era by two anonymous continuators. The Chronicle was first published in its entirety by William Ful-man in 1684.

A careful study of the second Continuator's account of the years 1459 to 1486, tells us a good deal about its author, who concludes his narrative by saying that he wrote it in ten days at Croyland, completing it on 30 April 1486. Fulman asserts that the Continuator was a Doctor of Canon Law, a Member of Edward IV's Council, and the unnamed envoy sent to Charles the Bold in 1471 mentioned in the Chronicle. Internal evidence suggests that the author was a royal servant, and often an eye-witness of the scenes he describes. It is difficult, for example, to read his account of the Council Meeting at which Clarence and Gloucester furiously disputed their claims to their wives' Neville inheritance, without believing he was present. Moreover, the author prided himself on his knowl-edge of affairs. During the course of his account of the oath of fealty taken to Richard's son in 1484, he mentions with evident irritation that it was 'drawn up by some persons to me unknown'. Whoever wrote the second Continuation stands revealed as possessing urbanity, learning, wit, perception and judgment.

No man better fits the bill as the Croyland author than Richard's Lord Chancellor, John Russell, Bishop of Lincoln, whose career resembles that outlined by Fulman, and whose character coincides with that displayed in the text. The Bishop, moreover, is known to have paid an episcopal visit to Croyland in April 1486, just when the work was written. All other Chronicles of 1483 give Russell a prominent place in proceedings, which is hardly surprising considering that the office of Lord Chancellor was the medieval equivalent of that of a modern Prime Minister. But the Croyland Continuator never so much as mentions him: a reticence which strongly suggests Russell's authorship. In all probability the Continuation was the work of a Croyland monk, who fitted the Chancellor's recollections into the Monastery's History.

The Continuator explicitly promised to set forth an accurate 'recital of the facts, without knowingly intermingling therewith any untruthfulness, hatred, or favour whatsoever'. On the whole, he appears to have succeeded in putting his precept into practice. If for no other reason than that he wrote within months of Richard's overthrow, he cannot be said to have succumbed to the malign influence of Tudor propaganda. At times, the Chronicler's obsession with accuracy could well be taken for pedantry. For example, he tells us that Hastings was beheaded 'on the thirteenth day of the month of June, being the sixth day of the week', and that the oath of fealty to the Prince of Wales in 1484 was sworn 'in a certain lower room' in the Palace of Westminster, 'near the passage which leads to the Queen's apartments'. Whenever the Continuator's statements can be verified he is seldom found to be wrong, and it therefore seems reasonable to assume that he is equally reliable when he cannot be cross-checked.

One of the earliest authors to write about Richard III was the antiquarian John Rous, who for forty years was Chaplain of the Chantry Chapel at Guy's Cliff near Warwick. In 1483 Rous produced a Latin and English version of a Chronicle Roll of the Earls of Warwick, patrons of his Chantry. The English text praised Richard extravagantly, in just such terms as he would himself have wished. But when Rous heard of the King's death at Bosworth, he deleted his name from the Latin Roll. Shortly before he died, he completed his 'Historia Regum Angliae', which did not appear in print until 1716. The work, dedicated to Henry VII, denounced Richard as a monster, born under an hostile star with 'unequal shoulders, the right higher and the left lower', who perished like antichrist after a cruel reign. Rous asserts in the course of his narrative that Richard was 'retained within his mother's womb for two years' and eventually emerged 'with teeth and hair to his shoulders'. The book appears to be based on two assumptions: that Warwick is the centre of the Universe, and that the principal purpose of writing history is to please patrons. But, nevertheless, it has some value. Rous presumably saw Richard during his visit to Warwick in August 1483, and wrote with authority about the Nevilles. Nor would it be reasonable to suppose that there are no authentic traditions in the ragbag of myths and gossip he preserves. The problem, as always, remains to distinguish fact from fiction.

The first full account of the Usurpation to appear in print was Polydore Vergil's *Anglica Historia* published in 1534. Vergil, an Italian priest born at Urbino, was sent to England in 1502, by Pope Alexander VI, as a collector of papal taxes. He remained in England for the next fifty years, and soon became friends with More, Colet and Erasmus. He had not settled long in a house by St Paul's Churchyard before Henry VII requested him to write a history of England from the Norman Conquest down to his own time. Vergil treated his theme in a more sophisticated way than was then customary. Indeed, his work was a deliberate reaction against monastic chronicles, which he describes as 'bald, uncouth, chaotic and deceitful'. He approached history in the spirit of the Renaissance, that is to say in a manner at once secular, sceptical and enquiring. Above all, he sought to tell the truth without fear or favour, a task he believed a foreigner was especially well qualified to perform.

Vergil was forced to base his account of the late fifteenth century on the recollections of Richard's surviving contemporaries. In some respects therefore his work possesses the character of an original authority. Among those he most probably consulted were Henry VII, Elizabeth of York, and Lord Stanley. Certainly one of his informants was close enough to Richard to notice his habit of biting 'his nether lip', and toying nervously with his dagger.

Attempts have been made to dismiss Vergil as 'the paid historian of the Tudors', who misrepresented facts 'to please his patrons' and 'to gratify his spite'. It is, of course, true that he wrote his History at Henry VII's request, and dedicated it to his son. But he was certainly not an obsequious echo of his Master's voice. On the contrary, he repeatedly showed his independence in thought, word and deed. His scant respect for legends of King Arthur, after whom Henry named his first born son, and from whom he claimed descent, hardly suggests a sycophant at work. The hostility Vergil displayed towards Richard III was the product of his research, not of a fawning desire to please the Tudors.

The *Anglica Historia* profoundly influenced the development of historical writing in England by encouraging a more critical approach. It is true it gave deep offence by its sceptical treatment of 'cherished national myths', which it provocatively attributed 'to the gullibility of the vulgar'. But that in no way discouraged other authors from plundering it remorselessly. Indeed, the interpretative pattern it imposed on the fifteenth century provided a framework for subsequent Tudor histories. Vergil was sometimes inclined to denounce Richard more vigorously than the evidence seems to justify, for instance in claiming he murdered Prince Edward of Lancaster in 1471, but such lapses do not seriously detract from the fidelity of his narrative.

The most influential of early histories of Richard was also the least reliable. Sir Thomas More's dramatic sketch, from which Shakespeare's portrait derives, was drawn with such literary power that 'his accusations linger, like inexorable demons, around the figure of the tormented king'. More began writing his 'History' in about 1515 but neither finished nor published it. It was not until 1557 that an authorative transcript was published by More's nephew, William Rastell.

The History of King Richard III begins with the death of Edward IV, and ends six months later before Buckingham's Rebellion. More never intended his book as *history* in the modern sense of the term. It was Rastell, not Sir Thomas, who gave the work its title. Some critics have even reproached More for failing to write like a nineteenth century historian, as if he were somehow to blame for failing to anticipate three hundred years of progress. More's portrait of Richard was intended as a homily, and the truth he sought was poetic not scientific. His 'History' is best understood as a sermon designed to exhibit an archetypal tyrant, to be held up as a mirror in which rulers might see how 'vice had been punished heretofore'.

Almost everything which Machiavelli praises in 'The Prince', More's book condemns. At times he enhances his warnings by adding imaginative touches to his narrative, so eager was he to expose the evils of absolutism. His main purpose in writing was to represent Richard as a 'personified vice', not to provide a faithful portrait of the last of the Plantagenets. His 'History' shares much in common with medieval morality plays, in which fidelity to fact is scarcely relevant. What matters, and what lends such pungency to his assault on the realpolitik of his age, is his 'peculiar loathing of tyranny'. It appears that his book was not only intended as an attack on despotism in general but on the Tudors in particular. In denouncing Richard III he obliquely reproached Henry VIII.

More's sense of humour was such that even his own family were sometimes left wondering whether he spoke in earnest or in jest. It was typical of him to end 'his life with a mock', remarking on the scaffold that a man 'might lose his head and have no harm'. Even his harrowing sermon on 'The Four Last Things' is relieved by light-hearted clowning. 'He thought nothing to be well spoken', wrote his contemporary Edward Hall, 'except he had ministered some mock in the communication'. Throughout his 'History' More pokes fun at scholarly credulity. For example, having solemnly retailed the merest gossip, he proceeds to attribute it to 'wise men' and 'credible' informants, and to draw absurdly confident conclusions from what he admits to be hearsay. There is no surer way to misinterpret More than to overlook his ever present irony and to accept literally what he intended as a joke.

Sir Clements Markham, writing in 1891, dismissed *The History of King Richard III* as a 'discreditable lampoon', whose unrelenting hostility to Richard casts doubt on its credibility. The book's opening sentence is not well calculated to encourage confidence in its accuracy, seeing that it asserts that Edward IV 'lived fifty and three years, seven months, and six days'. In fact, he died aged forty years, eleven months and twelve days. More's celebrated account of the murder of the Princes in the Tower is equally suspect, both because of its inconsistencies and because it reveals too much. It is not in the nature of mysteries to yield their secrets after thirty years of silence.

More's study of Richard III has rightly been seen as a milestone in historical literature. So vividly is it written that it seems to come from the pen of an eye-witness. But even more remarkable is the unity of its theme and its philosophical insight. Parts of the book could hardly be based on surer evidence, such as that of More's patron, the Earl of Surrey, who fought for Richard at Bosworth. Most important of all, the traditions embodied in the 'History' are those derived from the household of Archbishop Morton, whom More served as a page. Cavalier as he often was in handling facts, much of his narrative is substantiated by other authors and documents.

The History of King Richard III has variously been regarded as an authentic record of events, a magnificent tirade against tyranny evoked by Richard's career, and 'a melancholic and uncharitable work', maliciously designed 'to curry favour' with the Tudors. In so far as More's book derives its information from fifteenth century sources, its authority is as exceptional as Vergil's. Besides, as Erasmus said, More possessed one of the finest legal minds of his age, so his ability to sift evidence can scarcely be disputed.

Intractable as are the problems which More's 'History' poses, it cannot be disregarded. Whatever its faults it remains a work of genius. Edward Gibbon, writing for a French periodical, claimed that 'La Magnanimité, la probité, et le grand sens de cet auteur rendent son témoignage assuré'. There are compelling reasons for being more sceptical than Gibbon, but none for burning the wheat as well as the chaff. Edward Hall had sufficient independent information of his own to correct some of More's mistakes, but, nevertheless, thought him reliable enough to plagiarize him wholesale.

Some light is thrown on the reign of Richard III by various London chronicles. These parochial annals were chiefly concerned to record municipal affairs and only noticed national history when played on the London stage. Most of them handled evidence with uncritical innocence, and listed events without any attempt to interpret them. But at least their accounts are more or less contemporary, and come from spectators or those with walking on parts. The most notable example of the genre was published in 1938, under the title *The Great Chronicle of London*. Its author was Robert Fabyan, Master of the Drapers', whose account of events in the Capital in 1483 was written from first-hand knowledge. His description of Edward V's arrival in London in May of that year is drawn with a tailor's 'sharp eye for sartorial splendour'. The chronology of his work is, however, gravely defective, as was common with such histories. Fabyan also wrote *The New Chronicles of England and France* which was published in 1516. Despite the pretensions of its title it adds little to his previous work.

Documentary evidence for Richard's reign is disappointingly uneven. Less than ten letters have been preserved which mention the Usurpation, and details about the proceedings of Parliament are almost as sparse, apart from copies of Acts which still survive. On the other hand, we possess a mass of information about the exercise of crown patronage under Edward V and Richard III. An invaluable Register, catalogued as Harleian Manuscript 433 in the British Library, preserves letters, grants and other documents authorized by the King's personal signet seal. In the nature of things, however, the Harleian Register throws only occasional shafts of light into the darker recesses of Richard's secret intrigues.

It is impossible to provide a coherent account of Richard's reign without first deciding what to believe, doubt, or reject in conflicting traditions, and seeing that history is not an exact science this cannot be done by rule of thumb. Nevertheless, certain precautions can be taken when handling suspect evidence. First, the greatest reliance should be placed on those best qualified to testify, such as witnesses with first-hand knowledge of events. Secondly, independent testimony should be sought for unconfirmed assertions: a technique inevitably restricted by the interdependence of sources. Thirdly, allowance must be made for the distorting effect of malice, partiality, ignorance and deceit, while not forgetting that it is possible to be both prejudiced and right. Fourthly, before evidence is accepted, it must be consistent with all the known facts and inherently credible: a test which eliminates Rous' account of the birth of Richard III. It would be idle to pretend that the present narrative remorselessly follows these precepts, not for want of confidence in the principles outlined, but because it is harder to practise than to preach.

CHAPTER THREE

'The Young Prince'
1 April–28 April 1483

> Rivers: *Madam, bethink you, like a careful*
> *mother, of the young prince your son;*
> *send straight for him; let him be*
> *crowned; in him your comfort lives.*
> Shakespeare *Richard III* ii,2

Some time about Easter, which fell on 30 March in 1483, Edward IV became seriously ill. Precisely what was wrong with him nobody seemed to know. It was generally believed, however, that his insatiable appetite for wine and women had undermined his health. Towards the end of his life he became so grossly overweight that he may well have suffered a stroke. Mancini, who was in London at the time, heard that the King had 'allowed the damp cold to strike his vitals' while he was fishing from a small boat. Winston Churchill suggests that Edward succumbed to appendicitis, thereby providing as plausible a diagnosis as the absence of evidence permits.

When it became clear that the King was dying, it seemed only too likely that civil war would break out once again, but as long as he lived he remained master of the contending factions he had done so much to foster. Since Warwick's defeat in 1471, nobody had dared challenge him, except for his brother, Clarence: the lesson of whose fate was not lost upon those whose instincts for survival had been sharpened by years of strife. But once the crown passed to a boy of twelve, a savage struggle to obtain possession of his person, policy and patronage, was bound to follow. When government depended so much on the personality of the King, the reign of a child was calamitous.

Edward IV was largely to blame for the feuds which

destroyed his dynasty. The favours he showered on his wife's family incensed his own relations, who thought that the proper recipients of royal patronage were princes of the blood. His mother and brothers watched the Woodvilles foraging for grants, titles, and office, with a dismay scarcely diminished by wistful admiration. The Nevilles were so disgusted by the triumph of this family, whose growing power they saw as a challenge to their own, that they were driven to rebel. A considerable number of nobles, apart from those who surrendered to the temptation of marrying Woodvilles, spoke of the Queen's relations as insolent upstarts. Above all, what made them feared and hated was their outrageous success.

Should Edward IV die, and it soon became clear that he was unlikely to recover, the Woodvilles had little to fear in the new reign. For the past ten years Lord Rivers had been the Prince of Wales' Governor, and had presided over his court at Ludlow Castle. As President of the Council of Wales he controlled the Principality and the Marches. If any attempt ensued to take over the government, custody of the Prince was nine-tenths of the law. As if these advantages were not enough, King Edward, in the last months of his life, authorised his brother-in-law to raise troops in the Welsh Marches, the traditional Yorkist recruiting ground, and extended his power to sign warrants on behalf of the young Prince.

On 8 March 1483, Rivers instructed his agent, Andrew Dymmock of the Middle Temple, to consult Lord Dudley 'in all haste' about transferring 'such interest as I have in the Office of the Tower' to 'my Lord Marquis'. Lord Dudley, who retained the post of Constable of the Tower of London until his death at the age of eighty-six, was for many years too infirm to perform the duties of his office: hence effective command was delegated to a series of deputies. No records exist to show the precise nature of the 'interest' which Rivers transferred to Dorset, but by April 1483 the Marquis was in possession of the Tower, its soldiers and cannon, and the King's Treasure deposited therein for safekeeping. The Woodvilles believed that command of this crucial fortress would ensure control of the Capital.

As the moon shines with the borrowed radiance of the sun, so the power and glory of the Woodville family had its sole source in the King. Now that he was dying, their prospects depended on custody of his children. So long as Prince Edward was at Ludlow with his Uncle, and Prince Richard in London with the Queen, no-one could govern in their name. But if ever the boys were wrested from their grasp, the Woodvilles would face oblivion.

England in the fifteenth century put Sicily to shame when it came to blood feuds. The Queen's family was beset by enemies, chief amongst whom was the King's 'beloved servant, William Hastings'. The Queen's dislike of the Lord Chamberlain went back to 1464 when he attempted to drive too hard a bargain with her over a match between their children. Moreover, she blamed him for being a principal 'accomplice and partner' of her husband's 'privy pleasures'. The ferocious and squalid disputes which led Hastings and Dorset to threaten one another with capital charges, and to suborn witnesses to lend conviction to their accusations, were scarcely calculated to win a mother's heart or promote the interests of the Yorkist dynasty.

Struggles at Court for place and power were waged with deadly hostility. When Edward IV replaced Rivers by Hastings as Lieutenant of Calais in July 1471, the great House of Woodville swore by its nine Gods that it 'should suffer wrong no more'. Probably Hastings was the fitter man for the post, but Rivers was so infuriated by losing 'the best preferment in Christendom' that he and his family resolved to destroy the King's trust in the most faithful of his servants. So successful were their intrigues that Hastings spent part of 1477 in the Tower. Five years later he sought revenge by spreading scurrilous stories about Dorset and Rivers.

Nobody stood to lose more from the triumph of the Woodvilles than Richard Duke of Gloucester, whose interests were totally opposed to those of the Queen's family. The success of one faction required the ruin of the other. If the Queen's hopes depended upon the custody of her son, so did those of the Duke. Once the Woodvilles lost control of the Prince of Wales they would probably lose their lives in the bargain. By the same token, if they kept him in their hands, the prospect for their enemies remained bleak. Fear, rather than greed or ambition, was the prevailing mood, alluring as were the prizes for survival.

Richard can hardly be blamed for taking measures to avoid the fate to which his title seemingly condemned him. Two previous Dukes of Gloucester, both uncles of kings, had reputedly been slaughtered. The first, Thomas of Woodstock, was arrested in Calais in 1397 and supposedly poisoned by order of Richard II. The second, Humphrey, Duke of Gloucester, uncle to Henry VI, was arrested in 1447 on charges of treason. Five days later he died. The official version spoke of natural causes, but most people thought that he, too, had been murdered.

If Edward IV was responsible for making the Woodvilles over-mighty, the same may be said of his patronage of Richard. In 1471, after Warwick's attainder, he was given Neville properties in Northumberland, Yorkshire and Cumberland, including the Lordships of Sheriff Hutton and Middleham. In 1478, he was rewarded with a generous share of Clarence's titles and perquisites. In 1482, he was appointed Lieutenant of the North. Finally, in February 1483, he was granted the Wardenship of the Western Marches in perpetuity, and a vast hereditary Palatinate carved out of the border counties. Even Warwick the 'King-Maker' in all his glory had never enjoyed such power. Only when he was dying did Edward recognise too late that his reckless generosity to hostile branches of his family depended on the assumption that he 'himself should be able to rule both parties'.

On Monday, 7 April 1483, the King sent for such Members of his Council as were within easy reach of his Palace at Westminster. Propped up on pillows, he told them that for the sake of his children and the peace of the realm they should set old quarrels aside. It was not enough to profess to love his son if they hated one another. He went on to point out that the boy would need all the support and advice that they could give him. 'If you among yourself in a child's reign fall at debate, many a good man shall perish ere this land find peace again. Wherefore, in these last words that I ever look to speak with you, I exhort you and require you all, for the love that you have ever borne me, from this time forward, all griefs forgotten, each of you love other.' Then the King, 'no longer enduring to sit up, laid him down on his right side, his face toward them, and none was there present that could refrain from weeping.' So moved were they, that 'each forgave other and joined their hands together.' Their reconciliation was reminiscent of the 'Love Day' at St Paul's in 1458, both in the fervour with which the participants claimed to have composed their differences, and in the alacrity with which they demonstrated the insincerity of their professions. Unfortunately, deathbed histrionics were powerless to mitigate the consequences of a decade of ill-conceived policies.

Shortly before he died, Edward IV added some codicils to his will. As these have not survived there are doubts about what they said. His original will, drawn up at Sandwich in 1475, before he set sail for France, left elaborate instructions for completing St George's Chapel, in which he planned a magnificent tomb for himself. One of the 1483 codicils was supposed to have appointed the Duke of Gloucester 'Protector' to Edward V. But Rous, who had no inside knowledge, was the only fifteenth century writer to state positively that Richard was made Protector by 'ordinance' of 'the deceased King'.

When Edward IV's executors met for the first time at Lambeth Palace on 7 May they did not see fit to style Richard as 'Protector' in their minutes. Not until 14 May was he designated: 'Our dearest Uncle Richard Duke of Gloucester Protector of England.' Before that date, the names of Rivers and Dorset were scattered over official documents, in which they were styled 'Uterine Uncle' and 'Uterine Brother' of the King. As late as 18 May, a Bidding Prayer, used at a Convocation of the Clergy, ignored the Duke, but sought the protection of the Almighty for the young King and Elizabeth the Queen Mother.

Even if Edward IV had named Richard as Protector in his

will, he had little right to do so. In 1422, Parliament rejected Humphrey Duke of Gloucester's claim to act as Regent for his nephew, Henry VI, based on 'the last will of the King that was'. Such pretensions, they insisted, were 'neither grounded in precedent nor in the law of the land'. No sovereign was entitled to rule from beyond the grave 'without the assent of the three estates'. In the end, Duke Humphrey climbed down and accepted the lesser role of 'Chief of the King's Council' and 'Protector' of the realm. This precedent clearly established that the right to decide what form the government should take while Edward V was a child was a matter for Parliament and the Council, not the boy's father.

On Wednesday, 9 April, Edward IV died, three weeks before his forty-first birthday, 'sincerely repentant for his sins' and reverently receiving the sacraments of the church. 'Such was the most beseeming end of this worldly prince, a better than which could not be hoped for or conceived, after the manifestation by him of so large a share of the frailties inherent to the lot of Mankind. Hence, too, very strong hopes were afforded to all his faithful servants, that he would not fail to receive the reward of eternal salvation'.

Sir Thomas More tells a story to the effect that on the night Edward IV died, 'one Mistlebrook, long ere morning, came in great haste to the house of one Potter dwelling in Redcross Street without Cripplegate; and when he was with hasty rapping quickly letten in, he showed unto Potter that King Edward was departed. "By my troth, man," quod Potter, "then will my master, the Duke of Gloucester, be King."' More claimed to have learned this story from his father, who lived in Milk Street in the same ward as Potter.

Soon after his death, the King was laid on a board, 'all naked saving he was covered from the navel to the knees'. Mourners came from all over the City to take final leave of their Sovereign: Noblemen, Bishops, Courtiers, the Lord Mayor, and a horde of lesser dignitaries. Lord Howard, who had been sent for by the King only a few days before, arrived just in time to file past his corpse. The crowds came not merely to pay their last respects but to satisfy themselves that 'this noble and

victorious prince', who had so suddenly been 'taken from the
unstable glory of this world', had not been hastened out of it
by some treacherous malpractice. In that turbulent age, the
sudden death of a king in the prime of life was bound to arouse
suspicion, and many people believed that Edward must have
been poisoned.

One of the problems of minority rule is paralysis of government, and the words of Ecclesiastes were much in the minds
of Edward V's subjects: 'Woe to you, O land, when your King
is a child.' It was customary for a Council's mandate to die
with the King from whom its authority derived. Edward IV's
Council should therefore have resigned on 9 April. But as the
new King was too young to choose his advisers, it decided to
stay in office. Had it done otherwise, it is hard to see how the
country could have been governed.

'The Councillors of the King now deceased,' says the
Croyland Chronicler, 'were present with the Queen at Westminster', and decided the date upon which Edward V 'should
repair to London for the ceremonial of his coronation'. Immediately after the meeting, a letter was sent to Ludlow
announcing the accession of the Prince of Wales, and instructing Rivers to bring his nephew to London by the end of the
month. These things were necessarily done without consulting the Duke of Gloucester who was hundreds of miles from
court.

The news from London reached Ludlow on Monday, 14
April. Two days later, no doubt at his Uncle's dictation,
Edward V wrote to the Mayor of Lynn announcing his
impending departure so that he could be 'at our City of
London in all convenient haste by God's grace to be crowned
at Westminster'. The day fixed for his Coronation was 4 May,
the twenty-second anniversary of his father's accession. The
date of the ceremony was of more consequence than may at
first sight appear, for no sooner was the Coronation over than
the Protector's power lapsed. The sole purpose of that office
was to protect the realm until such time as a child King was
crowned. The precedent of Henry VI was once again decisive.
Before he was eight years old, Henry was crowned at West-

minster on 5 November 1429. Ten days later, the Protector, Humphrey, Duke of Gloucester, laid down his office on the 'advice and deliberation' of his Peers, who insisted that the 'Title of Protector and Defender ought to cease' once the King had sworn at his Coronation 'to protect and defend the Church and realm'. On the principle that promises made by godparents on a child's behalf at baptism are discharged at confirmation, so the duties of a protector ceased the moment the Sovereign was crowned and personally accepted the responsibility which had hitherto been exercised in his name.

Protectorates also came to an end when minors achieved their majority. Curiously enough, the precise year in which a King came of age was shrouded in obscurity. Henry VI did so in 1437 when he was sixteen, eight years after Gloucester had laid down his office. When Edward IV set up the Council of Wales in 1471 it was only required to act on his son's behalf until he was fourteen. The capacity of boys in the Middle Ages was more highly esteemed than later became the custom. Anybody who reached adolescence in the fifteenth century had already achieved a third of his probable life-span. At thirteen, Henry VI regularly performed political duties, minuting state papers in his own hand. It would have raised no problems for Edward V to have come of age in November 1484, on his fourteenth birthday. Those who argued that the King should be set aside to avert the evils of a long Minority exaggerated the damage to be expected in a year and nine months.

It has often been claimed that 'the convenient haste' with which Edward V told the Mayor of Lynn he intended to be crowned, provides proof of a Woodville Conspiracy to prevent the Duke of Gloucester securing control of the King. In so far as the Council at the time of the last King's death was dominated by Dorset and the Queen, the proposal – some called it a 'plot' – was clearly inspired by the Woodvilles. But to be fair to a family which has seldom had justice done to it, the Queen Mother was fully entitled to urge Rivers to bring her son to London as fast as he could come. It is not a crime to crown a King. Moreover, despite the 'convenient haste' with which Rivers was supposedly proceeding, his journey, in fact, could hardly have been more leisurely. He even waited ten days before starting so as to celebrate St George's Day at Ludlow. Whatever construction is put on the Queen's conduct, she was under no obligation to surrender control of her son, at imminent risk to herself, to him, and her family.

On 11 April, according to one London Chronicle, Prince Edward, 'then being about the age of twelve years, under the guiding of his uncle by the mother's side, called Lord Marquis Dorset, was proclaimed King by the name of Edward the Fifth.' Dorset, of course, was half-brother not uncle to the King, but the Chronicler may be right in believing he prompted the ceremony. That evening, Lord Howard dined with Hastings and gave the cooks twenty pence for their skill. It is barely conceivable that such artful politicians would have neglected to discuss how best to remove the King from Woodville influence.

When King Edward IV died, Richard was probably at Middleham, a few miles north-west of Ripon. The Castle stands on the southern slope of Wensleydale surrounded by moors and woods. It was begun in the twelfth century and its massive Norman keep has walls twelve feet thick. In 1461 it was the chief northern stronghold of Warwick the 'King-Maker', in whose household Richard learned the arts of chivalry. Here, as a boy, he met Anne Neville, who was brought up by the Countess under the same roof. Here, in 1473, his son Edward was born, and here, eleven years later, the young Prince died. Richard's decision to make Middleham his headquarters when he became Viceroy of the North was largely strategic but partly sentimental. Of all the rewards he was given on the restoration of Edward IV in 1471 it was the jewel of his Crown. Even today enough remains of this majestic fortress to show why it was once regarded as the Windsor of the North.

In 1478, Richard turned the Parish Church of Middleham, built by the Saxons and dedicated to the Blessed Virgin, into a College and Chantry, consisting of a Dean, six chaplains, four clerks and six choristers, charged with offering perpetual masses for the King and Queen, and for the 'good estate of my lady and mother, and of me, my wife and son'. Prayers were also to be said daily for 'the souls of the most illustrious Prince, Richard, formerly Duke of York, our father, and of our brothers and sisters, and of all the faithful departed.' Richard's College of Middleham was perhaps the most magnificent of his many religious foundations.

It is said that the Duke of Gloucester heard the news of his brother's death from Lord Hastings, who sent him 'letters and messengers' because of their 'long-standing friendship'. These advised the Duke 'to hasten to the capital with a strong force' and take 'the young King Edward under his protection and authority'. Even without such prompting, Richard was well aware that it was imperative for him to gain control of his nephews. At the same time, Hastings was probably in touch with the Duchess of York, whose niece, Catherine Neville, was his wife.

Besides replying to Hastings, Richard wrote 'most loving letters to Elizabeth the Queen, comforting her with many words, and promising on his behalf – as the proverb is – seas and mountains'. Among other soothing things he said was that she could rest assured of his 'duty, fealty, and due obedience to his King and Lord, Edward the Fifth'. Richard also wrote to the Council reminding them that he had been loyal to his brother Edward, 'at home and abroad, in peace and war, and would be, if only permitted, equally loyal to his brother's son'. He went on to ask them 'to take his deserts into consideration, when disposing of the government, to which he was entitled by law, and his brother's ordinance'. This letter had such 'a great effect on the minds of the people', that it 'was commonly said by all that the Duke deserved the government'.

While Richard was winning golden opinions from his letters to the Queen and the Council, he was singing another tune behind their backs. Those he regarded as 'ready to be kindled', he set 'afire' by insisting 'that it neither was reason nor in any wise to be suffered that the young King, their master and kinsman, should be in the hands and custody of his mother's kindred'. If Edward was left in their hands, they might without his knowing 'abuse the name of his commandment to any of our undoing'. It would be rash indeed to place reliance upon 'the late made atonement', or to believe that a contract made in an hour, 'should be deeper settled in their stomachs than a long accustomed malice many years rooted'.

Some time about 20 April, Richard attended a Requiem for Edward IV at York Minster, 'the same being accompanied with plenteous tears'. At the end of the service, he required 'all the nobility of those parts to take the oath of fealty to the late King's son.' Vergil remarks of this ceremony: 'himself was the first that took the oath, which soon after he was the first to violate'. Richard, in fact, had taken an earlier oath to his nephew, on 3 July 1471, when, with other Peers, spiritual and temporal, he signed a document in which he acknowledged that 'Edward Prince of Wales, Duke of Cornwall, and Earl of Chester', was the 'first begotten son of our sovereign lord'. On that occasion, he furthermore promised 'that in case hereafter it happen, you by God's disposition to outlive our said sovereign lord, I shall then take and accept you for the true, very, and righteous King of England etc., and faith and truth to you shall bear'. And so also swore the Archbishop of Canterbury and a host of eminent peers and prelates.

It has been argued that Richard would not 'have fettered himself and the nobility of the North with the obligations of an oath to Edward V, if, at that stage of his proceedings, he intended to supplant him as King'. Even in so unfastidious an age, men hesitated to break sacred pledges. In our own time, the oath of allegiance which the German armed forces took to Adolf Hitler, on 2 August 1934, the so-called 'Fahnenheid', long inhibited the Officer Corps from joining the Resistance. There are, of course, other possible explanations of Richard's conduct and motives. It could be that the ambition which later led him 'to wade through slaughter to a throne', was still dormant when he visited York. Alternatively, he may have hoped to court popularity and lull suspicion by ostentatiously displaying his 'natural affection towards his brother's children'.

While Richard was staying at York, he received an offer of support from his distant kinsman, Henry Stafford, Duke of Buckingham. The Duke's father had died in 1458 leaving him in the Wardship of the King. When his grandfather, the first Duke, was killed at the Battle of Northampton in 1460, young Henry succeeded to the title at the age of seven. In 1466, Edward IV arranged the boy's marriage to the Queen's sister Catherine Woodville. Ever after, the Duke resented his forced match to a lady 'he scorned to wed on account of her humble origin'.

Buckingham sent to York 'in the most secret wise he could' his trusted servant Humphrey Percival. At 'dead of night', when the Household was asleep, Percival was secretly brought to Richard and told him that 'in this new world' his Master would wait upon him 'with a thousand good fellows if need were'. After a further exchange of messages, the two Dukes wrote to Ludlow to discover 'on what day and by what route' the King proposed to set out for London. It was their wish, they said, to join him on his journey so that 'in their company his entry to the City might be more magnificent'.

Meanwhile, arrangements were being made in London for the funeral of Edward IV. He lay in state for eight days in St Stephen's Chapel, then the Chapel Royal of the Palace of Westminster, but later to become the meeting place of the House of Commons. The embalmed King, wearing shoes of red leather, wrapped in a white robe, and with the Cap of Maintenance on his head, was watched over night and day by Officers of State and Members of his Household. On Thursday, 17 April, his body was placed on a bier covered in Cloth of Gold and borne to Westminster Abbey, Lord Howard heading the procession carrying Edward's personal banner. A rich canopy of cloth, 'fringed with gold and blue silk', was carried over the corpse. The bier was escorted by the Lord Chancellor, Archbishop Rotherham of York, and a crowd of mourners including the Queen's son, Dorset, her brother, Sir Richard Woodville, Lord Hastings, Lord Stanley, and Sir William Stonor.

Next day the cortège set out for Windsor where the King

was to be buried in the Chapel he had helped to build as a monument to his dynasty. The bier rested overnight at Syon Abbey and set out on Saturday on the final stage of its journey. On the funeral chariot, drawn by six coursers, was a life-size 'similitude' of the late King, 'in habit royal, crowned with the very crown on his head', holding a sceptre in one hand and the orb in the other. The procession stopped at Eton before crossing the Thames and winding its way up the hill to St George's, where building was still in progress. Edward IV, despite his initial hostility to Henry VI's 'College of Our Lady of Eton', eventually looked on it more favourably. Indeed, he became so frequent a visitor that he kept a boat for his use moored by its banks. On this last visit, he was met by John Russell, Bishop of Lincoln, Provost Bost, who only a few weeks before had entertained him at the College, the Fellows in residence, the Head Master, David Haubroke, and the 'poor and needy boys of good character' who made up the body of scholars. As the Chapel bell tolled with forlorn insistence, the College dignitaries censed the corpse of the King who twenty years before had threatened to seize their endowments. That night the coffin rested on a 'marvellous well wrought hearse', placed in the choir of St George's. Amongst those who stood vigil by their late Sovereign were Lord Howard, Sir John Savage, John Cheyney, Master of the Horse, and William Colynbourne, an officer of the Duchess of York's Household.

At the burial service on Sunday, 20 April, masses were celebrated by Rotherham and Russell. After the coffin was lowered into the ground, the King's shield, sword and helmet were placed on his tomb, where they remained until plundered in 1642 by parliamentary troops. The service concluded according to custom with the officers of the late King's Household throwing 'their staves into the grave in token of being men without a master, and out of their offices'. Then the heralds likewise took off their coats of arms and threw them onto the coffin. In the Vestry, Garter King of Arms handed them 'rich embroidered coats', the outward emblems of their new allegiance. As they rejoined the Congregation, they shouted 'Le Roy est Vif! Le Roy est Vif!' If Edward IV's

Household were to regain the offices they had ceremoniously surrendered, it was to the reigning King they now had to turn. It might be supposed that when Norroy and Clarenceux King of Arms became 'Men without a Master', Edward IV's Council would also be disbanded. But because the King's government had to be carried on, and perhaps because power tends to perpetuate itself, the Council clung to office, despite the equivocal nature of its mandate. Between 9 April and 23 April, the late King's Councillors held several discussions, most of them after the funeral at Windsor. In the absence of precise dates for their meetings it seems best to consider the issues debated without regard to chronology. A number of pressing problems faced them in April 1483. How should the country be governed until the King came of age? How large should the escort be which accompanied him to London? Was it proper for the Council to make further decisions before the Duke of Gloucester joined it? Such grave issues demanded calm discussion, but unfortunately Westminster was a cauldron of fear, rumour and suspicion.

Three groups emerged in the Council during these April meetings: those totally committed to the Queen, such as Dorset and Archbishop Rotherham; those who remained uncommitted, like the Archbishop of Canterbury, Cardinal Bourchier, and Russell, Bishop of Lincoln; and those who were wholly opposed to the Woodvilles. Powerful as was this opposition – for which Lord Hastings kept a watching brief – it was under-represented at Westminster during the opening weeks of the reign. In so far as the Clergy had a concerted policy it was to support which ever party seemed likely to prevail. Bishops were primarily political appointments, and only too often their spiritual resources were as meagre as their consciences were agile.

The Council debated two proposals for administering the Kingdom during the royal minority. The first was that 'the Duke of Gloucester should govern because Edward in his will had so directed and because by law the government ought to devolve on him'. The second proposal, which eventually won the day, 'was that the government should be carried on by many persons among whom the Duke, far from being excluded, should be accounted the chief'. This plan commended itself to the Council because 'no regent ever laid down his office, save reluctantly and from compulsion, whence Civil War had often arisen. Moreover, if the entire government were committed to one man he might easily usurp the sovereignty.'

The Council's decision was later represented by Richard and his supporters as a plot to deprive him of his rightful place at Court: a claim with a long history. In 1387, in the reign of Richard II, a group of five 'Lords Appellant', including Thomas, Duke of Gloucester, secured the condemnation of the King's upstart favourites on the ground that they had poisoned his mind against the Royal Family. In 1450, Henry VI was petitioned to 'dismiss from him all the false progeny and affinity of the Duke of Suffolk', and 'to take about his noble person his true blood of his royal realm that is to say, the high and mighty Prince the Duke of York'. Two years later, Richard's father, in his Ludlow Manifesto, complained of his exclusion from the King's inner Council which he blamed on evil advisers. In 1460, Salisbury, Warwick, and the late King, then Earl of March, denounced Henry VI for his refusal to consult them. In 1469, Warwick returned to this theme, showing what mischiefs had ensued when kings 'estranged the great lords of their blood from their secret Council, and were not advised by them'. So when Gloucester's supporters in April 1483 accused the Woodvilles of just such offences, the very familiarity of the charges lent them a certain conviction.

Another matter the Council debated was the size of the escort the King should bring to London. Behind what appeared to be largely a matter of protocol, lurked a struggle for power. If Rivers arrived in London with a sizable army, raised in the Welsh Marches, the Woodvilles would reign supreme: a prospect which the majority of the Council regarded with dismay. What probably proved decisive was Hastings' threat to withdraw to Calais 'with all speed', unless the King set out with a 'moderate escort'. In the end, the

Queen was persuaded to restrict the royal retinue to two thousand men. More says that Richard prevailed upon her to compromise by telling her that too large an escort might lead to Civil War, and would break 'the amity and peace that the King her husband so prudently made between his kin and hers'. He further pointed out that if these things happened she and her family would bear the brunt of the blame: a possibility the Queen was unlikely to dispute. It seems more probable, however, that it was Hastings' ultimatum which led her to agree to limit the Ludlow contingent. The Yorkist rebellion against Henry VI in 1460, and Warwick's rebellion against Edward IV in 1470, had both started from Calais, so the Chamberlain's threat was unmistakably menacing. However great was his provocation, and however much he may have dreaded the prospect of Lord Rivers arriving in London with an army at his back, the fact remains that it was Hastings not the Woodvilles who first threatened to use force.

Some members of the Council suggested that they should postpone further discussion until the Duke of Gloucester joined them. Otherwise, they said, there was a risk that he would 'only accede reluctantly' to decisions reached in his absence, or even might 'upset everything' if he found them unacceptable. But Dorset replied impatiently, 'We are so important, that even without the King's Uncle we can make and enforce these decisions'. In the end, the Council agreed to confirm the proposal that Edward V should be crowned at Westminster on Sunday, 4 May, without consulting Richard.

The King and Rivers celebrated St George's Day, the festival of the Order of the Garter, at Ludlow Castle, on Wednesday 23 April 1483. Edward V had been admitted to the order when he was two, and six years later Rivers became a Knight. The Earl was famed throughout Europe for jousting and chivalry, so he owed his admission to the Order more to his own merit than his sister's prompting. Probably his love of pageantry and ceremonial helps to explain why he waited so long before setting out for London.

When all was at last ready, Edward V, with Lord Rivers, and his tutor, John Alcock, Bishop of Worcester, rode out of the Castle Gate down Broad Street and over Ludford Bridge, where twenty-four years before, his grandfather, the Duke of York, had been routed by Henry VI. The King was followed by a retinue of two thousand soldiers and servants and a long procession of carts, loaded with baggage, provisions, barrels stuffed with armour, and all the impedimenta of a royal household on the move. Instead of taking the direct road to London, through Evesham, Chipping Norton and Oxford, Rivers joined Watling Street a few miles west of Northampton. This detour was undertaken to enable the Duke of Gloucester to accompany the King on the last stage of his journey. Later it was alleged that Lord Rivers had tried to get to London before the Duke to win support in the Capital and crown Edward. But his dilatory departure and circuitous route hardly supports this contention. In fact, to judge from appearances, Rivers went out of his way to meet Richard's wishes.

Sometime after 20 April, the Duke of Gloucester set out on his journey south, accompanied by six hundred well mounted and well armed horsemen, mostly gentlemen of Yorkshire. He lingered at least for a day at Pontefract Castle, his official residence as Steward of the Duchy of Lancaster. On the afternoon of Tuesday, 29 April, Gloucester rode into Northampton, intending to join his nephew, Edward V, his brother-in-law, Lord Rivers, and his distant kinsman, Buckingham.

CHAPTER FOUR

'The Mighty Dukes'

29 April–4 May, 1483

Messenger: *Lord Rivers and Lord Grey*
Are sent to Pomfret, and with them
Sir Thomas Vaughan, prisoners.

Duchess: *Who hath committed them?*

Messenger: *The mighty dukes,*
Gloucester and Buckingham.

Shakespeare *Richard III* II.*4*

When the Duke of Gloucester reached Northampton he learned that the King was eleven miles down the road at Stony Stratford, a small Buckinghamshire town built where Watling Street crosses the Ouse. Since Roman times it had been a posting stage on the London road, and was long renowned for its inns. It is said that King Edward on 29 April lodged at the *Rose and Crown*, the remains of which are now concealed behind a modern frontage on the east side of the High Street. In 1464, his father rode out of the town on May morning to marry Elizabeth Woodville in the neighbouring parish of Grafton. The extravagant travellers' tales inspired by the hospitality of the 'Cock' and 'Bull' at Stony Stratford gave these two inns a place in our language.

Some time on 29 April, the Queen's second son by her first marriage, Richard Grey, joined his half-brother, the King. Seeing that he came from London, he may have been sent by the Queen to urge Rivers to hurry. If so, the King's journey that day from Northampton to Stony Stratford was presumably undertaken in response to her request.

Soon after the Duke of Gloucester arrived in Northampton,

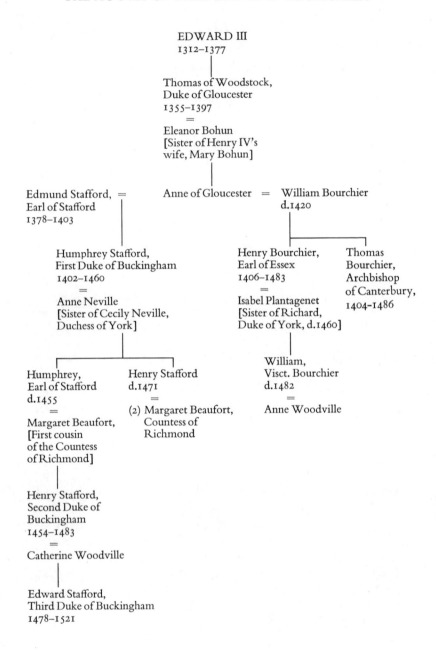

EDWARD III
1312–1377

Thomas of Woodstock,
Duke of Gloucester
1355–1397
=
Eleanor Bohun
[Sister of Henry IV's
wife, Mary Bohun]

Edmund Stafford,   =   Anne of Gloucester   =   William Bourchier
Earl of Stafford   d.1420
1378–1403

Humphrey Stafford,   Henry Bourchier,   Thomas
First Duke of Buckingham   Earl of Essex   Bourchier,
1402–1460   1406–1483   Archbishop
=   =   of Canterbury,
Anne Neville   Isabel Plantagenet   1404–1486
[Sister of Cecily Neville,   [Sister of Richard,
Duchess of York]   Duke of York, d.1460]

                                              William,
Humphrey,   Henry Stafford   Visct. Bourchier
Earl of Stafford   d.1471   d.1482
d.1455   =   =
=   (2) Margaret Beaufort,   Anne Woodville
Margaret Beaufort,   Countess of
[First cousin   Richmond
of the Countess
of Richmond]

Henry Stafford,
Second Duke of
Buckingham
1454–1483
=
Catherine Woodville

Edward Stafford,
Third Duke of Buckingham
1478–1521

Rivers returned to the city to 'submit the conduct of everything' to the Duke's 'will and discretion'. Rivers explained that the King had made his headquarters at Stony Stratford to make room at Northampton for the Duke and his escort. The Earl was received 'with an especially cheerful and joyous countenance', and that evening he and Richard had a convivial supper together. After a time, they were joined by Buckingham, who brought three hundred horsemen with him to Northampton: the city in which his grandfather died fighting for Henry VI. Eventually, they dispersed to their respective lodgings, or so Rivers imagined, for, in fact, the two Dukes, 'with a few of their most privy friends', spent most of the night conspiring together.

The Stafford family, of which Henry of Buckingham was head, owned extensive estates in twenty-two counties, and was especially powerful in Wales and the Midlands. Indeed, it was probably from Brecknock Castle that the Duke wrote offering to help Richard in the first days of the new reign. Few, if any, of his contemporaries could call upon greater military resources. It was said that his grandfather in 1454 ordered two thousand badges displaying the Stafford knot to distribute to his retainers. The founder of the family's fortune, Ralph Stafford, was given an earldom by Edward III in 1351. To support this honourable estate he abducted Margaret Audley, whose inheritance included the Marcher Lordship of Newport in South Wales, the Manor of Thornbury in Gloucestershire, and lands in several counties from Essex to Cornwall. Humphrey Stafford, the sixth Earl, was created Duke of Buckingham in 1444 in return for devoted service to the House of Lancaster. The second Duke was descended twice over from Edward III. His father was a great-grandson of Thomas of Woodstock, Duke of Gloucester. His mother, was a daughter of John of Gaunt's grandson, the second Duke of Beaufort. He was thus related to Edward V, the Duke of Gloucester, and Archbishop Bourchier. The Queen Mother, of course, was his sister-in-law, not that he relished the connection.

Edward IV's death opened new prospects for Buckingham,

whose catalogue of grievances against the King verged on the obsessive. Apart from his marriage to Catherine Woodville, which caused him so much anguish, he resented the patronage Edward IV bestowed on Lord Rivers in Wales, particularly as he saw himself as the natural ruler of a region so much of which he owned. When Edward IV died, the Duke was elated by the prospect that the Woodvilles would be dislodged, and that he might recover his rightful place in governing the Principality.

Of all the injuries of which Buckingham complained, the most galling was the loss of his Bohun Estates. Henry IV's wife was Mary de Bohun the Earl of Hereford's daughter. The Earl left his estates to be divided equally between Mary and her sister, Eleanor, Thomas of Woodstock's wife. So Buckingham, Woodstock's great-great-grandson, inherited Eleanor's share of her father's estates; while Mary's portion remained in Lancastrian hands, passing from Henry IV to his son and grandson. When Henry VI died, Edward seized all his possessions on the ground they were Crown Property. In vain, Buckingham asserted his reversionary right to Mary Bohun's estates, claiming that Henry VI had inherited them in virtue of being her grandson, not because he was king. Plainly Edward V would be as reluctant as his father to disgorge so rich an inheritance. Consequently, Buckingham's best hope of recovering this tantalizing legacy was through the good offices of the Duke of Gloucester.

Buckingham was most unpopular with his contemporaries, and those who knew him best tended to like him least. In many respects he resembled his seventeenth century namesake, George Villiers, Duke of Buckingham, of whom Dryden wrote in *Absalom and Achitophel*:

> Stiff in opinions, always in the wrong,
> Was everything by starts, and nothing long.

The Duke's greatest gift was eloquence, and few could rival the resource with which he found arguments to justify duplicity. But there was little else to commend this vain and wayward young man. His political instincts were chiefly destructive, and he staggered from one expedient to the next as if playing blind man's buff.

No record remains of what Gloucester, Buckingham, and 'their most privy friends' discussed into the early hours of Wednesday, 30 April. Nevertheless, it is possible to deduce what decisions they took from their subsequent actions. Buckingham, or some other confederate, probably brought the latest news from London, perhaps including information about the Queen's plans derived from her sister Catherine. If so, Richard's strategy may only have taken its final shape in the light of what he learned at this midnight conference. The early date fixed for the Coronation, the attempt to bring Edward to London with a considerable army, and his sudden departure for Stony Stratford as if to avoid his Uncle, were bound to provoke suspicion. Yet worse must follow when the King reached Westminster and joined his mother's household, for then the Queen, exercising the royal authority on her son's behalf, could exterminate her rivals. Unless her knavish tricks were confounded her adversaries seemed doomed.

There were three choices of action open to the Dukes. They could acquiesce in a Woodville Regency, presumably at the risk of their lives. They could resort to arms to settle the issue, but in so doing they would render themselves liable to the penalties of Treason. Finally, they could seize the King and govern in his name. Of these possibilities the last seemed the most attractive.

After only two or three hours sleep, the Dukes rose at daybreak and instructed their servants to saddle their horses and prepare for an early start. Meanwhile, guards were set on the road to Stony Stratford with orders to turn back travellers, thus ensuring that news from Northampton would not reach the King. Next, the city gates were locked on Gloucester's orders. When Rivers learned from his servants that he was virtually a prisoner, he boldly sought the Dukes and demanded to know what was happening. It at once became clear that they were more anxious to pick a quarrel than to answer awkward questions, and they vigorously denounced him for trying 'to set distance between the King and them'. No sooner did he begin to excuse himself than they ordered his arrest.

Whatever Rivers' intentions were in sending the King on to Stony Stratford – and the reason he gave for so doing might well be true – it proved a disastrous decision. Had he kept the royal escort together he could never have been disarmed, except possibly by a trick, for the King's forces outnumbered those of Buckingham and Gloucester by more than two to one.

Shortly after Rivers' arrest, the Dukes, accompanied by a 'number of gentlemen of the North, all clad in black', galloped down Watling Street as fast as their horses could carry them to intercept the King at Stony Stratford. They found him about to leap on horseback and continue his journey southwards. Richard greeted his nephew with the respect due to his Sovereign, uncovering his head and kneeling before him. The tone of his conversation, however, was a good deal less gracious. He began by 'expressing profound grief at the death of the King's father' which he attributed to 'companions and servants of his vices' who had 'ruined his health'. Such men, he said, 'should be removed from the King's side' to prevent them playing 'the same old game' with their new Master. He went on to accuse Lord Rivers of 'conspiring his death' by preparing ambushes for him on his journey to London. Fortunately, the confessions of accomplices had betrayed the plot. It was common knowledge, he furthermore claimed, that the Earl and others of his family 'had attempted to deprive him of the office of Regent conferred on him by his brother'. Consequently, for 'the sake of his own security', he had 'decided that these Ministers should be utterly removed.' He would himself discharge the duties of government as 'the King's father had approved'. In so doing, 'he would neglect nothing pertaining to the duty of a loyal subject and diligent protector.' Such measures were forced upon him 'as he knew for certain that there were men in attendance upon the King who had conspired both against his honour and very existence.'

The Dukes, as if to demonstrate the truth of what they said,

 o dūo Oliuer̄ kȳg · hūis ut̄j
a quam · et̄ ẟruia septim ·

Aliqʒ ꝓfessine · ac ilʒtūis Ẽolbaꝛdi
punꝗak̄ sectano · dignissim̄ admi

ꝓmogenū ꝛegī̄ henꝛici sext · et̄ sec
gentem registeno · et̄ huius sacri

issimaꝛum ꝛegum Ẽolbaꝛdi quaꝛ
collegꝰ amotes ā dn̄i 1489 et̄ posteꝛ

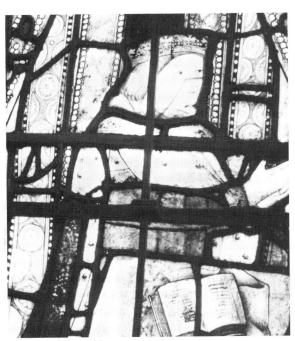

Above: From left to right,
these painted wooden
panels from St George's
Chapel, Windsor,
portray Henry VII, the
uncrowned Edward V,
Edward IV and Henry VI.

Stained glass portrait of
Edward V at Little
Malvern Priory.

Middleham Castle.

Sheriff Hutton Castle.

picked a quarrel with Richard Grey, accusing him and his family of plotting 'to rule the King and the realm' and 'to subdue and destroy' the traditional governing families. More mentions two further charges, made on this or a later occasion. First, that Dorset 'had entered the Tower of London, and thence taken out the King's Treasure'. Second, that Sir Edward Woodville, the Queen's dissolute brother, 'had put to sea in order to overawe the Kingdom'. 'These Dukes wist well', Sir Thomas adds, that both men were acting on instructions from the Council 'issued for good purposes'.

The young King was distressed by his Uncle's accusations against his Mother's family. They had been chosen, he said, by his father, upon whose prudence he relied, and experience had confirmed that they were 'good and faithful'. He 'had seen nothing evil in them' and wished to retain them, unless they were proved guilty. As for the manner in which the Kingdom should be governed, 'he had complete confidence' in the Queen and the Council. This proved too much for Buckingham who told the King that 'it was not the business of women but of men to govern'. Consequently, he would be well advised to relinquish his faith in his mother, and 'place his hope in his barons who excelled in nobility and power'. The King remained unconvinced, and professed himself ready to answer for the innocence of Lord Rivers and Grey, to which Buckingham replied that they had kept their dealings from his knowledge and that the charges against them were true. Eventually, Edward, 'perceiving their intention', surrendered himself to the care of the Duke of Gloucester. But he only did so because he recognized that the Dukes 'were demanding rather than supplicating'. For all their show of reverence he was as much their prisoner as was Lord Rivers.

Almost at once Richard's words were translated into deeds and several arrests were made in the King's presence, including those of Sir Thomas Vaughan and Grey. Sir Thomas was related to the Queen, and through her influence became her son's Chamberlain. In this role he played an important part in managing the Prince's Ludlow household. Amongst others arrested at Stony Stratford were Bishop Alcock and Sir Richard Haute. Alcock was greatly interested in the New Learning, and founded Jesus College at Cambridge. In 1473 he was appointed President of the Council of Wales, and in 1476 Bishop of Worcester. He was not imprisoned for long, as later in May he attended a meeting of Edward IV's executors. In 1485 he temporarily became Lord Chancellor, and a few years later was made tutor to Henry VII's son, Prince Arthur. The King's Treasurer, Sir Richard Haute, had Woodville blood on his mother's side of the family.

Before returning to Northampton, Gloucester issued a Proclamation ordering the King's escort to withdraw instantly 'and not approach any place to which the King might chance to come, under penalty of death'. It has been suggested that the royal forces would never have dispersed unless they had recognized Richard as Protector. As 'picked men', they 'can scarcely be imagined so pusillanimous as to have tamely abandoned their trust, if unlawful violence has been exercised against their royal charge'. On the other hand, Edward's troops were leaderless once Rivers was arrested. They were ordered to disband on pain of death, and were divided between two towns eleven miles apart. But, above all, they were duped. 'The Great Chronicle' says that Gloucester and Buckingham discharged the King's company under 'a dissimulated countenance', and Mancini tells us that 'the Welsh could not bear to think that owing to their stupidity their Prince had been carried off.'

The Duke of Gloucester may have convinced himself that his nephew was party to the 'conspiracy' of which he conceived himself to be the victim: thus ignoring the fact that the law of the land is administered in the King's name, and that policies can have no higher sanction than his assent. But setting aside the possibility that Edward connived at a scheme to delegate royal power to his mother's family, he left no one in any doubt that he deeply resented all that the Dukes had said and done since their meeting at Stony Stratford. In an effort to break his will, the Dukes dismissed his personal attendants, many of whom were old and trusted servants, and replaced them with men of their own. 'At which dealing he wept an was nothing content, but it booted not.'

The events of 30 April shattered the Queen's prospects. That morning her supremacy seemed assured. Dorset was in possession of the Tower and the late King's Treasure. Sir Edward commanded a fine fleet with which he could dominate London and the Channel coast. The Council had shown itself gratifyingly amenable to almost all her suggestions. Lord Rivers, the King's Governor, was expected shortly in London with two thousand troops. In four days time, her son would be crowned, thus finally disposing of Richard's claim to act as his Protector. Then suddenly, out of a cloudless sky, a storm gathered threatening death and destruction. Well might Lord Rivers have said in the words of Madame de Pompadour, 'Après nous le déluge'.

There has been some dispute over how long the news from Stony Stratford took to reach London. Presumably, both the Dukes and the Queen's friends would have despatched messengers to their associates at Westminster. The total distance they had to cover was fifty-two miles, following Watling Street through St Albans and Barnet. In the conditions of the late Middle Ages a horseman would expect to travel at least thirty-five miles a day if he saw no reason to hurry. Indeed, in the sixteenth century, Mary Queen of Scots rode twice that distance merely to see Bothwell, and in 1471 Edward IV marched his entire army that far to surprise Queen Margaret at Tewkesbury. In exceptional circumstances, such as the seizure of a King by his Uncle, greater feats were possible. In June, 1483, Sir Richard Ratcliffe took urgent orders from London to York, nearly two hundred miles apart, in just over four days: a journey the highwayman John Nevison was said to have undertaken in fifteen hours. Even more incredible were the claims made for Sir Robert Carey, an eager place-hunter, who was reputed in 1603 to have ridden from Greenwich to Edinburgh, a distance of three hundred and eighty-two miles, in under three days. Just as James VI was retiring for the night, Sir Robert stumbled into the royal presence, 'beblooded with great falls and bruises', to announce Queen Elizabeth's death.

In the light of such exploits it seems reasonable to suggest that messages from Stony Stratford reached London well before midnight on 30 April.

When the news of Richard's Coup spread through London people were 'wonderously amazed' by 'so outrageous and horrible' a deed, and no one was more dismayed, or had more to fear, than the Queen Mother, who now realized too late the mistake she had made in allowing herself to be dissuaded from 'the gathering of power about the King.' Had she insisted upon his coming to London with a larger escort, he could not have been captured, nor would her brother Anthony and her son Richard have been arrested, 'and sent no man wist whither, and to be done with God wot what'.

Late that Wednesday night and early the next morning, Dorset tried to raise troops to set the young King free. It soon became clear his appeals for help were meeting with scant success. Some were irresolute, others hostile, and many 'even said openly that it was more just and profitable that the youthful Sovereign should be with his paternal Uncle than with his maternal Uncles and uterine Brothers'. This flurry of military activity was not confined to the Marquis. Throughout the morning of 1 May, the adherents of both parties collected forces, some at Westminster 'in the Queen's name', and others elsewhere in London 'under the shadow of the Lord Hastings'. No fighting broke out, but there was 'great commotion and murmur', particularly in the City, which was as sensitive then as it is now to the faintest whisper of rumour.

The Queen, contrasting Richard's most loving letters with his seizure of her son, concluded she could not trust him, and fled to the Sanctuary of Westminster, taking with her the Duke of York, her daughters, and her brother the Bishop of Salisbury. The arrival of this party at midnight, with enough baggage to swamp a palace, must have challenged the resources if not the charity, of the Abbot, who suddenly found himself host to the Royal Family. The Queen knew his lodgings well as the King had been born there in 1470. By a strange chance she sought the protection of the Church on the very day nineteen years before that Edward IV had made her his wife and the Kingdom seemed at her feet. While she sat disconsolately on a pile of rushes, all around there was 'rumble, haste and business'. Servants with chests, coffers, and bundles on their backs, flew hither and thither, 'some going, some discharging, some coming for more', some breaking down walls to shorten their journey, and some, pretending to assist, helping themselves to the Queen's belongings.

According to More, Hastings received news of the Coup from a messenger sent by the Duke of Gloucester from Stony Stratford. In the light of this information, he addressed a gathering of 'Lords assembled together in London' in an effort to calm their fears. 'No man doubted or needed to doubt' Hastings' loyalty to King Edward. The steadfast devotion of his family to the House of York has been proved over four generations. So when he assured his fellow peers that Richard was 'fastly faithful to his Prince', and that Rivers had only been arrested to protect the Dukes, they were 'somewhat appeased'. Hastings promised the lords that those arrested would be impartially judged, and begged them not to resort to arms, pointing out that right would 'be on that side where the King is himself': which was precisely why the Dukes had seized him. It is possible that Hastings was only partly persuaded of the truth of what he was saying, but, nevertheless, he rejoiced in the fact that the transfer of power had been bloodless.

Almost the first use Richard made of the royal authority was to dismiss the Lord Chancellor, Thomas Rotherham, Archbishop of York, one of the late King's closest advisers. Because the Queen had helped to advance his career he was known to champion her interests. But a graver offence in Richard's eyes was the knowledge that the Archbishop 'would be faithful to Edward's heirs come what might'. More further alleges that Rotherham visited the Queen in Sanctuary early on 1 May and gave her the Great Seal. If this was indeed so, he clearly invited dismissal.

Some time on Friday, 2 May, Richard received news of London's reaction to his Coup, presumably from Lord Hastings. He was sufficiently encouraged by what he heard to set out for the City next day. Before leaving Northampton, he wrote to the Lord Mayor, Sir Edmund Shaa, announcing his intention to bring the King to London that very Sunday: the day previously planned for the Coronation. In the course of his letter, he attempted to allay 'a sinister rumour' current in the Capital, that he 'had brought his nephew not under his care, but into his power, so as to gain for himself the Crown.' He assured the Mayor that 'He had not confined his nephew the King of England, rather had he rescued him and the realm from perdition, since the young man would have fallen into the hands of those who, since they had not spared either the honour or life of the father, could not be expected to have more regard for the youthfulness of the son. The need had been necessary for his own safety and to provide for that of the king and kingdom. No one save only him had such solicitude for the welfare of King Edward and the preservation of the state. At an early date he and the boy would come to the City so that the Coronation and all that pertained to the solemnity might be more splendidly performed'. This letter was read aloud 'in the Council Chamber and to the populace', with the result that 'all praised the Duke of Gloucester for his dutifulness towards his nephews and for his intention to punish their enemies'. Nevertheless, those who recognised Richard's 'ambition and deceit, always suspected whither his enterprises would lead' and discerned that he sought 'to procure the goodwill of the people: hoping that, if by their support he could be proclaimed the only ruler, he might subsequently possess himself of the Sovereignty'.

Before starting out for London, Richard despatched his prisoners to Yorkshire. Grey was sent to Middleham, Sir Thomas Vaughan to Pontefract, and Rivers to Sheriff Hutton, a former Neville stronghold some ten miles north of York, which Richard acquired after Warwick's defeat at Barnet. It soon became his favourite northern residence, apart from Middleham. The Castle stood on a steep hill, defended by a double moat and surrounded by woods. Today, the gaunt remains of its corner towers are stark reminders of its former glory. Over the entrance gate may still be seen Richard's arms marshalled with those of Anne Neville.

The King, accompanied by the Dukes of Gloucester and Buckingham, set out from Northampton on Saturday, 3 May, and spent the night at St Albans. A scrap of parchment is preserved in the British Museum which appears to date from this visit. Across the top is written in bold, gothic style 'Edwardus Quintus'. Some way below is Richard's motto 'Loyaulté me lie' (Loyalty binds me) signed 'Richard Gloucestre', in a fine, italic hand. At the foot of the page is scrawled 'Souvente me souvene (Think of me often) Harre Bokynham'. Next morning, the King and the Dukes rode through Barnet to London accompanied by five hundred troops. They were met at Harringay by the Lord Mayor, the Aldermen robed in scarlet, and a large number of citizens wearing violet. The King was dressed in blue velvet but his Uncle preferred black. From Harringay, Edward was escorted to the City down Cheapside to St Paul's. As they rode through the crowds, the Duke of Gloucester made such a show of reverent humility to his Sovereign that many who previously suspected his designs became convinced of his loyalty. Again and again he pointed to his nephew proclaiming: 'Behold, your Prince and Sovereign Lord!' Howard hired a room near the Cathedral from which to watch the King's procession and toast his health in Malmsey.

That night that King lodged in the Bishop of London's Palace on the north-west side of old St Paul's where the present Chapter House stands. The building was connected to the Cathedral by a private door, and the coal house underneath it was used as a prison. The Palace was destroyed in the Civil War, and pulled down shortly after in 1650. For many centuries Kings had commandeered it when they stayed in the City: the Bishop retiring to Fulham to make room for his Sovereign. Henry VI regularly lodged there. When Henry VII reached London, fresh from his victory at Bosworth, he spent that night in the Palace at St Paul's, and Catherine of Aragon slept there on the eve of her wedding to Prince Arthur.

Richard did not remain under the same roof as his nephew

although he was only a short walk away. In 1476, he acquired the lease of a house in Bishopsgate, and it was there he held court in May, 1483. Originally, it had been built for Sir John Crosby, a prosperous wool merchant, who in 1471 was knighted by Edward IV for his part in resisting the Bastard of Fauconberg. Crosby leased the land from the Convent of St Helen's and began building in 1466. Crosby only just lived long enough to see his house, the tallest in London, completed. It was built round a courtyard, like an Oxford or Cambridge College. On the north side was the Great Hall, lit by an oriel window and roofed with an ornate scissor beam ceiling. Opposite was the Chapel. One side of the Quadrangle consisted of a high wall with an entrance into Bishopsgate. The whole design was exceedingly imposing and provided for gardens and outbuildings. However, it was a good deal too magnificent for Sir John's widow, who let it to Prince Richard. In the next century, it was leased to Sir Thomas More who seems not to have lived there himself, preferring the salubrious air of Chelsea. After the Dissolution of the Monasteries the Crown became ground landlord. Crosby's Place escaped the Great Fire of 1666 but was burned down soon after. The Great Hall, however, survived, and was subsequently put to a variety of uses. The East India Office temporarily took it over, Elizabeth Fry held a sale there to raise money for prisoners, and Mr Gladstone stored his finest claret in the chimney space. In 1908 it was carefully dismantled and rebuilt on its present site at the intersection of Cheyne Walk and Danvers Street: once part of Sir Thomas More's garden.

No sooner was Edward V installed in the Bishop's Palace, than the Duke compelled the Lords spiritual and temporal, and the Mayor and Aldermen of the City of London, to take an oath of fealty to the King. 'This, as being a most encouraging presage of future prosperity, was done by all with the greatest pleasure and delight'. It has been argued that the ceremony, like that held earlier at York, proves that Gloucester had no designs on the Throne. But the pleasure with which the oath was taken suggests an alternative explanation of Richard's motive for requiring it: his desire to lull people into the false belief that he wished his nephew to reign.

Richard knew how vital it was to persuade as many people as possible of the depravity of the Woodvilles in order to represent his own dubious actions as necessary counter-measures. For this reason, he sought 'at every turn to arouse hatred against the Queen and to estrange public opinion against her relations'. On their journey to St Paul's, the Dukes sent ahead four wagons loaded with weapons bearing the devices of the Queen's brothers and sons. According to More, this display of Woodville arms was intended as spurious proof of a plot to murder Gloucester and Buckingham. Heralds informed the crowds lining the streets: 'Lo, here be the barrels of harness that these traitors had privily conveyed in their carriage to destroy the noble lords withall'. But, as More remarks, it was 'no marvel' that arms should be found in the baggage from Ludlow, which 'must needs either be brought away or cast away'. It is true that 'much of the common people' were successfully duped, and said that the 'conspira-tors' deserved to be hanged. But it did not escape notice that if the Woodvilles had really plotted an ambush, they would rather have had their armour on their backs than packed up in barrels.

Mancini gives a different version of the story, for he under-stood the heralds to say that the arms had been gathered by the Duke's enemies and 'stored at convenient spots outside the capital, so as to attack and slay the Duke of Gloucester coming from the country'. It was common knowledge, however, that the weapons had been collected at the end of the late King's reign for use in the war against Scotland. In so far as Richard's charges were seen to be false, they 'exceedingly augmented' distrust of his designs.

Before reaching a verdict on Richard's conduct in the first month of his nephew's reign, we must first decide whether the Coup of 30 April was an appropriate response to a genuine conspiracy, or whether the so-called 'Woodville plot' was invented to justify the seizure of the King. Obviously the Dukes were entitled to act as they did if they really believed there were plans afoot to murder them, and they certainly found a rich crop of reasons to show that the Woodville threat was real. It was argued that the early date fixed for the Coronation was designed to terminate Gloucester's authority, as, indeed, it probably was. It was claimed that the plan to bring Edward V to London with a formidable military force was an obvious attempt to overawe the Capital. It was further-more said that the Queen and her kin were eager to deprive Richard of the Protectorate, 'to rule the King', and 'subdue the noble blood of the realm'. Most serious of all, Rivers and his associates had prepared ambushes on the road to London to murder Gloucester and Buckingham. This dastardly scheme was supposedly betrayed by accomplices, but Richard proved strangely coy to submit these vital witnesses to the rigours of Court proceedings. It cannot be utterly fanciful to detect a hint of malicious humour in Richard's accusations. At the very moment he charged the Woodvilles with conspiring to over-throw him, he was himself in the process of plotting their destruction. Such effrontery might seem amusing were it not for its deadly intent.

There can be no doubt that the Woodvilles feared Richard and tried to oppose him, but that does not necessarily mean they plotted to seize or kill him. The evidence Richard pro-duced to prove their guilt would not have hung a dog. The balance of probability favours the contemporary view that his accusations were designed to distract attention from his own intrigues. When the pot calls the kettle black it has probably caught sight of its reflection in a looking-glass. The Croyland Continuator believed that Rivers, Vaughan and Grey were innocent. More said that their fault was 'only that they were good men, too true to the King'. Mancini saw their arrest as proceeding from Richard's resolve to rid himself of every 'source of danger'. Vergil maintained their true offence was to thwart the Duke's ambition, and Rous insisted they never so much as contemplated the crime with which they were falsely charged.

Soon after Edward's arrival in London, the Council met at the Bishop's Palace, and Richard urged them in vain to prosecute Rivers for treason. The majority refused to be persuaded that there was any case to answer, and very properly observed that treason involved offences against the King of which the Earl was innocent. Because Richard finally seized the Crown, it is tempting to see his entire career as directed towards that end. Nevertheless, in April 1483 he had done nothing more than seek his own safety in a swift pre-emptive bid. But, for all that, the majority of his early historians believed that he plotted to seize the Throne the moment his brother died. Shakespeare traces the source of his ambition back to 1460, when Richard was only eight. On 'A Plain before Sandal Castle', the young Prince tells his father:

> How sweet a thing it is to wear a crown;
> Within whose circuit is Elysium,
> And all that poets feign of bliss and joy.

Four years later, the precocious youth dreams of sovereignty for himself, 'like one who stands upon a promontory, and spies a far off shore where he would tread.' Apart from the eccentricity of his chronology, Shakespeare followed the best authorities in portraying Richard's bid for power as long premeditated. It would be wrong, however, to suppose that it was only in retrospect that Richard was thought to covet the Crown the moment his brother died. Mancini, for instance, mentions a rumour current in London, sometime early in May, that the Duke of Gloucester intended to make himself King. It cannot therefore be wholly unreasonable to assume that the course he finally chose attracted him from the first.

CHAPTER FIVE

'King's Games'

5 May – 13 June 1483

And so they said that these matters be Kings'
games, as it were, stage plays, and for the
most past played upon scaffolds. And they
that wise be would meddle no farther.

Sir T. More *History of King Richard III*

Richard's seizure of Edward V created as many problems as it
solved. If the precedent of 1422 was followed, Richard could
only expect restricted powers, much as he would have preferred
full royal authority. To add to his problems, Sir Edward
Woodville had put to sea in command of a powerful fleet, the
Council's support could never be taken for granted, and he
could not but dread the approach of the Coronation. Under
these circumstances, he could depose the King, if need be by
Civil War; he could try to extend the Protectorate; or he could
seek to have the Coronation postponed. For some weeks he
seems to have kept each of these options open.

During the first fortnight of May, the Council met almost
daily at the Bishop's Palace to discuss such matters as the
Protectorate, Rotherham's successor as Lord Chancellor, the
new date for the Coronation, when Parliament should meet,
where the King should reside, and whether to try Lord Rivers
for treason. Now that the Woodvilles were in disarray, the
Council began to re-group around former loyal servants of the
late King, Gloucester's personal adherents, and those who
tended to trim their sails to whatever breeze prevailed. Edward IV's followers numbered among them Hastings, Stanley, Rotherham and Morton. The most prominent of
Gloucester's supporters were Buckingham, Northumberland, Howard and Lovell. The 'Trimmers' were led by

Archbishop Bourchier and Bishop Russell of Lincoln. At least for a time these groups agreed on most issues and such loyalties as divided them were not apparent.

The Council's first task was to settle how the country should be governed during what remained of the King's Minority. Mancini describes the Duke of Gloucester as seizing the initiative. 'Having entered the City the first thing he saw to was to have himself proclaimed, by authority of the Council and all the Lords, Protector or Regent of the King and realm.' The powers which the Council agreed to confer on him were precisely those bestowed on Duke Humphrey in 1422. Since this precedent greatly enhanced their authority, they naturally found it attractive. Besides, experience had taught them how rash it could be to commit the government to one man who might use his power to 'usurp the sovereignty'.

The earliest existing documents describing Richard as 'Protector' are Commissions of the Peace, dated 14 May 1483. When some days later Edward V sent a letter to the Master of King's Hall, Cambridge, requiring him to offer Hugh Fraunce the next vacant Fellowship, he did so 'by thadvise of oure derrest Oncle the duc of Gloucestre protector and defensor of this oure Royaume during oure yong Age'. Sir Thomas More was greatly intrigued by the incongruity of applying the term 'Protector' to a prince who supposedly murdered the nephews entrusted to his care. A favourite image of early writers was that of lambs entrusted to a wolf.

On 10 May, the Council appointed John Russell, Bishop of Lincoln, to succeed Rotherham as Lord Chancellor. He was partly chosen because he was known to be uncommitted to faction. In no sense can he be regarded as one of Gloucester's partisans. On the contrary, it was said that he accepted office 'much against his will'. Prebendary Simon Stallworth, who was on the Bishop's staff, told Sir William Stonor that the Lord Chancellor had 'much business and more than he is content withal'. By virtue of his Office, the Lord Chancellor was a foremost Member of the Council, Chief of the King's Secretariat, and next in precedence after the Royal Family to the two Archbishops. But in spite of his high position, Russell was something of an outsider in Richard's government: disqualified, no doubt, by his probity.

Russell was educated at Winchester and New College, became Keeper of the Privy Seal in 1474, Bishop of Lincoln in 1480, and Chancellor of the University of Oxford in 1483. One of Caxton's earliest printed works was a speech he made in 1470 when he presented the Garter on Edward's behalf to Charles the Bold of Burgundy. He died in 1490 and was buried in Lincoln Cathedral. More describes him as 'a wise man and a good and of much experience and one of the best learned men undoubtedly that England had in his time'. That Russell alone of all Richard's officials received such unstinted praise from Sir Thomas suggests he was not the Protector's most fervent admirer.

The Council showed some indecision in fixing a new date for the Coronation. At first they appear to have chosen Tuesday, 24 June, the Feast of the Nativity of St John the Baptist, but then to have changed to 22 June, perhaps because Edward IV had been crowned on a Sunday. On 5 June, some fifty letters were sent out ordering various gentlemen to assemble at the Tower of London on 18 June 'to receive the noble order of Knighthood at our Coronation, which, by God's grace, we intend shall be solemnized the twenty second day of this present month at our Palace of Westminster'. It appears from the accounts of Piers Curteys, Keeper of the Great Wardrobe, that Coronation robes were made for Edward V, including a 'short gown, made of two yards and three quarters of crimson cloth of gold', lined with black velvet; 'a long gown, made of six yards of crimson cloth of gold, lined with six yards of green damask; a doublet and a stomacher, made of two yards of black satin etc; besides two footcloths, a bonnet of purple velvet'; and 'gilt spurs, with many other rich articles and magnificent apparel for his henchmen and pages'.

Custom required that the Council's arrangements to govern the realm during Edward V's Minority should be sanctioned by Parliament, and it was consequently decided to hold one on 25 June after the Coronation. A Writ of Summons, dated 13 May, decreed that a Parliament should be held at Westminster on Wednesday 25 June, 1483, to discuss 'certain arduous and urgent business, concerning the state and defence of this kingdom of England and the English Church'. Lord Howard received his Writ on 17 May and paid three shillings and four pence to the man that brought it.

The Bishop of London's Palace had only been intended as a temporary residence for the King. The need consequently arose to find somewhere more suited to his needs. The Palace of Westminster was considered, as was the Hospital of St John, the English Headquarters of the Knights of St John of Jerusalem, on the west side of Smithfield. 'But the Duke of Buckingham suggested the Tower of London; which was at last agreed to by all, even those who had been originally opposed thereto'. This decision was reached about 10 May and acted upon soon after, as is shown by a grant given 'at our Tower of London on the nineteenth day of May in the first year of Edward V'.

In the Middle Ages the Tower of London served as a fortress, prison, and palace, not to mention zoo. It was also the home of the Treasury, the Mint, and the Crown Jewels. The royal residence was on the south side of the White Tower, facing the river. Charles II was the last King to make use of it before it was finally pulled down. According to custom, Kings lodged in the royal apartments before setting out to Westminster to be crowned. In 1483 the Tower had not achieved the ominous reputation it soon acquired, in spite of the recent murders of Henry VI and the Duke of Clarence. It is inconceivable that the Council would have consented to Buckingham's proposal if it had seemed in any way sinister.

The Council remained obdurate over the trial of Lord Rivers and his associates. Gloucester hoped to charge them with treason but met with strong resistance. Several Councillors were sufficiently chivalrous to feel some sympathy for the Queen and her relations. The Croyland Chronicler, who was no doubt one of them, mentions the concern felt over 'the detention of the King's relations and servants in prison; besides the fact that the Protector did not, with a sufficient degree of considerateness, take measures for the preservation of the dignity and safety of the Queen'. Considering how unpopular the Woodvilles were, this regard for their welfare suggests a dawning awareness that the Duke of Gloucester was every bit as ambitious as those he had dispossessed, and a good deal more powerful. The Councillors who opposed the condemnation of the prisoners advanced cogent arguments to establish their innocence, pointing out that Edward III's Statute of Treason of 1352 restricted the crime to compassing the death of the King, Queen, or Prince of Wales. Of such heinous offences Lord Rivers was not guilty. In so saying, the Council showed its respect for the law and its willingness to thwart Richard.

Some of the earliest grants of the Protectorate distributed lands and offices belonging to the Woodvilles. On what legal grounds they were forfeited it is impossible to say. No member of the family had been tried in a Court of Law, indeed the Council had cleared them of accusations of treason. Nevertheless, Rivers' Manor of Woodham Martin was handed to Robert Bell, and his office of Chief Butler was given to Lord Lovell. Alfred Cornburgh received Sir Thomas Vaughan's post as Controller of the Coinage of Tin in Devon and Cornwall, and two estates belonging to Dorset were handed over to Sir Richard Huddleston. Gratifying as it might be to watch the Woodvilles suffer, such arbitrary confiscations set a disturbing precedent.

Nobody questioned Richard's right as Protector to exercise royal patronage. The greatest beneficiary of his bounty was the Duke of Buckingham, of whom it might justly be said: 'Unto everyone that hath shall be given'. Whether the magnitude of his reward was the measure of his avarice, or of Richard's opinion of his loyalty, the authority bestowed upon him by a series of grants in May 1483 was virtually without precedent. He was appointed Chief Justice and Chamberlain of North and South Wales for the rest of his life, besides being made Constable and Steward of some fifty Castles and Lordships in the Principality and Marches. In addition to such vice-regal powers, he was given extensive authority in Dorset, Somerset, Wiltshire, Shropshire and Hereford, including the right to muster troops. These things were done as the grant expressed it: 'considering the faithfulness, energy and circumspection of our well-beloved kinsman'. Northumberland, Howard and Catesby enjoyed less lavish patronage, and Hastings was merely confirmed as Lord Chamberlain and Master of the Mint, but was not otherwise rewarded.

The last weeks of May and the first fortnight of June were troubled and confused, and rival groups met secretly and separately, committing hardly anything to paper. There was little authoritative news but rumour abounded. Like those who lived through these bewildering times, historians are obliged to resort to sheer guesswork.

It is clear that during this period Richard must often have contemplated the policy he finally adopted: to depose his nephew and make himself King. But he also considered, or affected to consider, an alternative plan. Some time between 13 May when writs were issued to summon Parliament, and 17 June when they were rescinded, the Lord Chancellor, Bishop Russell, drafted a speech to be delivered at its opening on 25 June. Its theme was the need to continue the Protectorate until Edward V came of age. The Chancellor's so called 'sermon' was the medieval equivalent of the modern 'Speech from the Throne' in which government policy is outlined. The main purpose of summoning Parliament, he wrote, was to confirm the Protector's authority 'till ripeness of years and personal rule be concurrent together'. But until that time, 'the power and authority of my lord protector is so behoveful and of reason to be assented to and established by the authority of this high court, that among all the causes of the assembling of Parliament in this time of year, this is the greatest and most necessary first to be affirmed'. Russell's draft ended with a dramatic flourish in which he imagined the young King addressing Gloucester in these improbable terms: 'Uncle, I am glad to have you confirmed in this place, you to be my protector in all my business. Ita fiat, amen'. It would seem, therefore, that the Chancellor, acting on Richard's instructions, proposed to extend the Protectorate beyond its customary lifespan.

Russell's address was to be delivered three days after the Coronation, yet not one word does it say about Edward being crowned. As the Protector's authority ordinarily ceased the moment the service was concluded, the omission is remarkable. One explanation of this oversight could be that the Bishop prepared his 'sermon' in the certain knowledge that the ceremony would never take place. The draft contains a further hint that he worked on this assumption as it includes an apology for summoning Parliament in June. In fact, had the King just been crowned, there could hardly have been a better moment to meet.

In the last months of Edward IV's life it appeared probable that war would break out with France. It seemed even more likely after his sudden death that Louis XI would exploit the confusion caused by Edward V's Minority to attack Calais and English ships in the Channel. By the end of April, the French had 'made the seas unsafe' and had even landed on the south coast and carried off such booty as they could find. These raids were attributed to Philippe de Crèvecouer Sire d'Esquerdes, or, as the English preferred to call him, Lord Cordes. This gallant and enterprising officer was above all a patriot who wanted to see France supreme in Europe, and 'so sore longed for Calais that he would commonly say that he would gladly lie seven years in hell, so that Calais were in possession of the Frenchmen'. Towards the end of April, before Richard reached London, the Council ordered Sir Edward Woodville to meet the French challenge.

The Protector could never feel secure while Sir Edward remained at sea with a powerful fleet, and, as it was commonly believed, part of the late King's Treasure. With the Queen in Sanctuary at Westminster, and Rivers a prisoner at Sheriff Hutton, Woodville hopes depended on the Navy. Fauconberg's exploits in 1471 showed how dangerous such a force could be. During the second week of May, the Protector, 'with the authority of the Council', published a proclamation denouncing Sir Edward Woodville 'as an enemy to the State if he did not disband his fleet'. A period of grace was appointed to allow masters of ships, officers, soldiers and crew to desert, after which time they would be treated as outlaws and their property confiscated. Tempting rewards were offered to anyone 'taking Edward alive or dead'. On 10 May, Sir Thomas Fulford and John Hallwell were ordered 'to rig them to sea in all haste and to go to the Downs among Sir Edward and his company'. Presumably they were supposed to persuade the Navy to mutiny and to offer deserters pardons. On 14 May, further orders were issued to Edward Brampton 'to go to sea with ships to take Sir Edward'. He too was authorized to offer pardons, except to a few named ringleaders. Brampton was well chosen for the task. He began life as a Jew but became a Christian, calling himself Edward after his godfather, the late King. In 1471 he fought at Barnet and Tewkesbury, and two years later was sent to join the siege of St Michael's Mount, which the Earl of Oxford had captured. Oxford's garrison was suborned with fair promises, and, despite having 'victuals enough till mid-summer', was forced to surrender in February 1474. Brampton could therefore boast previous experience in seducing men from their loyalties.

Two of the most formidable ships under Sir Edward's command were on loan from Genoese merchants trading in London. When their Captains learned of the Council's Proclamation, they resolved to return to port for fear that they would otherwise risk 'losing their wares and imperilling their countrymen'. These two vessels were manned by Genoese sailors, among whom Sir Edward had put a 'sprinkling of picked English troops' to ensure loyalty. One of the Genoese Captains, deciding to forestall possible resistance, ordered his crew to prepare a lavish dinner 'with delicious wines and victuals'. He then exhorted his English guests, with an eloquence they found irresistible, to drink deep to banish the boredom of the voyage. This they did with such zest that they were strewn all over the decks 'sodden with wine'. Sir Edward's troops, like those of the Duke of Wellington three centuries later, apparently only 'enlisted for drink'. When the Genoese Captain invited these 'picked' men to go below deck to sleep in peace, they meekly complied. Shortly after, they were 'called up one by one from below the hatches and trussed up with ropes and chains'. So successful was this stratagem that it was copied by the other Genoese Commander. No sooner had the Italians overcome their English guards than they 'began to sound trumpets and horns', and send messages to the other Captains 'that they would obey the Protector and the Council'. Their example proved infectious, and most of the fleet resolved to return home, except for the Falcon and Trinity which 'fled with Edward to the Breton Coast'. Only when Henry VII became king did these two ships reappear in royal service.

Soon after the surrender of Sir Edward's fleet, the Council began to show signs of division. Some Councillors were growing suspicious that the Protector was becoming too powerful and too ambitious. Now that his enemies were crushed, his pre-eminence seemed less justified and more threatening. Moreover, there were a number of people who felt that their claim on Richard's gratitude had not been sufficiently recognized. Hell knows no fury like a suitor scorned. If some people nursed imagined injuries, Lord Hastings possessed a genuine grievance. It could hardly have escaped his notice that Richard had shown him no sign of his indebtedness. Estates were showered upon Buckingham, Howard, and Lovell in a dozen counties, but Hastings had not received a single acre. His principal concern, however, was less his own neglect than his fear that the Protectorate might be prolonged, or, worse still, the young King deposed.

The opposition to Richard which surfaced in the last week of May, was inspired by suspicion of his intentions, concern for the King's welfare, and apprehension about the small group of favoured friends upon whom he increasingly relied. Before Richard's appointment as Protector, the late King's companions had been at the centre of affairs, but now men like Buckingham and Howard threatened to relegate them to the periphery of politics. Towards the end of May, the Council began to confer in separate groups. Various meeting places have been mentioned: the Tower, Crosby's Place, the Star Chamber at Westminster, Barnard's Castle, and Morton's official residence, Ely Place. It is possible that the Council met in separate groups to expedite business by sharing out work. Most observers, however, believed that the Protector's Meetings at Crosby's Place, to which few were invited and whose proceedings were kept secret, spent more time conspiring against the State than conducting its business. Sir Thomas More says that while some of the Council assembled in one place to make plans for the Coronation, 'as fast were they in another place contriving the contrary', but Mancini believed that it was Hastings, Morton and Rotherham who took the initiative to meet in each other's houses.

Morton studied law at Balliol to qualify as an ecclesiastical lawyer, and soon earned a reputation for scholarship and piety. He began his career as a Lancastrian, but after Henry VI's death became one of Edward IV's most valued advisers. Mancini described him as 'a man of great resource and daring', who had 'been trained in party intrigue' over many years. In 1479 he became Bishop of Ely, and four years later consoled the King on his deathbed. His career suffered a setback in 1483 when it became clear to the Protector that nothing would shake his allegiance to Edward V, but he flourished exceedingly under Henry VII having helped him to win the Throne. Within six years, he was appointed Archbishop of Canterbury, Lord Chancellor and a Cardinal. In the seventeenth century, Sir George Buck, one of Richard III's earliest protagonists, described the Bishop as 'not only a seditious and treacherous man' but also 'a covetous, bloody, cruel and ambitious' prelate. but Sir Thomas More, who remembered the Bishop well having served as a page in his household, described his master as distinguished by 'prudence and virtue'. His knowledge of law and experience of affairs was profound, 'in wit he was incomparable, and in memory wonderful excellent'.

More tells a story about Lord Stanley warning Hastings 'that he much misliked these two several councils', and protesting that 'while we talk of one matter in the one place', we little know 'whereof they talk in the other place'. But Hastings dismissed such fears on the ground that his trusted agent,

William Catesby, could be relied on to keep him informed about what was discussed at Crosby's Place. Many Londoners shared Lord Stanley's disquiet, 'though they neither wist what they feared nor wherefore'. More likened their mood of anxiety to the sea before a storm, which 'without wind swelleth of himself sometime before a tempest'.

There is nothing to show at precisely what moment Richard resolved to usurp but it seems probable that he made up his mind soon after 5 June when his wife joined him at Crosby's Place. It would be hard to conceive of a Neville persuading him not to aspire to the Throne. As the Coronation drew nearer, so his danger increased, and the crisis came to a head a fortnight before the ceremony.

Some time early in June, Richard arranged for Hastings to be sounded, probably by Catesby. Precisely what proposition was put to him nobody ever divulged, but presumably his reaction was sought to Richard becoming King. Catesby was certainly well qualified to act as an intermediary, being both Hastings' agent and a legal adviser to Buckingham. He came from a Lancastrian family with estates in Northampton and Warwick. Early in his career, he made a powerful marriage to Lord Zouche's daughter, Margaret, whose mother was a companion of the Queen, and godmother to the King. Catesby became one of Richard's inner council, an 'Esquire of the Body', and Chancellor of the Exchequer. In 1605, his descendant, Robert Catesby, played a prominent part in the Gunpowder Plot. More claims that Catesby never actually sounded Hastings, but, nevertheless, told the Protector that he remained steadfastly loyal to Edward V, and had spoken such 'terrible words' in response to his enquiries that he dared not proceed further. What may have led Richard to hope that so chivalrous a knight as Hastings would agree to betray the King was the supposition that no prudent man would reject a tempting bribe. In the eighteenth century, Sir Robert Walpole once remarked 'Every man has his price', but then, remembering Sir John St Aubyn, added, 'except the little Cornish baronet'.

During May and June, the Protector did everything in his

power 'to mollify the multitude with largesse and liberality', so 'enflamed' was he 'with desire to usurp the Kingdom'. Almost every day, he conferred 'in most crafty and subtle manner', with peers, politicians and merchants, in an effort 'to win the hearts of his adversaries with gifts, rewards, and promises', sounding out how they were 'affected', and 'saying always that he did not seek the Sovereignty, but referred all his doings to the profit of the realm', thereby 'covering and cloaking his desire' under 'the colour and pretence' of the public interest. By such means, 'he enveigled the minds of the Nobility', apart from those who knew 'from the beginning what mark he shot at'.

On Tuesday, 10 June, Richard wrote a letter to John Newton, Mayor of York, which turned out to be the prelude to a new and critical intrigue. 'The Duke of Gloucester', it began, 'Brother and Uncle of Kings, Protector, Defender, great Chamberlain, Constable and Admiral of England. We greet you well, and as you love the welfare of us, and the welfare and surety of your own selves, we heartily pray you to come to us in London in all the diligence you possibly can, after the sight hereof, with as many as you can defensibly arrayed, there to aid and assist us against the Queen, her bloody adherents and affinity, who have intended and daily do intend, to murder and utterly destroy us and our cousin, the Duke of Buckingham, and the old royal blood of this realm, and as is now openly known, by their subtle and damnable ways forecasted the same, and also the final destruction and disinheritance of you and all others the inheritors and men of honour, as well of the north parts as other countries, that belong to us; as our trusty servant, this bearer, shall more at large show you, to whom we pray you give credence, and as ever we may do for you in time coming fail not, but haste you to us hither.'

'The trusty bearer' mentioned in the Protector's letter was Sir Richard Ratcliffe, who set out for York on 11 June and reached the City four days later on Sunday, 15 June. Ratcliffe, like many of Gloucester's close advisers, came from Yorkshire, and seems to have met him first in Warwick's household. His shrewd understanding and experience of the world was well concealed by his blunt and coarse manner. Edward IV knighted him at Tewkesbury, and he served under Richard in the campaign in Scotland of 1482. More speaks of him as Gloucester's agent in 'lawless enterprises', and as being 'as far from pity as all fear of God'.

In the fifteenth century it was a common practice to add 'credences' to letters: confidential verbal instructions or explanations entrusted to their bearer. The Mayor's Clerk at York noted in his records the tenor of Ratcliffe's message. 'The credence of the which letter is that such fellowship as the City may make defensibly arrayed, as well of horse as of foot', shall assemble on Wednesday 25 June at Pontefract, 'there attending upon my Lord of Northumberland, and so with him to go up to London, there to attend upon my said Lord's good grace'.

Only one other letter which Ratcliffe carried north, seeking help from the Protector's adherents, is known to have survived. It was addressed to Ralph, Lord Neville, heir of the Earl of Westmorland: one of the group of Nobles whom Edward IV had antagonised by pursuing his family's advantage at their expense. Just as the Protector looked to him for military support, so he looked to Richard to redress his grievances. 'My Lord Neville,' wrote Richard, 'I recommend me to you as heartily as I can; and as ever ye love me and your own weal and security, and this realm, that ye come to me with that ye may make, defensibly arrayed, in all haste that is possible; and that ye give credence to Richard Ratcliffe, this bearer, whom I now do send to you, instructed with all my mind and intent. And, my Lord, do me now good service, as ye have alwaye before done, and I trust now so to remember you as shall be the making of you and yours. And God send you good fortunes. Written at London, eleventh day of June, with the hand of your heartily loving cousin and master, R. Gloucester.' In these hasty but revealing lines Richard appealed to a rich assortment of sentiment, ranging from devotion for his 'loving master' to undisguised self-interest.

There was no sign whatever in London of the fearful conspiracy which Richard so vividly described to the Mayor of York. The day before the letter was written Stallworth told Stonor he had nothing to report. As for the Queen and her 'bloody adherents', they were either in Sanctuary or in prison: not the best places from which 'to murder and utterly destroy' the Protector with nine hundred men to guard him.

Various suggestions have been put forward to explain why Richard made this sudden appeal for help. According to one theory it was a desperate response to his discovery of a plot by Lord Hastings. But 'if immediate action had to be taken, the help sought was clearly too far away to arrive in time'. It could be that Richard intended to overawe Parliament. Admittedly his army would arrive a few days late, but the fact it was known to be on its way would presumably have sufficed. Vergil believed that the force was required to prevent 'commotion' among the 'commonality' when 'they should see the Crown bereft from Prince Edward'.

News that a Northern army was marching south reached London by 21 June. That very day, Stallworth told Sir William Stonor: 'It is thought there shall be twenty thousand men of my Lord Protector and my Lord of Buckingham in London this week, to what intent I know not but to keep the peace.' The Croyland Chronicler, recalling, no doubt, the dreadful day in 1461 when Queen Margaret's army passed within six miles of his Abbey, causing terror and panic throughout the Lincolnshire fens, wrote of 'Multitudes of people making a descent from the North to the South, under the especial conduct and guidance of Sir Richard Ratcliffe'. Fabyan offers a more realistic estimate when he says that the Northerners numbered four thousand. But even a force that large, particularly when added to the nine hundred troops already in London, was enough to cause consternation.

Some time on 12 June, two separate Council Meetings were arranged for the morning of Friday, 13 June, which was not regarded as a day of ill omen in the Middle Ages. Vergil stresses the portentous aspect of events by describing them as taking place 'about the day before the Ides of June'. One meeting took place at Westminster under the Lord Chancellor, and the other, presided over by Richard, at the Tower.

121

According to Vergil, the reason why Russell and 'the residue of the nobility' were not invited to the Protector's meeting was that he did not wish them to be 'present at such an outrageous and foul spectacle'. Those specially required to attend included Hastings, Rotherham, Stanley and Morton, besides 'many others whom he trusted to find faithful either for fear or benefit,' such as Buckingham and Howard. Hastings seemingly walked into the trap without a care in the world, much as Rivers had done when he met the Dukes at Northampton. Mancini described the Lord Chamberlain as struck down by 'a friend he had never doubted'.

The Council Meeting at the Tower began at about eight o'clock in the morning. The majority of those present were such as Gloucester 'knew would favour his cause'. More says that the Protector arrived an hour late, and having apologized for oversleeping asked Morton to send for a mess of strawberries from his garden at Ely Place. While these were being fetched, he temporarily withdrew. Several accounts of the Tower meeting describe the Protector as having secretly placed armed men in an adjoining room ready to rush in the moment a signal was given. Vergil refers to them as 'a sort ready to do a mischief', and lists them as Charles Pilkington, Robert Harrington, and Thomas Howard, John Howard's son. Mancini claims that the meeting took place in the 'innermost quarters' of the Tower, and that Richard gave Buckingham command of the soldiers ready to answer his summons.

The moment Richard returned, it was clear from his 'wonderful sour, angry countenance' that something was seriously wrong. When he sat down in his place, 'frowning and frothing and gnawing on his lips', his councillors were 'much dismayed', marvelling 'what thing should him ail'. He told them that the Queen and 'Shore's wife' had 'wasted his body' by witchcraft, a charge he went on to establish by describing his symptoms. 'My Lords,' he said, 'I have procured you all to be called hither this day that I might show unto you in what great danger of death I stand; for by the space of a few days past, neither night nor day can I rest, drink, nor

eat, wherefore my blood by little and little decreaseth, my
force faileth, my breath shorteneth and all the parts of my
body do above measure, as you see (and with that he showed
them his arm) fall away; which mischief verily proceedeth in
me from that Sorceress Elizabeth the Queen, who with her
witchcraft hath so enchanted me that by the annoyance thereof
I am dissolved.' More describes Richard as plucking up 'his
doublet sleeve to his elbow upon his left arm' to show the
injury he had allegedly suffered. 'No man was there present,'
he continues, 'but well knew his arm was ever such since
birth'. Telling as is this objection, it presupposes that Richard
was born deformed which is open to serious doubt.

More is the sole source of a story that the Protector accused
'Shore's wife' of being the Queen's accomplice. 'Jane', as she
was mistakenly called by later writers, was, in fact, christened
'Elizabeth' sometime about 1450. Her father was John Lambert, a Warden of the Mercers, and her mother was Amy
Marshall, a prosperous grocer's daughter. Elizabeth married a
goldsmith, William Shore, whose family came from Der-
byshire. It was not a propitious match. When, or how, she met
Edward IV is not known, but whether out of 'respect for his
royalty, the hope of gay apparel', or the prospect of ease and
pleasure, she became his mistress. William Shore discreetly
retired to Antwerp leaving his wife to the King. In 1476, she
began an action for nullity of marriage on the ground of her
husband's impotence and her desire 'of being a mother and
having offspring'. After Edward IV died, she bestowed her
favours on Lord Hastings and later Dorset. Although Richard
never proceeded with the accusation that 'she went about to
bewitch him and that she was of counsel with the Lord
Chamberlain to destroy him', he handed her over to the
Church on the charge 'herself could not deny' that she had
broken the Seventh Commandment. 'For this cause, as a
goodly continent prince, clean and faultless of himself, sent
out of heaven into this vicious world for the amendment of
men's manners', he ordered the Bishop of London, Thomas
Kemp, 'to put her to open penance'. Writing a week after the
Tower council, Stallworth informed Sir William Stonor,

'Mistress Shore is in prison: what shall happen to her, I know not'.

Richard's charges of witchcraft must be seen in their fifteenth century context. In 1484, Pope Innocent VIII issued a Papal Bull which initiated a frenzied revival of persecution lasting for two centuries. The practice of burning witches continued in England into the eighteenth century, and the law permitting it was not repealed until 1734. It would be wrong, therefore, to imagine that the first stirrings of the scientific spirit of the Renaissance had any immediate effect upon beliefs which claimed biblical authority. Edward V was the only English King in the fifteenth century who was not supposed to have been the victim of witchcraft. Henry VI was reputedly wasted by enchantments. Henry V's stepmother, Joan of Navarre, was accused of instigating a Franciscan friar to kill the King by sorcery. In 1441, the Duke of Gloucester's second wife, Eleanor Cobham, was sentenced to life imprisonment by Archbishop Chichele on charges of witchcraft, heresy and treason. In particular, she was accused of wishing Henry VI dead so that she might become Queen. In 1477 two associates of the Duke of Clarence were hanged, drawn and quartered for treasonably imagining the death of Edward IV 'by necromancy and other means'. When Richard, on 13 June, revived his attacks on the Queen Mother, he accused her of the only crime she could have committed within the confines of Sanctuary.

Hastings, who was accustomed to speak 'very freely' to the Protector, said that if the Queen and Shore's wife were found guilty they should, of course, be punished. But Richard replied he would not be fobbed off 'with "ifs" and with "ands". I tell thee they have so done, and I will make good on thy body traitor.' At that moment, he 'clapped his fist upon the board a great rap' and someone outside the Council Chamber shouted 'Treason: Treason.' At which signal, armed men rushed in and filled the room. 'And anon the Protector said to Lord Hastings:

"I arrest thee, traitor."
"What me, my Lord?" quod he.
"Yea, thee, traitor," quod the Protector.'

Mancini says that Hastings was killed at the moment of arrest. 'Thereupon the soldiers, who had been stationed there by their Lord, rushed in with the Duke of Buckingham and cut down Hastings on the false pretext of treason'. In reality, he was mistaken in supposing that the Lord Chamberlain died immediately. Such might have been the Italian practice but Richard preferred to observe the proper formalities. Nevertheless, Hastings was only given a few moments to make his last confession before being led out to Tower Green, where Lady Jane Grey was to meet her end some seventy years later. There he was beheaded on 'a squared piece of timber' intended for repairs. All accounts are agreed that Hastings was put to death 'suddenly without judgment'. Under the provisions of Magna Carta he had the right to be tried by his Peers, and since they were already summoned to meet in twelve days time there need have been little delay in prosecuting him. The fact that he was executed 'at once, without any process of law or lawful examination', was both arbitrary and tyrannical.

During the scuffle in which Lord Hastings was arrested, Stanley received a wound in the head, possibly inflicted by Robert Middleton with whom he had a private quarrel. 'The Great Chronicle' speaks of his face being 'grazed a little with some weapon'. But More heightens the drama, describing how Middleton let fly at Stanley, who shrank at the stroke to prevent his head being 'cleft to the teeth', and fell under the Council table with blood streaming about his ears. It was widely believed that Stanley would have shared Hastings' fate but for Richard's fear that his son, Lord Strange, would seek revenge by stirring up rebellion. Within a fortnight, Stanley was set free and restored to favour.

The Protector might well be apprehensive of the power of the Stanleys who wielded enormous influence in Cheshire and Lancashire. Thomas Stanley, the head of the family, was born in 1435. As a young man he married Eleanor Neville, the Earl of Warwick's sister and Richard's first cousin. In 1459 he began his notable career as a trimmer by remaining aloof at the Battle of Blore Heath, despite desperate appeals for help from both sides. The following year he fought for Henry VI at

Northampton but changed allegiance after the Yorkist victory at Towton. When Henry VI was temporarily restored in 1470, Stanley committed himself to the Lancastrian cause with so many reservations that Edward IV forgave his squeamish flirtation and made him a Privy Councillor. About 1482, he married once more, this time Lady Margaret Beaufort, widow of Edmund Tudor, Earl of Richmond. After his stepson, Henry Tudor, attempted to overthrow Richard in October 1483 his days seemed numbered. But such was his political agility that he extricated himself from this debacle as nimbly as in 1459 and 1470. Through all the changes and chances of a fleeting world, Stanley contrived to sustain himself in office under seven successive régimes. Looking back over fifty troubled years he could boast like the Abbé Sieyès after him: 'I survived'. The Bishops of York and Ely, who were arrested at the same time as Lord Stanley, were saved from execution out of respect for their holy orders. Rotherham was temporarily kept in custody by Sir James Tyrell, while Morton was sent to Brecknock Castle as the Duke of Buckingham's prisoner.

The news of Hastings' sudden execution, and the arrest of three of the late King's most trusted councillors, spread through the city, partly because the Protector sent his servants to shout ' "Treason, treason", throughout the whole town'. At first, 'the citizens, taking the rumour to be true, began to cry out likewise.' But when they began to understand 'by terrible speech bruited abroad the truth of the matter, then began every man on his own behalf to fear the heart of inward enemies, and to look for nothing else but cruel slaughter or miserable flight'.

The Duke of Gloucester, in the hope of allaying suspicion, ordered a herald to parade through London proclaiming 'that the Lord Hastings, with divers other of his traitorous purpose', had, that very morning, conspired to slay the Protector and the Duke of Buckingham during the Council Meeting at the Tower, in order to rule 'the king and the realm at their pleasure', and rob or kill whom they pleased. Much of the Proclamation was concerned with slandering the Lord Chamberlain, accusing him of being 'an evil counsellor to the King's father, enticing him to many things highly redounding to the minishing of his honour and to the universal hurt of his realm, by his evil company, sinister, procuring, and ungracious example'. His vicious mode of life, especially his liaison with Shore's wife, 'which was one also of his most secret counsel of this heinous treason, with whom he lay nightly, and namely the night last passed next his death', had contributed to his 'unhappy ending'. Hastings' execution without the semblance of a trial was justified on the grounds that delay 'might have encouraged other mischievous persons, partners of his conspiracy', to attempt to set him free, 'whose hope now being by his well deserved death politicly repressed, all the realm should by God's grace rest in good quiet and peace'.

So short a time elapsed between Hastings' execution and the reading of the Proclamation, 'that every child might well perceive that it was prepared before', particularly in view of the fact that it was elaborately composed and contained so much matter. A merchant was said to have commented on the breathtaking speed of its production that it must have been written by prophecy: a jest which was close to the mark seeing that Richard had written to York on 10 June to tell them of some such plot. Catesby may possibly have had a hand in producing the Proclamation. Shakespeare makes his Scrivener say:

> Eleven hours I have spent to write it over,
> For yesternight by Catesby was it sent me.

The Protector's attempt to justify himself was greeted with scepticism and derision. 'With us there is much trouble', wrote Stallworth 'and every man doubts the other'. At first, says Mancini, 'the ignorant crowd' believed the official version of events. But soon 'the real truth was on the lips of many, namely that the plot had been feigned' in the hope that the Dukes might escape the odium of their crime. Shakespeare's Scrivener summed up the public mood.

> Who is so gross,
> That cannot see this palpable device?
> Yet who's so bold, but says he sees it not?

The death of Hastings was 'generally lamented', particularly by those 'who favoured King Edward's children' and had 'reposed their whole hope and confidence' in him. As the most prominent of the late King's Household, he appeared to guarantee the continuity of government. Nearly everyone agreed, in the words of 'The Great Chronicle', that he was 'murdered for his truth and fidelity' to his Master. Regret for his passing was mingled with fear of the manner of it. 'Now perceived they well, that Duke Richard would spare no man so that he might obtain the Kingdom.' Probably the tribute which most faithfully reflected the views of Hastings' contemporaries was that of Sir Thomas More. 'Thus ended this honourable man, a good knight and a gentle, of great authority with his prince, of living somewhat dissolute, plain and open to his enemy', and constant to his friends. His real crime was not conspiracy but refusal to conspire, and his head was 'smitten off' because the Protector 'knew well that he would not assent unto his wicked intent'.

In his will, signed on 27 June 1481, Hastings wrote in his own hand: 'The King of his abundant grace for the true service that I have done hath offered me to be buried in the College or Chapel of St George at Windsor in a place by his Grace assigned' and he expressed his desire that when he died he should be interred near his Sovereign. This wish was granted, and his body lies on the north side of the chancel of St George's close to Edward IV's chantry. His faithfulness unto death was the noblest aspect of that relationship between Lord and Retainer which was dubbed 'Bastard Feudalism' in the nineteenth century. This inelegant phrase does scant justice to a perfectly legitimate refinement in the concept of 'Good Lordship'. There was not a hint of depravity in the Lord Chamberlain's notion of allegiance, which made him Edward's faithful retainer, as Earl of March, Duke of York, and King of England, and which led to his execution on Tower Green because it was known he would never betray the son of his Sovereign Lord.

The Protector decided not to proceed against Hastings by means of a retrospective Act of Attainder, in spite of the fact

A contemporary portrait of Richard III, which once belonged to the Paston family.

The Princes in the Tower, as portrayed by Millais in 1878.

that he was supposedly guilty of so serious a treason that it had been necessary to execute him without trial. In a grant given under his sign manual and seal on 23 July, Richard took Catherine Hastings under his protection, agreeing 'to be good and gracious Sovereign Lord to the said Catherine as our well-beloved cousin and widow'. The grant pardoned her late husband's 'offences', and gave her the wardship of 'Edward son and heir of the said William during his nonnage'. Richard could hardly have acted otherwise, as even he might have found it difficult to prove the Lord Chamberlain's guilt if he was, in fact, innocent. Without an Act of Attainder only Hastings' offices could be distributed. Of these Catesby was given the lion's share, having climbed 'over the body of his patron'.

In 1480, Hastings had begun to build a fortified Manor House at Kirby Muxloe, four miles west of Leicester. This moated 'castle' was constructed of brick, at that time an innovation. Probably he picked up the idea when he fled to Bruges with Edward IV in 1470. The Gate House and West Tower were completed when news of his execution reached Leicestershire and all work stopped. The Castle is 'something of a toy, but stands at the beginning of the development of the Tudor house'. Recently a number of arguments have been advanced to show that Hastings was not executed on 13 June as commonly supposed, but a week later on 20 June. The fact that building ceased at Kirby Muxloe in the middle of June suggests that the traditional date has much to commend it.

Richard justified the coup of 13 June on the ground that he acted in self-defence. His only crime, so he said, was to counter a conspiracy to murder him: a telling plea provided the plot was genuine. But almost all writers closest to the event, express, or imply, scepticism. Mancini summed up the common view when he described Hastings as put to death 'on the false pretext of treason'. Nevertheless, several historians have accepted the Protector's allegations at face value, or have found other reasons for believing Hastings guilty. Horace Walpole argued that the events of 13 June were Richard's response to 'absolute necessity and the law of self-defence': a contention long before exploded by Milton in *Paradise Lost*.

> So spake the Fiend, and with necessity,
> The tyrant's plea, excused his devilish deeds.

John Stow, writing in 1580, tells of a plot in July 1483 to release Edward V while his guards were distracted by a fire. It is the fate of traditions to become detached from their chronological setting, so Stow's story could conceivably refer to an attempt by Hastings to rescue the young King. One other hint has been seen as pointing to the existence of some such conspiracy. George Cely, a prosperous fifteenth century wool merchant, scribbled a mysterious note on the spare leaf of a document which reads as follows: 'There is great rumour in the realm. Chamberlain is deceased in trouble. The Bishop of Ely is dead. If the King, God save his life were deceased; the Duke of Gloucester were in any peril; if my lord prince, which God defend, were troubled; if my Lord Howard were slain.' These incoherent jottings, which look like a first response to rumours circulating on 13 June, have appeared to some to suggest that Hastings and his friends were involved 'in a widespread and dangerous conspiracy which somehow threatened the life of the King and the safety of his brother'. Whether such rumours were spontaneous, or officially inspired, it is impossible to say, but as Morton survived until 1500 not all Cely's fears proved well founded.

The only vestige of evidence that Hastings employed Elizabeth Shore as an intermediary in his intrigues with the Woodvilles, comes from Richard's remarks of 13 June as reported by More. Sir Thomas himself was highly sceptical, and mentions that most of those who heard Richard's charges thought that the Queen would 'of all folk, least make Shore's wife of counsel, whom of all women she most hated, as that concubine whom the King, her husband, most loved'.

Even assuming, for the sake of argument, that Hastings stands convicted, it is hard to see what his crime is supposed to have been. In so far as he conspired he did so on Edward's behalf, probably with his knowledge and consent. Plotting to save the King from a so-called 'Protector' is not an indictable offence. But it is, of course, treason to plan to seize the Throne.

The revival of the most degrading features of renaissance politics by twentieth century totalitarian states, with their corrupt intrigues, midnight assassinations and sudden lawless executions, has made the tyrants of the late Middle Ages a great deal more credible to us than they were to the Victorians. In the eighteenth century, Horace Walpole, bred in the traditions of the Enlightenment, insisted that the Tudor view of Richard III was unacceptable because no man could be so wicked. We know better now. Those who have lived under the shadow of Hitler and Stalin cannot but feel a sense of déjà vu as they contemplate Richard's exploits.

The execution of the Lord Chamberlain and the arrest of a former Lord Chancellor, naturally intimidated the King's supporters, as was no doubt the intention. Once Richard had seemingly sacrificed Hastings for standing in his way, no-one felt safe. The Croyland Chronicler succinctly summed up the result of this savage coup. The strongest supporters of the new King being thus removed 'without judgment or justice, and all the rest of his faithful subjects fearing the like treatment, the two dukes did thenceforth just as they pleased'.

CHAPTER SIX

'This Palpable Device'

14 June–22 June 1483

Who is so gross,
That cannot see this palpable device?
Yet who's so bold, but says he sees it not?

Shakespeare *Richard III* III.6.

The most dangerous of Richard's enemies still at large after 13 June was Dorset, who seems to have joined the Queen on the dispersal of Sir Edward's fleet, and to have left Sanctuary after Hastings' murder. Richard made 'narrow and busy search' in an effort to find him, but the Marquis proved as elusive as ever. Spies reported 'that he was hiding in the adjacent neighbourhood', so orders were given to surround 'the already grown crops and the cultivated and woody places' in the vicinity of Westminster with troops and dogs, and they 'sought for him, after the manner of huntsmen, by a very close encirclement: but he was never found.'

Throughout May, efforts were made to persuade the Queen to leave Sanctuary. As long as she sought the protection of the Church her distrust of the Protector was bound to damage the government's reputation. In an attempt to remove this scandal and reproach, sedulous attempts were made to persuade her that neither she nor her children were in any danger. The Minutes of the Council of 23 May record vigorous efforts by the Protector, Buckingham, and the Archbishop of Canterbury, to allay her fears. But eventually negotiations foundered and nothing further was done until after Hastings' death.

On the morning of Monday, 16 June, the Protector again held a Council to discuss the release of the Duke of York. The

Councillors met in the Star Chamber at Westminster, much chastened by recent events. Mancini was in no doubt about Gloucester's motive in seeking to get Prince Richard into his grasp. Even if Edward V was deposed, he 'foresaw that the Duke of York would by legal right succeed'. Sir Thomas More was equally emphatic that the Duke's true reason for negotiating his nephew's release was the boy's claim to the Throne. 'The Protector so sore thirsted for the finishing of that he had begun, that he thought every day a year till it were achieved, yet durst he no further attempt as long as he had but half his prey in his hand, well witting that if he deposed the one brother, all the realm would fall to the other, if he either remained in sanctuary' or was smuggled out of the country. Naturally, this was not the reason he gave the Council when seeking their approval, and it is proof of his resource that he contrived to present them with so many specious arguments.

Richard persuaded the Council that those who hated and maligned him had mischievously prevailed on the Queen to seek Sanctuary, as if they were 'wicked, wretched and desperate naughty persons'. By giving the impression that 'we went about to destroy them, and that all our doings tended to violence', she had brought 'exceeding great dishonour to us and the whole realm'. Richard warned the Council that he looked to them to provide a remedy 'for this womanish disease creeping into our Commonwealth'. It was, he said, 'a heinous deed of the Queen, and proceeding of great malice towards the King's counsellors, that she should keep in sanctuary the King's brother from him'. This she had done for no other purpose than 'to bring all the lords in obloquy and murmer of the people, as though they were not to be trusted with the King's brother'. So long as the Queen refused to leave the Abbot's lodgings, it redounded 'greatly to the dishonour both of the King's highness and of all of us that hath been about his grace, to have it run in every man's mouth, not in this realm only, but also in other lands (as evil words walk far) that the King's brother should be fain to keep sanctuary'.

The Protector further argued that it would be highly improper 'that the King should be crowned in the absence of his brother, who on account of his nearness of kin and his station ought to play an important part in the ceremony'. But, of course, it was not merely the Duke of York's absence which would give offence. 'What a sight I pray you shall it be to see the day wherein the King shall be crowned, if, while that the solemnity of triumphant pomp is in doing, his mother, brother, and sisters remain in sanctuary?' Besides, said the Protector, Prince Richard 'was held by his mother against his will' and ought to be set free. Sanctuaries had been founded as 'a place of refuge, not detention, and this boy wanted to be with his brother'. The King, 'in his tender youth', could not happily live for long solely 'in the company of ancient persons'. He ought to associate with boys of his own age, and he could hardly have a more suitable companion than the Prince. Finally, if the Queen persisted in the pretence that her son required the protection of the Church, there 'is not one amongst all the people who may not justly be in fear of himself, and think that all majesty of law is already violated'.

The Council, suspecting 'no subtlety', thought the Protector's advice both 'meet and honest', and agreed to send a deputation to the Queen to try once more to persuade her to leave Sanctuary. Richard told them that even if they failed to 'withdraw her from her opinion', they must at least ensure that she handed over her son 'so that he may be present at his brother's Coronation'. It was agreed that these negotiations should be conducted by a delegation consisting of the Archbishop of Canterbury, the Bishop of Lincoln, the Duke of Buckingham, Lord Howard, and 'sundry other grave men'.

Cardinal Bourchier, Archbishop of Canterbury, was born in 1404 and died in 1486, having lived through all, or part, of the reigns of Henry IV, Henry V, Henry VI, Edward IV, Edward V, Richard III and Henry VII. He was a great-grandson of Edward III, his mother's father being Thomas of Woodstock, Duke of Gloucester. His eldest brother, Henry Bourchier, first Earl of Essex, married Edmund Duke of York's daughter Isabel. Their son, William, Viscount Bourchier, married Anne Woodville, Queen Elizabeth's sister. Before he was thirty, Thomas was appointed Bishop of

Worcester, but soon cast longing eyes on the richer see of Ely. As a young prelate he was so absorbed in ecclesiastical intrigue that he had little time to spare for pastoral duties. While Henry VI was out of his mind in 1454, Bourchier was appointed to succeed Cardinal Kemp as Archbishop of Canterbury. The following year he was made Lord Chancellor but only retained the post for a few months. His dismissal was engineered by Margaret of Anjou who distrusted his Yorkist sympathies. Bourchier, having been alienated from the Lancastrians by the savagery of the 'Parliament of Devils', crowned Edward IV and remained loyal to him thereafter. In 1456 the Archbishop began building Knole as a country residence in Kent, where he later entertained in princely fashion. It was there that the Prior of Croyland first tasted a currant. In his declining years, Bourchier tried to withdraw from politics. He refused to officiate, for example, at Edward IV's funeral, on the ground he was too frail to travel to Windsor. Nevertheless, he reluctantly consented to attend the Protectorate Councils, and the ease with which he was apparently beguiled shows how sound was his instinct to retire. During his career he crowned three Kings: Edward IV, Richard III and Henry VII.

The Protector suggested that if the Queen proved obstinate, 'then shall we, by mine advice, by the King's authority,' fetch out the Duke of York and conduct him to the Tower to join his brother, in whose company he would be 'so well cherished' that the whole world would see that only the malice and perversity of the Queen had ever kept them apart. Bourchier agreed to do his utmost to secure the Prince's release, but would not consent to take him against his mother's will, which 'would be a thing that should turn to the great grudge of all men and high displeasure of God if the privilege of that holy place should now be broken'. These courageous words were the prelude to pusillanimous actions. In the end, the Prince was handed over and no blows were struck. But the Queen only parted with her son because she dared not do otherwise. Her decision was voluntary in the sense that she chose to avoid bloodshed. The Archbishop must have been amazingly ingenuous if he thought that it was his pleading, rather than the armed men at his back, which prevailed on this obdurate woman.

Buckingham remained unconvinced by the Archbishop's reasoning, and argued that it might become necessary to seize the Prince to prevent the Queen from sending him 'out of the realm'. Sanctuaries, he said, merely encouraged 'thieves, murderers, and malicious, heinous traitors: as though God and St Peter were the patrons of ungracious living'. The Duke of York had committed no crime and had no conceivable need of the Church's protection. 'Verily, I have often heard of sanctuary men' but never before of 'sanctuary children'. If it became necessary to take the Prince from his mother by force, no harm would be done, because the boy's life and liberty could 'by no lawful process stand in jeopardy'. Most of the Council agreed with the Duke that if Prince Richard was 'not delivered, he should be fetched', but they, nevertheless, hoped that force would not prove necessary.

The delegation headed by the Archbishop was accompanied by an intimidating array of armed men. Mancini says that the sanctuary was 'surrounded with troops' and it was only because 'the Queen saw herself besieged' that she agreed to surrender her son. The Croyland Chronicler, who was probably a witness of the scene, says that 'a great multitude' came by 'water to Westminster armed with swords and staves'. Lord Howard's account book shows an entry on 16 June making payment for eight boats 'up and down from Westminster'. Stallworth, writing within four days of the event, states that 'on Monday last there was at Westminster a great plenty of harnessed men' to secure the deliverance of the Duke of York. Under these circumstances, there can be little doubt that the Queen, who had resisted all previous entreaties, only consented to surrender the Prince because of a blatant threat of force. Even then she yielded to the Council's minimum demand and neither she nor her daughters agreed to leave Sanctuary.

Had the Queen felt confident that the armed men, so much in evidence during the course of negotiations, would respect the privileges of the Church, she might have refused to hand

Prince Richard over. Her misgivings, of course, were totally justified as their orders were to violate Sanctuary if all else failed. Besides, what other inference was to be drawn from the presence of so many troops? It is true that in earlier times the rights of Sanctuary had been treated as inviolate. Mancini wrote of 'ancient observance' which from 'religious awe or from fear of the people' none dared transgress. It was not even lawful for Kings to drag men out of Sanctuary against their wills. But customs, he said, had changed in recent years. Since the time of Henry VI, 'whether religion has declined, or the people's power diminished and that of the sovereigns vastly increased, Sanctuaries are of little avail against the royal authority'. A notorious instance of the violation of Sanctuary took place in 1471, when the Duke of Somerset and ten or so prominent Lancastrians took refuge in Tewkesbury Abbey after the battle. Nevertheless, they were dragged out on the orders of Edward IV and beheaded in the Market Place. The King's apologists claimed that the Abbey possessed no franchise entitling them to harbour traitors, but Somerset's fate showed how dangerous it could be to rely on the Church's protection. Moreover, it was not only the Queen who foresaw the possibility of bloodshed. So did the Archbishop, whose principal reason for undertaking his mission was 'to prevent a violation of sanctuary'. The most telling argument he almost certainly deployed was that to hand over the Prince was the lesser of two evils.

Bourchier began by telling the Queen that he had been sent by the Council to require her to release the Duke of York so that he might join his brother who longed for his companionship. She replied that the Prince had 'been so sore diseased with sickness' that she dared not trust him to another's care. The Archbishop warned her that many people believed that it would not be wrong to remove the boy by force, 'which if you finally refuse to deliver him, I verily think they will'. When he perceived 'that the Queen began to speak biting words against the Protector', he assured her that if she handed over her son to him personally, 'he durst lay his own body and soul in pledge' for the boy's safety and honour. The Queen, recognizing that the choice before her was either to accept this promise or provoke the Prince's seizure, 'kissed and blessed him, turned her back and wept and went her way, leaving the child weeping as fast'. Mancini agrees with More that the Queen finally capitulated 'trusting in the word of the Cardinal of Canterbury'.

Most accounts of the negotiations to release the Duke of York suggest a resort to fraud as well as force. *The Great Chronicle* refers to 'manifold feigned fair promises', and Vergil writes of bringing about by 'sleight' the plan to secure the Prince. Bourchier's role is particularly hard to fathom. The Croyland Chronicler, anxious no doubt to vindicate the Cardinal, speaks of him being 'compelled to appeal to the good feelings of the Queen', and all were agreed that he 'thought nor intended none harm'. Nevertheless, his astounding credulity implies a confusion of mind which only age can excuse. Three days before Bourchier extracted Prince Richard from Sanctuary, the Protector had treacherously executed one of the King's most trusted servants: the prelude as many believed to his seizing the Throne. But apparently the Archbishop saw nothing sinister in the fate of Hastings, or in the purpose inspiring his own mission. For a man who had held high office through fifty years of ruthless political intrigue, and had furthered his own career with exceptional tenacity, such uncharacteristic simplicity may best be explained as senility. Few men were less of a holy innocent than the Archbishop. A knave he might well be but a fool he was not. It is true that in troubled times he displayed a suppleness of conscience and flexibility of allegiance which said much for his will to survive but less for the strength of his principles. Nevertheless, his contemporaries refused to believe he acted as Richard's willing accomplice. As they saw it, he was shamefully deceived and acted in good faith. If so, the passing years had blunted the edge of a mind which had once been as sharp as a butcher's knife.

The Archbishop conducted the Duke of York from the Abbot's lodging to Westminster Hall, where Buckingham was waiting to escort him to the Star Chamber to meet his uncle. The Protector received the Prince at the door of the Council Chamber 'with many loving words'. 'Now welcome, my lord,' he is quoted as saying, 'even with all my heart'. The Protector and Archbishop then conducted the released captive to his brother in the Tower 'out of which after that day they never came abroad. And so was the innocent child pulled out of his mother's arms'.

At about the same time as the Protector took Prince Richard into custody, he gave orders that the Duke of Clarence's son, Edward, Earl of Warwick, then a boy of eight, should be brought to London to live in his Household. The Duke and Duchess of Gloucester were the child's nearest relations. The Duke was his paternal uncle, and the Duchess was his mother's only sister. Both the 'King-Maker's' daughters died before they were thirty and both produced delicate sons. Edward was said to be so 'simple' that he could not distinguish a hen from a goose. When the wretched youth was executed in 1499, culpable only of being Clarence's heir, he had little idea what was happening. It is possible that his trouble was less hereditary than the product of long confinement 'out of all company of men and sight of beasts'. Warwick's claim to the Throne was better than that of his uncle, unless, as was later argued, his father's attainder debarred him from the succession. For this reason, the Protector 'feared that if the entire progeny of King Edward became extinct, yet this child, who was also of royal blood, would still embarrass him'.

After 16 June, the Dukes 'acted no longer in secret, but openly manifest their intentions'. Either that day, or the next, writs were sent out postponing the Coronation and the opening of Parliament. The die was cast and secrecy no longer possible. Having removed potential enemies and secured rival claimants, Richard was eager to seize the crown with all possible haste 'ere men could have time to devise any way to resist'. The initiative was bound to remain his during the first few days of stunned confusion, when 'no man wist what to think nor whom to trust'. Moreover, the 'lords of the realm', many of whom were already in London for the Coronation and Parliament, were 'out of their own strengths'. A nobleman's power lay in his castles and retainers. In the county from which he came his word was law. It was said of the inhabitants of Northumberland that they knew no prince but a Percy. But many of the mightiest Barons were strangers in Westminster, and were jostled like anyone else in the streets of the capital. Indeed, their country habits often attracted ridicule. Richard ordered such noblemen as arrived at Court with the escorts 'their title and station demanded', to send their retinues home, explaining by way of justification that he had to allay the fears of London merchants 'lest so great a concourse of men in a wealthy city might turn to plundering against the will of their masters'.

The moment Richard decided to become King it became necessary for him to stop the Coronation of Edward V on 22 June: hence the writs issued to cancel the ceremony in the Abbey and the opening of Parliament. This decisive step was presumably endorsed by the Council at its meeting on 16 June. Only two copies of these writs of 'supersedeas' have survived, and neither bears the date of issue. Nevertheless, internal evidence suggests that they were sent on 17 or 18 June. York received its writ on 21 June, as the City Council's minutes record: 'At this day a supersedeas was directed to the Sheriff for the Parliament, so it shall not need to any citizen to go up to the City for the Parliament'. To reach York by 21 June, the writ must have left London by 18 June at the latest. On the other hand, the ceremony can hardly have been cancelled before 16 June: the day Bourchier persuaded the Queen Mother to release Prince Richard to attend the Coronation.

More claims that the Protector only told Buckingham of his plan to depose the King after he had 'imprisoned the Queen's kinsfolks and got both her sons into his own hands.' The Duke apparently had serious misgivings about breaking his oath of allegiance, but was eventually prevailed upon to do so by being told 'that the young King was offended with him' for his family's sake, and would seize the first chance of revenge. Recognizing that he was too far committed to turn back, Buckingham resolved to profit from his predicament, and agreed to help the Protector depose the King in return for a grant of the Bohun estates of which Edward IV had deprived him. The last known document bearing Edward V's signature is dated 17 June. Mancini reported that after Hastings' execution 'all the attendants who had waited upon the King were debarred access to him.' Then, shortly after his brother joined him, the Princes 'were withdrawn into the inner apartments of the Tower proper, and day by day began to be seen more rarely behind the bars and windows, till at length they ceased to appear altogether'. The King's doctor, John Argentine, was the last attendant left him. Argentine, a great collector of books and manuscripts on medicine and theology, reported 'that the young King, like a victim prepared for sacrifice, sought remission of his sins by daily confession and penance, because he believed that death was facing him'. The doomed youth showed signs of exceptional promise. In particular, 'his special knowledge of literature' enabled him 'to discourse elegantly, to understand fully, and to declaim most excellently from any work whether in verse or prose that came into his hands, unless it were from among the more abstruse authors. He had such dignity in his whole person, and in his face such charm, that however much they might gaze he never wearied the eyes of beholders'.

Mancini left England in July 1483 but even before he departed there were fears for King Edward's safety. 'I have seen many men', he wrote, 'burst forth into tears and lamentations when mention was made of him after his removal from men's sight: and already there was a suspicion that he had been done away with,' but 'by what manner of death, so far I have not at all discovered.'

By Sunday, 22 June, the day originally fixed for Edward's Coronation, Richard was undisputed master of London. The nobles had meekly obeyed his instructions to send their retinues home. He had nothing whatever to fear from the London Train Band. Sir Edmund Shaa, the Lord Mayor, had promised him the support of the Aldermen and City 'upon trust of his own advancement'. The only soldiers in the capital were under his command. In a few days time he expected his troops from the north. During the last ten days of June, the King's loyal supporters were powerless to prevent his deposition because Richard disposed of such overwhelming power.

The citizens of London were mostly hostile but helpless spectators of Edward's overthrow. Nor were the nobles in any mood to resist for they clearly perceived 'that Duke Richard would spare no man so that he might obtain the Kingdom'. It is true that the Protector 'sought with all diligence to win unto him the chief of the nobility by large gifts and fair promises'. But in so far as he succeeded in obtaining their support they were 'seduced rather for fear than hope of benefit'. Mancini portrays the leading men of the day as terrorized into submission. The nobles, he wrote, 'warned by the example of Hastings', and seeing themselves 'surrounded and in the hands of the Dukes', came to the conclusion that it 'would be difficult and hazardous to resist'. Their inaction should rather be seen as rejecting suicide than signifying consent.

Before Richard could take possession of the Crown, he had to devise some excuse for deposing the reigning King. Otherwise, 'he knew well', there was a grave risk of an uprising 'for defence of liberty and conservation of the royal right'. So, after 'revolving many matters in his mind, at last he bethought himself of a device whereby the people, being seduced by a certain honest pretence, should the less grudge at his doings'. Amongst those whom Richard consulted were the Lord Mayor, and his brother, Dr Ralph Shaa, 'a divine of great reputation among the people' for learning and eloquence. It seems almost certain that the strategy he ultimately pursued was one he suggested himself. Like so many people apparently seeking advice he was less eager for enlightenment than to have his opinions endorsed. In his 'secret conference' with Dr Shaa, he maintained 'that his father's inheritance ought to descend to him by right, as the eldest of all the sons which Richard, his father, Duke of York, had begotten of Cecily his wife; for as much as it was manifest enough, and that by apparent argument, that Edward, who had before reigned, was a bastard, that is, not begotten of a right and lawful wife'. He therefore begged Shaa 'to instruct the people thereof in a sermon at Paul's Cross, whereby they might once in the end acknowledge their true liege Lord'.

According to More, the bastardy charge was not merely directed against the late King but also his children, by way of double indemnity. The 'invention' devised for deposing the King 'rested in this: that they should allege bastardy, either in King Edward himself, or in his children, or both, so that he (Edward IV) should seem disabled to inherit the Crown by the Duke of York, and the Prince (Edward V) by him'. But, of course, 'to lay bastardy in King Edward sounded openly to the rebuke of the Protector's own mother, which was mother to them both; for in that point could be none other colour but to pretend that his own mother was one adulteress'. In an effort to circumvent this embarrassment, aggravated by the Duchess' arrival in London for her grandson's Coronation, Richard proposed to handle the matter obliquely, 'as though men spared in that point to speak all the truth for fear of his displeasure. But the other point, concerning the bastardy that they devised to surmise in King Edward's children – that, would he, should be openly declared and enforced to the uttermost'.

Presumably Richard accused his brother of being a bastard and his mother an adulteress because there were no other grounds for dispossessing his nephew. Previous Kings had been deposed for incompetence or tyranny. Henry IV accused Richard II of constitutional irregularities, and Edward IV denounced Henry VI for losing France, for trusting worthless favourites, and for giving away crown lands. But Edward V could hardly be set aside as incapable of ruling, or blamed for any of the evils of the age: unless youth is a crime. There was only one way for Richard to clothe his naked bid for power and that was to suggest that the King had no right to the Throne.

Accusations of bastardy were common political currency during the late Middle Ages, and they did not need to be true to serve their purpose. Richard II was reputed to be the son of a French Canon in the Black Prince's Household. The Duke of Somerset was widely believed to be the true father of Margaret of Anjou's son, Edward, Prince of Wales. Lancastrian propaganda insisted that Lionel, Duke of Clarence disowned his daughter, Philippa, and that consequently the claim of her Mortimer descendants to the Crown was spurious. The rumour that Edward IV was the son of a foreign archer was put about by Warwick the 'King-Maker' in 1469. Six years later, Charles the Bold, scornfully referred to his brother-in-law as 'Blayborgne', the supposed surname of his French father. In 1478, George, Duke of Clarence, was tried for exploiting this story for treasonable purposes, and charged with 'falsely and traitorously' intending to disinherit the King and his issue, and 'exalt himself and his heirs to the regality and Crown of England', upon 'the falsest and most unnatural coloured pretence that man might imagine'. In particular, he had 'untruly noised, published and said, that the King our sovereign lord was a bastard and not begotten to reign upon us'. It was enough for a member of the Royal Family to be born overseas for the slander of bastardy to arise, on the assumption that no foreigner was to be trusted: especially with women. Edward IV was born at Rouen and was never allowed to forget the taint this was thought to imply. In 1482 the Duke of Albany claimed the throne of Scotland on the ground that his brother James III was born out of wedlock.

Not a single contemporary writer believed that Richard's accusations of bastardy were anything other than a 'palpable device' to give some 'colour' to his designs on the Throne. More speaks of the sand upon which the Protector built in pretending that Edward V was not lawfully King. Nevertheless, 'that invention, simple as it was', provided him with a pretext for seizing the Crown. So contemptuous was Mancini of Richard's wild accusations that he did not deign to refute them, but his scepticism is plain in his scornful reference to the corruption of 'preachers of the divine word', who did not blush to say in their sermons 'in the face of decency and all religion, that the progeny of King Edward should be instantly eradicated, for neither had he been a legitimate king, nor could his issue be so. Edward, said they, was conceived in adultery and in every way was unlike the late Duke of York, whose son he was falsely said to be, but Richard, Duke of Gloucester, who altogether resembled his father, was to come to the throne as the legitimate successor'. An account of Edward V's reign written about 1490 describes Richard as 'having himself crowned on fraudulent grounds', and Rous speaks of him as having 'feigned a title to the Crown for his own advancement'. Not until Buck in the seventeenth century began the task of salvaging Richard's reputation did any historian take the charge seriously.

In the late fifteenth century, few people could read or write, and printing was rare. Views were of necessity exchanged by word of mouth. The best opportunity for political propaganda was offered by the pulpit. Sermons fulfilled the functions now performed by broadcasting and newspapers. Every Sunday the Church's captive congregations embraced the majority of the nation, and no pulpit was more influential than that at St Paul's Cross, which was patronised by the Court and the great men of the City. It stood in the open air, on the north-east side of the Cathedral. The preacher faced the transept and was flanked on his left by the chancel. Nothing now remains of this once celebrated landmark, although the site is marked by an octagonal outline in the paving. The pulpit itself was constructed of timber but was mounted on stone steps and capped with a lead covered canopy. In 1643 the Long Parliament ordered its destruction, not because its structure was crumbling but because it was put to subversive use. A two tier open gallery backed onto the north wall of the chancel and enabled exalted personages to hear sermons without having to mingle with the populace. It was from Paul's Cross that George Neville, Bishop of London, proclaimed Edward IV's title to the Throne on 4 March 1461. Nine years later, Warwick's Chaplain preached a sermon from the same place denouncing him as an Usurper and reminding his congregation of their allegiance to Henry VI. These precedents helped make the St Paul's sermon 'a recognised instrument of revolution'. As the last two Kings had both been deposed with the Church's blessing, it seemed only equitable that Edward V should enjoy the same privilege.

The Protector presumably chose 22 June for Shaa's sensational revelation because it was the first Sunday following the release of the Duke of York. Obviously nothing would have persuaded the Queen to hand her son over voluntarily if she had known that he and his brother were about to be disinherited. Two other factors show how carefully the sermon was timed. The approach of the Northern army coincided with this crucial phase of the Usurpation, and Elizabeth Shore's recent public penance was calculated to draw attention to Edward's evil ways and hence to throw doubt on the legitimacy of his sons.

The text of Shaa's sermon was taken from the third verse of the fourth chapter of the Book of Wisdom. 'But the multiplying brood of the ungodly shall not thrive, nor take deep rooting from bastard slips, nor lay any fast foundation.' What this meant, the preacher explained, was that although bastards might wrongfully inherit other men's lands for a season, God in his grace and wisdom 'provideth that it continueth not in their blood long, but the truth coming to light, the rightful inheritors be restored, and the bastard slip pulled up ere it can be rooted deep'. That such was indeed the way in which Providence worked he proved with a wealth of examples from the books of the Old Testament. He next sang the praises of the Protector's father, the late Duke of York, and reminded his listeners that by the Act of Accord of 1460 Parliament had not only acknowledged his rightful claim to the Crown but had entailed the succession upon the Duke and his heirs. Shaa then came to the nub of his argument that neither Edward IV nor Clarence 'were lawfully begotten, but gotten unlawfully of other persons by the adultery of the Duchess their Mother'. The late Duke's close friends, who knew his family most intimately, believed that his sons Edward and George 'more resembled other known men than him'. But the Lord Protector, Shaa claimed, 'that very noble prince, the special pattern of Knightly prowess, represented the very face of the noble Duke, his father. This is the father's own figure, this his own countenance, the very print of his visage, the sure undoubted image, the plain express likeness of the noble Duke, whose remembrance can never die while he liveth'.

Vergil agrees with More that Dr Shaa laid great stress on the fact that Edward IV did not resemble his father, 'for he was high of stature, the other very little; he of large face, the other short and round. Howbeit, if such matters were well considered, no man could doubt but Richard was the Duke's true son, who by right ought to inherit the realm'. Those who had some regard for the Duchess of York's honour insisted that Edward IV resembled her Neville relations many of whom were giants among men.

Shaa's charges against the late King and his mother left his audience 'wonderous vehemently troubled in mind' and 'abashed with the shamefulness of the matter'. They hardly knew which was worst, 'the rashness, foolhardiness and doltishness of the preacher', or the 'madness of Richard's wicked mind, who would not see how great shame it was to his own house and to the whole realm, how great dishonour and blot, to condemn, in open audience, his mother of adultery, a woman of most pure and honourable life; to imprint upon his excellent and good brother the note of perpetual infamy; to lay upon his innocent nephews an everlasting reproach'. Some of those who heard Shaa's accusation were 'aghast with the outrageous cruelty of the horrible fact', and 'in great fear of themselves because they were friends to the King's children'; while others began 'to bewail the misfortune' of the Princes in the Tower 'whom they adjudged now utterly undone'. Such was the scandal caused by the Protector's allegations that half a century later Charles V's Ambassador to the Court of Henry VIII alluded to them in the course of a correspondence with Thomas Cromwell. Vergil, writing with the authority of one who could well have derived his information from Henry VII's Queen, the Duchess of York's grand-daughter, says that Cecily 'being falsely accused of adultery, complained afterwards in sundry places to right many noble men, whereof some yet live, of that great injury which her son Richard had done her'.

Shaa's accusations against the Duchess appear to have been

withdrawn, for two days later different reasons were found to disinherit the King. Presumably her indignant rejection of this atrocious calumny explains the change. Few wives could have been more faithful than the Duchess, who preferred the rigours of campaigning with her husband to separation. She was, moreover, a lady of exceptional piety who took the vows of the Sisters of St Benedict. Nobody could have been less convincingly cast in the role of an adulteress. It looks very much as if Richard desperately sought some legal excuse to reject his nephews' claim to the Throne. Having seized on the ill-considered idea of alleging his brother's bastardy, he instructed Shaa to preach his sermon. Impetuosity was one of the less fortunate characteristics he inherited from his father. But confronted by his outraged mother, and the hostile reaction of those who heard the charge, he shifted his attack, alleging that the late King's marriage was uncanonical, and hence none of his children legitimate. It does not say much for the wisdom of the initial strategy that it proved necessary to abandon it so soon.

Shaa's reputation was totally shattered by his infamous sermon. When he finished speaking his congregation 'stood as they had been turned into stone'. Those who had previously admired his 'learning and natural wit', were amazed he should play any part in 'such a business'. His subsequent fate provided a salutary warning for meddlesome prelates who shared his zeal for dabbling in politics. More says that when he returned home that Sunday he 'never after durst look out for shame, but kept him out of sight like an owl'. His friends reproached him so bitterly that he soon acknowledged his error, and, after a few months, apparently died of remorse.

CHAPTER SEVEN

'*A World of Cares*'
23 June–6 July 1483

Gloucester: *Will you enforce me to a world of cares?*
Call them again: I am not made of stone,
But penetrable to your kind entreaties,
Albeit against my conscience and my soul.

Shakespeare *Richard III* III.7

The hostility which greeted Dr Shaa's hastily contrived sermon showed how difficult it was to persuade people that Richard's title to the Throne was better than the King's. Having set sail on the wrong tack, and having encountered some dangerously choppy water, it was vital to change direction. The new course the Protector intended to steer was designed to avoid the reef which had shattered Shaa's reputation. Hardly anything more would be said of his mother's adultery, but a great deal would be made of his brother's unlawful marriage. This time it was left to Buckingham to explain. The Lord Mayor, Sheriffs and Aldermen, and the Judges and Magistrates of the City, were ordered to assemble on the morning of Tuesday, 24 June, to hear the Duke justify Richard's title to the Throne. This momentous meeting took place in the Guidhall, which had been built earlier in the century to rival Richard II's Westminster Hall. Since then, it has twice been threatened with destruction: by the Great Fire of 1666 and by the Blitz in 1940. The present building, although much restored, preserves its original crypt, porch and walls, and remains the scene of the Lord Mayor's Banquet. When Buckingham arrived at the Guildhall on 24 June, 'accompanied with divers Lords and Knights', he found the Mayor and Aldermen assembled at the east end with an expectant crowd of citizens gathered before them.

In the Middle Ages consent was regarded as being the essence of marriage. Betrothal was deemed to be just as binding as vows made in church, and Ecclesiastical Courts could annul a 'second' marriage if a pre-contract was proved. Henry VIII twice availed himself of this nicety of canon law to sever an irksome tie: when Anne Boleyn was accused of being pre-contracted to Northumberland, and when he got rid of Anne of Cleves on the ground of her previous betrothal to Francis, Duke of Lorraine.

The gist of Buckingham's argument was that Edward IV's marriage to Elizabeth Woodville in 1464 was bigamous, and hence Edward V was a bastard. The late King, so he claimed, 'was legally contracted to another wife to whom the Earl of Warwick had joined him'. Indeed, the Earl, acting on Edward's instructions, 'had espoused the other lady by proxy'. It was certainly true that in 1463 Warwick started negotiations for a marriage alliance between Princess Bona of Savoy, Louis XI's sister-in-law, and Edward IV. But if Buckingham was right in saying that these negotiations were successfully concluded, it is singular, to say the least, that the injured party raised no objection to the Woodville marriage. For nineteen years nothing was said, and then two days before the Protector deposed his nephew, Buckingham suddenly told the world that the boy's mother had never been lawfully married. So timely a revelation, for which Warwick or Clarence would have paid a king's ransom, strains coincidence beyond the limits of probability.

It was not enough for Buckingham to dismiss the claim of the Queen's children to the Throne without also demolishing that of the Duke of Clarence's son, Edward, Earl of Warwick. There would be little point in deposing Edward V merely to make his cousin King. Buckingham therefore went on to show that Warwick 'had been rendered ineligible for the crown by the felony of his father: since his father after conviction for treason had forfeited not only his own but also his son's right of succession.' Once these flaws were recognised, it necessarily followed that 'the only survivor of the royal stock was Richard, Duke of Gloucester, who was legally entitled to the Crown'. Buckingham then proceeded to argue that Richard's 'previous career and blameless morals would be a sure guarantee of his good government', but warned his audience that he would probably 'refuse such a burden', unless entreated to undertake it.

More exalts Buckingham's Guildhall speech into one of those elaborate orations which adorn classical histories, but for all his literary licence his narrative rests on authentic traditions. Not only was he familiar with the work of London Chroniclers, who witnessed the scenes they described, but his father, Sir John More, whom he acknowledges as one of his sources of information, was almost certainly present at the Guildhall that 24 June.

According to More, Buckingham told his audience that he had come to offer them what they had long desired: Law, order, and security. He then blamed the late King for most of the evils of the age, from foreign and civil war to a profligate court. He went on to speak of Shore's wife, 'a vile and abominable strumpet', whom the King had given a greater share in government than 'all the Lords in England'. There was no woman anywhere, he said, 'young or old, rich or poor', in whom Edward 'anything liked, either person or favour, speech, pace or countenance, but without any fear of God or respect of his honour, murmer or grudge of the World, he would importunely pursue his appetite and have her, to the great destruction of many a good woman and great dolour to their husband and their other friends'.

Buckingham next argued that Edward V's claim to the throne was specious. While not abandoning Shaa's contention that Edward IV was a bastard, he merely remarked in passing that it was not for him to enlarge upon a matter which could not but be offensive to the Protector whose 'filial reverence to his Mother' was common knowledge. He proceeded to claim that 'for lack of other issue lawfully coming of the late noble prince, Richard, Duke of York, to whose royal blood the crown of England and of France is by the high authority of Parliament entailed', the 'most excellent prince, the Lord Protector' was the rightful successor to the Throne.

The weight of the Duke's attack was directed against Edward IV. None of the late King's children he argued had been 'lawfully begotten, for as much as the King was never lawfully married unto the Queen their mother'. But here Buckingham – or perhaps Sir Thomas More – named Dame Elizabeth Lucy as the lady to whom Edward IV was supposedly pre-contracted. As Dame Elizabeth was one of the most notorious of Edward's mistresses, the story was not implausible. The King called her his 'witty concubine', and she was almost certainly the mother of his natural son Arthur Plantagenet, whom Henry VIII in 1523 created Viscount Lisle. Her character, however, was not such as to suggest that the King would have needed to promise to marry her before enjoying her favours. Buck calls her a 'wanton wench', perfectly 'willing and ready to yield herself to the King and his pleasures without any conditions'. Buckingham concluded his speech by inviting his audience to demonstrate their support for his proposal to make the Protector King, a request to which he would 'more graciously incline' if he knew that the petition found favour with 'the worshipful citizens of this the chief city of the realm'.

The Duke's appeal was received in sullen silence. As Shakespeare expressed it, 'The citizens are mum, say not a word'. Buckingham, however, had expected a great shout of 'King Richard! King Richard!' to soar to the rafters of the Guildhall. Indeed, he had been given to understand that the Mayor had previously rehearsed just such an outburst. But instead 'all was hushed and mute'. 'Marvellously abashed' by this frigid response, he asked the Mayor what it meant. Sir Edmund could only suggest that the audience had failed to grasp the force of the Duke's arguments. So Buckingham 'somewhat louder' went over the matter again, 'in other order and other words, so well and ornately, and nevertheless, so evidently and plain, with voice, gesture, and countenance so comely and convenient that every man much marvelled that heard him and thought that they never had in their lives heard so evil a tale so well told'. But for all his eloquence, the citizens stood 'as still as midnight' and not a whisper was heard.

In a despairing effort to break this 'marvellous obstinate silence', the Duke required his 'dear friends' to answer one way or another whether they intended 'to have this noble prince, now Protector', to be their King or not. Thus challenged, 'the people began to whisper among themselves secretly', and the sound was like that 'of a swarm of bees'. And then, at long last, some servants of Richard and Buckingham, supported by a group of rowdy apprentices, 'began suddenly at men's backs to cry out as loud as their throats would give, "King Richard! King Richard!" and threw up their caps in token of joy.' Buckingham deftly seized the opportunity by proclaiming it to be a 'goodly cry and joyful to hear, every man with one voice, no man saying nay'.

Shakespeare, closely following More, represents the Duke as telling Richard how he exploited this carefully rehearsed charade.

> Some followers of mine own
> At the lower end of the hall hurled up their caps,
> And some ten voices cried 'God save King Richard!'
> And thus I took the vantage of those few,
> 'Thanks, gentle citizens and friends!' quoth I,
> 'This general applause and cheerful shout
> Argues your wisdom and your love to Richard.'

The early Chroniclers were agreed that the Guildhall address was magnificently eloquent. Fabyan wrote of Buckingham's 'sugared words of exhortation' and particularly commended the Duke for speaking 'without any impediment or spitting'. *The Great Chronicle* remarked that such as heard him 'marvelled and said that never before that day had they heard any man, learned or unlearned, make such a recital or oration as that was'. It is a measure of the unpopularity of the policy recommended that so persuasive a speech fell on deaf ears.

On Wednesday, 25 June, the day appointed for the opening of Parliament, a number of members of both Houses petitioned the Protector to accept the Crown. The activities of this self-constituted 'Grand Council' owed much to Buckingham's direction. In order to give 'some semblance of constitutional legitimacy' to deposing Edward V, Richard 'could not entirely abandon the precedents of 1327, 1399 and 1461'. On these occasions, usurping Kings had obtained Parliament's approval of their titles. Thus the petition of 25 June became a precious argument on Richard's behalf, which he exploited to the utmost. Nevertheless, there are grounds for believing that the Assembly which offered him the Crown had no constitutional standing. The Parliament which met in January 1484 and settled the Crown on Richard and his issue, had such serious misgivings about its predecessor that it acknowledged in the preamble to its Royal Title Act that the Bishops, Peers and Commoners who drew up the June Petition were not then 'assembled in form of Parliament', and that consequently 'divers doubts, questions and ambiguities' had arisen.

According to Richard's argument, as his brother's rightful heir, he should have begun his reign on 9 April. That being so, the Writs to summon a Parliament in May 1483 were issued by an imposter. It therefore follows that the Assembly of 25 June was unlawfully convened and its Petition worthless. Parliament could not have things both ways. If, as it asserted, Edward V was no true King, then it, by the same token, was no true Parliament. Richard himself fully recognized this crucial flaw in his argument, and desperately struggled to resolve it. But the more he made of the Petition inviting him to accept the Throne, the more he was faced by the awkward fact that the Assembly possessed 'neither constitutional authority nor a right to speak for the Kingdom'.

The Petition which the Assembly presented to the Protector has not survived, but a version of it was incorporated in the Royal Title Act of January 1484, which presumably resembled the original fairly closely. In its final form, the Act provides the fully developed official vindication of Richard's Usurpation. The Croyland Chronicler reports a rumour current at the time, 'that the address had been got up in the North, whence such vast numbers were flocking to London'. It may not be too fanciful to suggest that there are hints in the spelling and wording of the Petition that a northerner had some hand in it.

The Petition began with a tendentious summary of the reign

of Edward IV, designed to discredit the Woodvilles, and to contrast Richard's blameless career with that of his dissolute brother. It wistfully recalled a legendary golden age of charity, peace and concord. But then Paradise was lost, 'the counsel of good, virtuous and prudent persons' was ignored, and 'insolent and vicious' favourites ruled the realm. Above all, Edward IV's 'ungracious pretensed marriage (as all England has cause so to say) made betwixt the said King Edward and Elizabeth, some time wife of Sir John Grey, Knight, late naming herself and many years heretofore Queen of England', was the cause of mischiefs as various 'as murders, extortions, and oppressions, namely of poor and impotent people, so that no man was sure of his life, land nor livelihood, nor of his wife, daughter nor servant, every good maiden and woman standing in dread to be ravished and defouled'. Such was the everyday currency of fifteenth century protest, and most of these things had been said by Warwick of Edward IV, by Edward of Henry VI, and by Henry IV of Richard II. But in 1484 the invective was directed against the late not the living King, as Edward V could hardly be blamed for this catalogue of iniquities.

The 1484 version of Parliament's Petition, instead of naming Princess Bona, or Elizabeth Lucy, as the wife to whom 'King Edward stood troth plight', cast a third person for the role: Lady Eleanor Butler, daughter of the 'Old Earl of Shrewsbury'. Lady Eleanor was born in 1435 and married Sir Thomas Butler while still a girl. Her husband died when she was in her mid-twenties. Buck describes her as 'a very fair and noble lady', who inspired the King's most 'fervent and vehement' affection. But only too soon he discarded her, at which she was 'greatly grieved and lived a melancholic and heavy and solitary life ever after'. How she died 'is not certainly known, but it is out of doubt that the King killed her not with kindness'. It is possible that Lady Eleanor's name was substituted for that of Dame Elizabeth Lucy in the 1484 version of the Petition for fear that Arthur Plantagenet might claim the Throne. After all, if the late King was lawfully married to Dame Elizabeth, it was difficult to avoid the conclusion that her son was his rightful heir. One further reason has been suggested for what looks like the last minute introduction of Lady Eleanor's name. If the Petition of June 1483, in fact, mentioned Princess Bona, the French Court might well deny the story. Hence the need to find a less vulnerable name. A not inconsiderable advantage of the liaison described in the Act of 1484 was that neither of the parties supposedly involved was alive to refute the charge.

One of the first measures of Henry VII's Parliament in 1485 repealed the Act of 1484 confirming Richard's title, and ordered the destruction of all existing copies of the document. Naturally, Henry VII was anxious to suppress aspersions about the legitimacy of Elizabeth of York, his future Queen. Because so many copies of the Act were burned, and because its handling of the pre-contract was so objectionable to the Tudors, no sixteenth century writer mentioned Lady Eleanor. It was only when Buck in the reign of James I listed the allegations of the 1484 Act that her name appeared in print.

Philippe de Commynes, one of Louis XI's most trusted counsellors, says in his Memoirs that Richard first heard of his brother's betrothal from Robert Stillington. Stillington, despite humble origins, rose to be Bishop of Bath and Wells and Lord Chancellor. But in 1478 he fell from favour and spent some weeks in the Tower. He had been closely associated with Clarence, whose cause he may have defended with too much zeal. According to Commynes, Stillington told the Duke of Gloucester early in 1483 'that King Edward, being very enamoured of a certain English lady, promised to marry her, provided he could sleep with her first, and she consented. The Bishop said that he had married them when only he and they were present. He was a courtier so he did not disclose this fact but helped to keep the lady quiet'. It is difficult to decide which was the more dishonourable, his initial silence or his subsequent disclosures. The Bishop's career after Bosworth shows him to have been an ambitious and crafty intriguer. Soon after the Battle he was arrested and then pardoned, but in 1487 was once more dabbling in treason, this time supporting Lambert

Simnel's conspiracy. For the third time he was imprisoned, and died shortly after.

If Commynes was right in believing that Stillington helped Richard to discredit Edward V, his motives are plain to discern. He had long nursed a rancorous grievance against the Queen and her Woodville relations. He deeply resented the fact that Edward IV had deprived him of the Lord Chancellorship in 1475. It was said that he hoped to marry his bastard son to Elizabeth of York, and finally, as Commynes expressed it, 'this wicked Bishop kept thoughts of revenge in his heart' for the time he spent in the Tower in 1478. Nor would a man so eager for high office in Church and State have failed to appreciate that once Richard became King he would have the means of rewarding those who had helped him to win the Throne. Few people would be more deserving of his gratitude than a priest prepared to risk his immortal soul by offering false witness.

The most compelling reason for rejecting the story of Edward IV's precontract is that there is not a shred of evidence to support it. It was based on a series of assertions, almost certainly invented, intended to justify the unlawful deposition of the rightful King. The Petition is remarkable for supplying no proof whatever of its charges, professing them to be matters of common knowledge, and offering 'hereafter, if and as the case shall require', to provide sufficient proof 'in time and place convenient'. There is no record that this promise was kept, or that witnesses were examined. Francis Bacon, one of England's most illustrious lawyers, dismissed the charge as a 'fable' long since 'exploded'. Not a single writer who lived through the Usurpation was any less sceptical, and all were agreed that Richard 'had himself crowned on fraudulent grounds'. More refers to the story of Edward's prior betrothal as nothing more than a 'convenient pretext' for deposing Edward V, and Rous describes the arguments deployed on Richard's behalf, as 'feigned for his own advancement'. When Mancini discusses the consultations which followed Buckingham's Guildhall appeal, he is at pains to stress that what finally persuaded the nobles to acquiesce in the Usurpation was not the force of his argument, but the fact that 'the alliance of the two Dukes' would be 'hazardous to resist'.

In so far as the Royal Title Act of 1484 denounced the marriage of Edward IV, it exceeded its jurisdiction. Laymen were not qualified to meddle in matrimonial matters, which were principally regulated by ecclesiastical law. Had Richard seriously believed that the King was illegitimate, he should have submitted evidence to a Church court. His failure to do so suggests scant confidence in his claim. When Henry VIII divorced Anne of Cleves in 1541, he followed the proper procedure. First, he applied to the Convocations of York and Canterbury to pronounce on her prior betrothal, and then, on the strength of their verdict, requested Parliament to annul his marriage. But he was on sure ground in alleging her pre-contract.

It is evident that in Richard's lifetime few people took his bastardy charges seriously. The rulers of Europe would hardly have contemplated marriage alliances with Edward's daughters had they reason to doubt they were lawfully begotten. Nor would Englishmen have rejoiced in the match between Henry Tudor and Elizabeth of York if they had thought her illegitimate. Finally, even assuming that the pre-contract took place precisely as stated in the 1484 Act, it could not justify Edward V's deposition. Lady Eleanor Butler died in 1468, two years before the birth of the Prince of Wales. Marriage vows last 'till death do us part', but not beyond the grave. It was consequently useless to cite a terminated contract as proof that the King was the child of a bigamous union.

Richard, having disposed of Edward's children, had still to reject the Earl of Warwick's claim. This he had little difficulty in doing, because, so he said, the boy was disabled from succeeding by the Act of Attainder passed against his father. But, in fact, the 1478 Act merely deprived Clarence's issue of the 'honour, estate, dignity and name of duke', and said nothing whatever about excluding them from the Throne. Moreover, both precedent and law established that acts of attainder did not, and could not, prevent a man being King. Henry V and Edward V were the only two Kings of the House of Lancaster and York who were not attainted at some time in their lives. The fact that Henry IV, Henry VI, Edward IV and Richard III himself, reigned despite attainders, exposed the flaw in the theory that Warwick was somehow debarred.

On the same day that the so-called 'Parliament' agreed on its Petition to the Protector, Lord Rivers, and most of those arrested with him on 30 April, were beheaded at Pontefract Castle. It is probable that the order for their execution was sent north on 17 June with the Writs of Supersedeas cancelling the Coronation and opening of Parliament. It is hardly conceivable that such instructions could have been given unless it had also been decided to make the Protector King. Rous alone suggests that the 'conspirators' were given some form of trial, with Northumberland presiding as Chief Judge, but he agrees with other contemporary chroniclers that they were 'innocent of the deed charged against them'.

The sentence of Rivers, like that of Hastings, was totally unconstitutional, because it ignored his legal right to trial by his Peers in the High Court of Parliament. He received the news of his impending execution on 23 June, and at once made a will requesting to be buried next to his nephew, Richard Grey. He also composed a ballad on the Mutability of Fortune: a subject on which he wrote with authority. There was 'no redress', he proclaimed, for the 'unsteadfastness of this world', and as it was vain to try to resist fate, he was 'willing to die'. The philosophical resignation inspiring his lament was in keeping with his temperament, but also owed much to the medieval image of Fortune's Wheel on which men revolve from the summit of wealth and power to the depths of shame and despair.

On 24 June, while Buckingham was addressing his audience in the Guildhall, Rivers was making his last journey from Sheriff Hutton to Pontefract, where Richard II had also met his end. The Castle stood on a commanding hill, and was a formidable royal fortress. All that is left of it now is one of its towers and the outlines of its foundations. Nothing else remains to evoke its awesome past as the site has become a Municipal Park: ordered, trim and soulless. Sir Richard Ratcliffe supervised the executions which took place on the last day of Edward V's reign. The spectacle was witnessed by the army which Richard had summoned earlier in the month. The prisoners were not suffered to speak from the scaffold, 'lest their words might have inclined men to pity them and to hate the Protector'. More says they were beheaded 'without judgment, process, or manner of order', for no better reason than that 'they were good men, too true to the King and too nigh to the Queen'. Their headless corpses were buried naked in the Monastery at Pontefract. The hairshirt which Rivers was found to be wearing became a relic of the Carmelite Friars at Doncaster who hung it for many years before an image of the Virgin. 'Of all Richard's victims he was the noblest and most accomplished'. But like Hastings he stood in Richard's way and like Hastings therefore he had to die.

On Thursday, 26 June, 'the Mayor and all the Aldermen and Chief Commoners of the City, in their best manner apparelled, assembling themselves together, resorted unto Baynard's Castle', where the Protector had taken up residence, to offer him the Petition inviting him to be King. 'To which place repaired also, according to their appointment, the Duke of Buckingham, with divers noblemen with him, besides many Knights and other gentlemen'. Baynard's Castle, or 'York House' as it was sometimes called in the late fifteenth century, rose like a Venetian palace from the Thames. The building was designed round a courtyard, flanked by hexagonal towers. It was situated close to the outlet where the Fleet Ditch ran into the Thames, a little to the east of the present Mermaid Theatre. Originally, the Castle was built by Ralph Baynard, one of William the Conqueror's captains. It was rebuilt after a fire in 1428 by Humphrey Duke of Gloucester, and passed to Henry VI on the Duke's attainder. Soon after, the King either gave or sold the property to Richard Duke of York who made it his Town house. After his death, the Duchess continued to live there, and it was in the Great Hall of the Castle that Archbishop Bourchier in 1461 invited Prince Edward of York to accept the Throne. Nothing remains of the Castle today as it was gutted in the Great Fire of 1666, but the

Lithograph, 1842, by Thomas Shotter Boys, of the interior of Guildhall.

Richard's handwritten postscript about Buckingham's rebellion in a letter of
12 October 1483 to the Lord Chancellor, Bishop Russell.

Hastings' castle at Kirby Muxloe.

Pietro Torrigiano's bronze sculpture of Henry VII and Elizabeth of York in Westminster Abbey.

name is preserved in a nearby public house. Excavations on the site in 1972 uncovered its foundations. Mancini says that Richard had 'purposely betaken himself' to his mother's house so 'that these events might not take place in the Tower where the young King was'. Presumably he somehow contrived to persuade her that Dr Shaa was solely responsible for the scandalous sermon preached at Paul's Cross. It is difficult to believe that she would otherwise have forgiven him so soon.

Buckingham spoke on behalf of the assembled company, begging the Protector to 'behold the long continued distress and decay' of the realm, 'and to set his gracious hand to the redress and amendment thereof by taking upon him the Crown, according to his right and title lawfully descended unto him'. Richard, at first, professed his reluctance to bear 'the golden yoke of Sovereignty'. Nor, so he said, would the 'love he bore unto King Edward and his children' allow him to set his nephew's claim aside. Shakespeare well perceived the calculation which led him to feign unwillingness.

> Cousin of Buckingham, and sage grave men,
> Since you will buckle fortune on my back,
> To bear her burthen, whe'er I will or no,
> I must have patience to endure the load:
> But if black scandal or foul-faced reproach
> Attend the sequel of your imposition,
> Your mere enforcement shall acquittance me
> From all the impure blots and stains thereof . . .

Regardless of Richard's posturing, and his pretence that the last thing he wanted was power, he eventually allowed himself to be persuaded. It was generally agreed, said Buckingham, that 'King Edward's line should not any longer reign upon them': although heaven knows what the young Prince had done to provoke this desperate resolve. Unhappily, if Richard persisted in refusing their offer, they would be forced to invite 'some other nobleman' to take the Crown. The Duke's words much moved the Protector, who otherwise, 'as every man may wit, would never of likelihood have inclined thereunto'.

The carefully stage-managed ceremonies by which the Protector became King, closely followed the pattern of Edward

IV's inauguration. Both brothers had their titles proclaimed in a service at St Paul's. Both were begged to accept the Crown at Baynard's Castle. Both formally began their reigns by seating themselves in the Marble Chair of King's Bench in the Great Hall of Westminster Palace. Both endeavoured to fortify their claims by appealing to the ancient tradition of election as well as primogeniture. But, if More is to be believed, Richard's 'mockish election' availed him nothing. 'There was no man so dull but he perceived well enough' what lay behind these antics. More draws an analogy between the real world and a stage. The audience at a play know perfectly well that the actor who assumes the role of a sultan is in fact only a shoemaker. But not one of them would be so foolish as to 'call him by his own name while he standeth in Majesty', for fear of being hit on the head for 'marring the play'. In just the same way, the subjects of Richard III perceived the truth but did not dare acknowledge it.

On 26 June, after assenting to 'Parliament's' Petition, 'The King's said highness, notably assisted by well near all the lords spiritual and temporal and the commons of this realm', rode to the Palace of Westminster, and there, in 'honorable robes apparelled, within the Great Hall, took possession and declared that the same day he would begin to reign'. Westminster Hall was originally built by William Rufus at the close of the eleventh century, but was almost totally reconstructed between 1397 and 1399. No sooner was the work approaching completion than Richard II, whose chief glory it was, was deposed by Prince Henry of Lancaster, his own first cousin, who persuaded the three estates to meet under its magnificent hammer-beam roof and sanction his seizure of the Throne. Besides sessions of Parliament, the Hall was also used for judicial proceedings. Richard's own brother, Clarence, was tried there for treason in 1478. Unlike the rest of the Palace of Westminster it somehow survived the fire of 1834, and in recent times has witnessed the lying-in-state of King George VI and Sir Winston Churchill. In 1224 Henry III ordered three judgment seats to be placed in it for the Court of King's Bench, the Court of Common Pleas, and the Court of Chancery. The

King's Bench, or 'Sedes Regalis', was made of marble and was placed at the upper end of the Hall on the right-hand side. In 1680, during the reconstruction of the Palace, it was removed to make way for a door. The *Great Chronicle* refers to it as 'the King's Chair or place where all Kings take first possession'. The climax of a Sovereign's secular enthronement was the moment he seated himself on the King's Bench. In 1460, the Duke of York had dismayed his fellow peers by presuming to place his hand on its sacred surface. But when his youngest son 'obtruded himself into the marble chair', no-one dared object. During this ceremony, Lord Howard stood on Richard's right hand, and the Duke of Suffolk, his sister Elizabeth's husband, on his left.

The new King delivered a 'long oration' to those present, particularly addressing his remarks to the Judges and Magistrates in his audience. He began by declaring his intention to reign from that day onwards, and went on to say that the chief duty of a King was to administer the laws effectively. To that end, he exhorted the legal profession to conduct itself 'in right straight manner, justly and duly without delay or favour'. He concluded by expressing his wish to achieve concord throughout the realm, and assured his audience 'that he did put out of his mind all emnities and that he there did openly pardon all offences committed against him'.

From Westminster Hall, Richard proceeded to the Abbey, where he was presented with the sceptre of St Edward. After receiving the sacrament at the shrine, he was 'conveyed to the choir and was set there while Te Deum was sung in a feigned manner by the monks'. From the Abbey, he rode to St Paul's Cathedral and was received throughout the journey 'with great congratulations and acclamation of all the people', at least according to his own account of the proceedings. That night he lodged in the Royal Palace at Westminster, and the following day was 'proclaimed throughout the city, King of England, by the name of Richard III.'

The absence of opposition to Richard in June 1483 may seem remarkable, particularly in view of his subsequent unpopularity. But the coups by which he seized the Throne were so sudden and swift that there was no opportunity to oppose them until it was too late to do so effectively. By 26 June, the choice before those who deplored the Usurpation was whether to acknowledge that Richard had successfully made himself King, or to risk all on behalf of a boy who might well be dead. Moreover, time-servers could always justify opportunism as a pious submission to Providence. By the same token, it profited a man little to defend a dynasty which God no longer appeared willing to sustain.

The Garrison at Calais took an oath of fealty to Edward V soon after it heard of his father's death. On learning that their Captain, Lord Hastings, had been executed as a traitor, they wrote to the Protector to discover what was happening. On 28 June, instructions were sent explaining that two days earlier the Protector had become King, and that consequently the Garrison should transfer its allegiance to him. Calais, of course, was not alone in taking an oath to Edward V. Similar oaths had also been taken 'in divers places in England, by many great estates and personages being then ignorant of the very true and sure title which our sovereign lord that now is, King Richard III, hath to the Crown of England'. In other words, even if Edward V had mistakenly been acknowledged as King on 9 April, the Duke of Gloucester should by rights have succeeded his brother. 'That oath notwithstanding, now every good true Englishman is bound, upon knowledge had of the said very true title, to depart from the first oath, so ignorantly given to him to whom it appertained not; and therefore to make his oath anew, and owe his service and fidelity to him that good law, reason, and the concord assent of the Lords and Commons of the realm, have ordained to reign upon the people, which is our said sovereign lord King Richard III'.

The instructions went on to refer to the Petition presented to the Protector on 26 June, in which, it was claimed, his 'sure and true title is evidently shewed and declared'. Much was also made of the approval of the 'Lords Spiritual and Temporal and the Commons of this realm'. The document was an ingenious mixture of specious casuistry, demonstrable falsehoods, calculated omissions, and half-truths. No mention, of course, was made of the deception and duress by which 'assent' was won. As for the popular enthusiasm claimed for the Usurpation, it escaped the notice of other observers. When Richard 'exhibited himself in the streets of the City', wrote Mancini, 'he was scarcely watched by anybody, rather did they curse him with a fate worthy of his crimes.'

Richard spent the two days following the Westminster ceremonies in planning his Coronation fixed for 6 July, making appointments, and rewarding those who had helped him to seize the Throne. On Friday, 27 June, at Baynard's Castle, Russell handed back the Great Seal to Richard, who thereupon re-appointed him Lord Chancellor and returned it to his keeping. The next day, Buckingham was made Great Chamberlain and Constable of England, Catesby was created Chancellor of the Exchequer, and Lord Howard Earl Marshal and Admiral of England. Hope of reward had been the principal inspiration of many of Richard's supporters and he was not so rash as to disappoint them. Buckingham was generously endowed with 'castles, lordships, manors, lands and tenements' in Shropshire, Hereford, North and South Wales and the Welsh Marches. Lord Howard was created Duke of Norfolk: a title to which he was heir, provided the Duke of York was dead, or deprived of his rights. He was furthermore given estates in several counties to support his dukedom, and his son, Sir Thomas Howard, was made Earl of Surrey. Others rewarded included Brackenbury, Catesby and Lovell. Most of the property thus distributed belonged to the Crown, but some to the Woodvilles.

On the same day that Richard rewarded his followers, he conferred the title of Prince of Wales on his only legitimate child, Edward, Earl of Salisbury, then ten years old. In explaining his reasons for so doing, he stated his belief that 'among the provinces subject to us none requires separate and immediate rule under us as much as the principality of Wales, because of its remote position and because of the language and customs of the people'. Consequently, 'following the footsteps of our ancestors, we have determined to honour our dearest first born son Edward and do make and create him Prince of Wales and Earl of Chester.'

The Northern force, which Richard sent for on 10 June, and which witnessed the executions at Pontefract on 25 June, finally reached London on 1 July, where it was joined by fresh levies which Buckingham had sent for from Wales. The mere knowledge that Richard's army was marching south sufficed to exert a powerful influence on events in London, which the two Dukes had anyway dominated from the moment they entered the City on 4 May. The number of troops expected from the North was much exaggerated in prospect. Stallworth mentioned a figure of twenty thousand expected to reach the Capital soon after 22 June. In fact, the forces which eventually mustered on Finsbury Fields consisted of about four thousand men. They were surprisingly ill equipped, and the terror inspired by their approach turned to contempt on their arrival. Fabyan describes them as wearing 'their best jacks and rusty salettes with a few in white harness not burnished to the sale'. Nevertheless, the very fact that they had reached London diminished the risk of hostile demonstrations during the Coronation. Richard went out to meet them at Finsbury where they were drawn up ready for inspection in a great circle. After passing bare-headed around their ranks, he thanked them for their loyalty. Immediately after the Coronation the army was sent home.

On 4 July, Richard and his Queen proceeded in state down the Thames from Westminster to the Tower from which it was customary for Kings to set out for their Coronation. In spite of the overwhelming military resources at Richard's disposal, he still feared the possibility of disturbances, and considered it necessary to issue a Proclamation 'forbidding any person under penalty of death, on account of any old or new quarrel, to make any challenge or affray whereby the peace might be broken, or any sedition or disturbance of the peace within the City of London'. He further 'commanded that no man, under pain of imprisonment, should take any lodging in the city or suburbs, except by appointment of the King's harbingers'. Finally, 'Everyone was to be in his lodging by ten o'clock at night; and the carrying of glaives, bills, long and short swords and bucklers was prohibited'. It is strange that such precautions had to be taken if the King really believed what he told the Calais Garrison about the 'great congratulation and acclamation of all the people in every place'.

Soon after reaching the Tower, Richard invested seventeen gentlemen with knighthoods and released most of those held prisoner since 13 June. Archbishop Rotherham, on whose behalf the University of Cambridge had interceded, was allowed to return to his diocese. Stanley was not only set free but appointed Lord Steward of the King's Household. Morton alone was considered too dangerous to be given his liberty, and was sent to Brecknock Castle under Buckingham's custody. During the night of 4 July, two Kings slept in the Tower of London for the only time in its history: although possibly Edward V slept the sleep of the dead.

On Saturday, the King rode in state from the Tower to the Palace of Westminster. As he passed along the two mile route, 'he greeted all onlookers, and himself received their acclamations'. Richard was attended by an impressive number of nobles, including three Dukes, nine Earls and twenty-two Lords. Their presence certainly seemed to demonstrate the support of the peerage for changing the succession. The King wore a blue doublet wrought with nets and pineapples, over which was a purple cloak trimmed with ermine. He was escorted by seven henchmen wearing short white gowns of cloth of gold and crimson doublets. The Queen's mantle matched the henchmen's gowns and was trimmed with Venice gold and furred with ermine. Peter Curteys, Keeper of the Wardrobe, had been obliged to pay his tailors bonuses to complete the royal garments in under a week. But the most splendid spectacle of all was Buckingham, wearing a blue velvet cloak blazened with his device of golden cart wheels.

The Coronation service on Sunday 6 July began with a procession from Westminster Hall to the Abbey, the King and Queen walking barefoot on a specially laid carpet. They were led by numerous priests, abbots and bishops, so that a river of mitres and crosiers could be seen weaving its way through the crowds. The Cardinal Archbishop of Canterbury, who had claimed to be too old to bury the late King, shuffled behind a Cross held high by the Bishop of Rochester. Following these dignitaries of the Church Militant came the greatest nobles of the land, bearing their symbols of office or royal insignia. Northumberland carried the pointless sword of mercy: a quality not much in evidence at Pontefract ten days before. Lord Stanley bore the mace of Constable, Kent and Lovell naked swords of justice, and Surrey the sword of State in a rich scabbard. Next came the Duke of Norfolk, Earl Marshal of England, holding the Crown in his hands,

> Within whose circuit is Elysium
> And all that poets feign of bliss and joy.

The King's brother-in-law, the Duke of Suffolk, carried the sceptre, and Suffolk's son, the Earl of Lincoln, the Orb. Richard, wearing a coat and surcoat of crimson satin and a purple velvet robe furred with ermine, was supported by the Bishop of Bath and Wells, whose timely revelations were said to have opened his eyes to his right to the Throne. The Barons of the Cinque Ports held a gorgeous canopy over his head and his train was carried by the Duke of Buckingham. A drove of assorted noblemen made up the tail of the King's procession.

Buckingham was later rumoured to have been incensed by the humble role assigned to him at the Coronation. He particularly resented the fact that the Duke of Norfolk had been appointed to act as High Steward, and it vexed his proud spirit to play the part of a page to the man he had made King. More says that Buckingham left the Coronation banquet 'feigning himself sick; and King Richard said it was done in hatred and despite of him'. Nor did it escape notice that his wife, the Queen Dowager's sister, Catherine, was nowhere to be seen.

Queen Anne's procession was almost as magnificent as that of the King. The Earl of Huntingdon walked before her bearing her sceptre, and the Earl of Wiltshire her Crown. Her robes matched those of her husband, and her train was carried by Lady Margaret Beaufort, now Lady Stanley, who two years later returned to the Abbey to see her son crowned. The royal pair were escorted from the West Door to Chairs of State placed in St Edward's shrine where they sat and listened to 'divers holy hymns' being 'solemnly sung'.

Regarded sacramentally, the climax of the Coronation is not crowning but anointing. Following the hymns, Richard and his Queen stripped themselves to the waist before the High Altar so that holy oil could be poured over their backs, breasts, shoulders, palms and hair. The ampulla containing the sacred oil was enclosed in a golden eagle garnished with pearls and precious stones. Happily, this splendid relic survived destruction during the Commonwealth and remains part of the royal regalia. The oil preserved in it was reputed to have been presented to Archbishop Becket by the Virgin Mary. From then onwards, Kings were no longer obliged 'to buy their oil at the apothecary's but had it brought direct from Heaven'.

After being anointed, the King and Queen were arrayed in fresh robes of cloth of gold and crowned by Archbishop Bourchier. Richard was then presented with the Orb and Sceptre, while a Te Deum was sung which must have been heard by the Dowager Queen from the Abbot's lodging nearby. Next, Mass was said and the royal pair received the Sacrament kneeling before the High Altar. The service concluded, they returned in the same order of procession to the Palace of Westminster, this time carrying their regalia.

Before the Coronation Banquet, which started at four o'clock, the King and Queen retired to their apartments while the Duke of Norfolk rode into the Hall and cleared it of spectators. The seating arrangement for the great Coronation Feast paid meticulous regard to the precedence of the guests. The King sat at the centre of a table raised on a dais. The Bishop of Durham was placed on his right and the Queen on his left. It was customary for the Archbishop of Canterbury to be given the place of honour but Bourchier returned to Lambeth. Perhaps he was too exhausted to remain, or perhaps he intended a gesture of reproach. Mancini described him as crowning Richard 'unwillingly'. The ladies sat at a long table in the middle of the Hall, at another sat the Lord Chancellor presiding over members of the House of Lords, and 'at a table next to the cupboard sat the Lord Mayor and Aldermen'. There were 'divers other tables, whereat also many noble and worshipful persons sat and dined'. Richard ate off plates of gold, the Queen off gilt, and others who sat at the royal table off silver. Amongst those who served the dishes set before the King were his two boyhood companions, Sir Robert Percy and Lord Lovell.

When the second course was served, the King's Champion, Sir Robert Dymmock, rode into the Hall, dressed in full armour on a horse trapped with white and red silk. His hereditary office was created by William the Conqueror who conferred it on Marmion from whom it had descended through the female line to the Dymmocks. Sir Robert proclaimed in defiant tones that if any man there present 'should say that King Richard III was not lawfully King, he would fight him with all utterance', and he threw down his gauntlet as proof of that intent. The only response to his challenge was a shout of 'King Richard! Long live King Richard!' When the Champion had repeated his offer in different parts of the Hall, he was given a gilded bowl, the ancient fee for his service. Then Garter King-at-arms proclaimed the King's styles and title while other heralds scattered a hundred pounds of largesse. At last, as it began to grow dark, the King and Queen retired to their apartments in the Palace. Apart from Edward V, the most notable person absent was the newly created Prince of Wales. No explanation was offered. Possibly he was ill, or perhaps it was feared that the sight of the boy might prove too dangerous a reminder of his namesake in the Tower.

The unsurpassed magnificence of Richard's Coronation was no doubt designed to disguise the grave defects of his title. Nevertheless, he was now an anointed King and God's Lieutenant on Earth. His subjects had no other choice but to offer him their allegiance or risk the penalties of treason. It is easy to see why Richard spared no cost to put on this glittering pageant, but harder to understand how honourable men could deign to support the charade.

CHAPTER EIGHT

'Young Edward Lives'
7 July–25 December 1483

Richard: *Young Edward lives; Think now what I would speak.*

Buckingham: *Say on, my loving lord.*

Richard: *Why, Buckingham, I say I would be King.*

Buckingham: *Why, so you are, my thrice renownéd lord.*

Richard: *Cousin, thou was not wont to be so dull.*
               Shall I be plain? I wish the bastards dead.

Shakespeare *Richard III* IV.11

Just over a fortnight after the Coronation Richard set out on a Royal Progress. The meagre military escort which accompanied him on his journey suggests that he did not expect opposition. But he was not so foolish as to believe that he could hope to survive for long on nothing more than grudging acquiescence. The reign of Henry IV showed what fate had in store for usurpers: a weary round of conspiracies and rebellion. Unless he won positive and widespread support he risked being overthrown. It was for this reason that he decided to make a tour of his kingdom and woo the hearts of his subjects. Once people saw for themselves how eager he was to redress grievances and to amend wrongs, they would recognize the wisdom of those who had offered him the Crown. One grave obstacle, however, stood in the way of his bid for popular favour. Unlike Henry IV, or, indeed, his own brother, he could not justify his seizure of the Throne on the grounds of previous misgovernment. They had been able to rely on powerful support from those antagonized by Richard II or Henry VI. But everyone knew that Edward V was innocent of blame. So Richard's Usurpation was seen as a crude bid for power, and nothing but sympathy was felt for the boy he dispossessed.

In the Middle Ages Kings were expected to maintain their royal estate with princely ostentation. Men judged them by the splendour of their Courts, the lavishness of their hospitality, and the number of attendants who accompanied them on their journeys. Nobody understood better than Edward IV the value of display. Admittedly, it was no hardship for one so vain to appear in fine clothes and dazzling jewels. Nor did he ever weary of dancing, feasting and jousting. He even revived the old custom of wearing the Crown on great occasions. Richard's magnificent Coronation showed that he too recognized the importance of pageantry, and the noble retinue which followed him on his Progress could hardly have failed to exalt the royal image. He began his journey from Windsor accompanied by five bishops, his nephews Lincoln and Warwick, Lovell, Lord Stanley, and a splendid array of peers, knights and officers of the Household. Nobody could have seen this great cavalcade pass by and not have felt awed by its majesty. The Duke of Buckingham accompanied the King for most of the first part of the journey, but the Queen did not join him until the Court took up residence at Warwick.

The royal party reached Oxford on Thursday, 24 July, after a brief visit to Reading. The King, in fact, was a Cambridge man at heart, as he soon revealed by his patronage and appointments. The Bishop of Lincoln, John Russell, was the only Oxford man he appointed to high office. Moreover, his generous gifts to King's and Queens' were unmatched in the older University. But none of these things were apparent in July 1483, and Richard did his utmost to make himself agreeable. Throughout his stay he lodged at Magdalen, and was entertained by William Waynflete, Bishop of Winchester, the founder of the College. On Friday, the King attended two disputations held in Magdalen Hall. One of those who debated before him was William Grocyn, then relatively unknown, but later famous as the friend of More, Erasmus and Colet. During his stay, Richard visited several other Colleges and patiently listened to torrents of florid rhetoric. Such was his desire to please that he scattered largesse with abandon. Grocyn was presented with a buck and five marks, while the scholars of Magdalen received wine and venison. After Richard left the College, Waynflete had the words 'Vivat Rex in aeternum' written in its register. As it happened, the aged Bishop outlived the King and witnessed the triumph of Henry Tudor.

From Oxford, the royal party moved north to Woodstock, where Richard was able to gratify the townspeople by a generous gesture at little cost to himself. Edward IV, during one of his visits to the town, annexed a large tract of neighbouring land by an arbitrary exploitation of the law. Much as this improved his hunting it grieved those who found themselves deprived of 'a great area of the country'. Richard now restored this land to its former use, to the delight of the local inhabitants.

After leaving Woodstock for Gloucester, he stayed at Minster Lovell. The Manor House had been rebuilt in the early part of the century by Francis Lovell's grandfather, William Lovell. It was arranged round a quadrangle on the banks of the River Windrush, near the church which Henry VI gave to his College of Our Lady of Eton. The church is still in use, but only the ruins of the Great Hall and the south-west Tower remain of the Manor. Francis Lovell was not only created a Viscount by the King, but Chamberlain of the Household and Chief Butler of England. Somehow he evaded capture after Bosworth, and reappeared fighting for Lambert Simnel at Stoke. Legend has it that he escaped once more from the battlefield and hid in a cave or vault. In 1708, when a chimney was being repaired in the southwest Tower of Minster Lovell, an underground room was revealed. It was found to contain a skeleton sitting at a table, on which was a pen, paper and book. Lovell's descendants believed that at long last they had found where he had concealed himself.

One mysterious vestige of the King's visit, is a letter he sent from Minster Lovell 'To the Right Reverent Father in God our right trusty and well-beloved the Bishop of Lincoln, our

Chancellor of England'. It referred in a somewhat cryptic manner to an 'enterprise' lately undertaken by 'certain persons' now 'in ward'. The Chancellor was instructed to arrange a commission 'to sit upon them, and to proceed to the due execution of our laws in that behalf'. It has been suggested that those arrested had conspired to release the Princes from the Tower, or their sisters from Sanctuary. It seems unlikely, however, that so important a plot would have left no other trace. But whatever the nature of the sedition mentioned, it was evidently serious, coming as it did only three weeks after Richard's Coronation. Considered in retrospect, it looks suspiciously like one of those preliminary tremors which precede political earthquakes.

After leaving Minster Lovell, Richard crossed the Cotswolds and made for Gloucester. When Queen Margaret besieged the City in 1471 it told her that it was the Duke of Gloucester's town and would only open its gates to the King or his brother. It was now rewarded for its loyalty by being created an independent county with its own Lord Mayor and Sheriffs. Moreover, Richard, eager as ever to win popularity, declined its offer to help to defray the cost of his Progress, 'affirming that he would rather have their love than their treasure'. Before continuing his journey north, he took leave of Buckingham, who set off home for Brecon with the Bishop of Ely.

On 4 August, Richard visited the scene of the Battle of Tewkesbury and the tomb of the Duke and Duchess of Clarence behind the altar in the Abbey. While in the town, he promised to repay a considerable debt which the Duke owed the monastery. After a brief visit to Worcester, the King reached Warwick Castle on 8 August, where alarming reports reached him of threatened risings on behalf of Edward V. There was, of course, no longer any acceptable reason he could give for detaining his nephews in the Tower, and it may be that rumours of plots to free them finally convinced him that they were better dead. If More is to be believed – and it must be admitted that his version of the Princes' murder is exceedingly suspect – it was during the King's visit to Warwick that he ordered Sir James Tyrell to see that the boys were dispatched.

Dr Johnson once told Boswell that he could repeat an entire chapter of Horrebow's *Natural History of Iceland* from memory. It was chapter seventy-two 'concerning snakes' which read as follows: 'There are no snakes to be met with throughout the whole island'. If the present chapter was strictly confined to what can be proved about the fate of Richard's nephews, it would rival Horrebow for brevity. All it could safely say would be: 'There is no conclusive evidence to establish when or how the Princes died'. It is one of the wonders of the world that such oceans of ink have been spilled on a subject about which so little is known.

Concern began to be felt for the Princes when they disappeared from sight. For a short time after the Duke of York joined his brother on 16 June, the boys could be seen 'shooting and playing in the garden of the Tower'. But soon they were, as we saw, in its 'inner apartments' and 'began to be seen more rarely behind the bars and windows, till at length they ceased to appear altogether'. Before Mancini left England in the early part of July, he heard rumours that Edward V 'had been done away with'. Be that as it may, one thing seems certain. From the moment 'the Prince and his brother were put under sure keeping', they 'never came abroad after'.

The great majority of Englishmen in 1483 were convinced that the Princes had been murdered on their Uncle's orders. It was a matter of 'common fame', wrote Fabyan, 'that King Richard had within the Tower put unto secret death the two sons of his brother Edward IV'. A surviving deposed King inevitably constituted a threat to his supplanter, which is presumably why Edward II, Richard II, and Henry VI, perished mysteriously soon after losing their thrones. It is hardly surprising therefore that Edward V was thought to have suffered the same fate. This conviction was not confined to Englishmen. The French Chancellor, Guillaume de Rochefort, told the States General at Tours, in January 1484, that the Princes had been 'killed with impunity' and the Crown 'transferred to their murderer'; and Philippe de Commynes says in his Memoirs that Louis XI would have nothing to do with Richard, believing him to be 'extremely cruel and evil', and holding him responsible for having 'the two sons of his brother, Edward, put to death'. Some writers have chosen to represent such allegations as propaganda, invented to vindicate Henry VII; but on grounds of mere chronology it is impossible to describe the evidence of Mancini, de Rochefort, and Louis XI as that of Tudor hacks.

When rumours began to circulate that the Princes were dead, Richard ordered his troops to surround Westminster, and the neighbourhood of the Abbey 'assumed the appearance of a Castle or fortress'. One possible explanation of the decision to put the Sanctuary under siege is that Princess Elizabeth of York had acquired a new importance as rightful Queen of England.

The Rebellion which broke out in October 1483 on behalf of Henry Tudor, won the support of the Woodvilles and other prominent Yorkists. It is inconceivable that they would have helped him unless they felt sure that the Queen's sons were dead. In 1487, when Lambert Simnel impersonated Warwick, Henry VII spoiled his game by parading the real Earl through London 'in the most public and notorious manner that could be devised'. In precisely the same way, it was open to Richard to silence 'whispering among the people' by producing his nephews. That he did not avail himself of so decisive an opportunity suggests they were dead.

Early historians of Richard's reign believed that King Edward's children 'were rid out of this world' but nobody claimed to know precisely how they died. 'Some said they were murdered between two feather beds, some said they were drowned in Malmsey, and some said they were pierced with a venomous potion'. Sir Thomas More is unique in offering a circumstantial narrative of 'the dolorous end of these babes' which has passed into English folklore. Richard, says More, decided to have his nephews murdered because people believed their claim to the Crown was better than his own. Accordingly, 'he sent one John Green, whom he specially trusted', with a letter of credence to Sir Robert Brackenbury, acting Governor of the Tower. The letter ordered Sir Robert to 'put the two children to death' but this he declined to do. The King was at Warwick when he heard of Sir Robert's refusal to carry out his instructions. On the advice of a 'secret page', he sent for Sir James Tyrell, and sought his help in this 'mischievous matter'. Tyrell proved a willing minion, and set out for London with a letter commanding Brackenbury to surrender the keys of the Tower for a night. Sir James then hired Miles Forest, 'a fellow fleshed in murder before time', and John Dighton, 'his own horse keeper, a big, broad, square, strong knave', to murder the Princes. About midnight, when the boys were asleep, these two villains 'came into the chamber and suddenly lapped them up among the clothes', and 'keeping down by force the featherbed and pillows hard unto their mouths' smothered them, until 'they gave up to God their innocent souls'. After the youths' struggles had ceased, 'they laid their bodies naked out upon the bed and fetched Sir James to see them. Which, upon the sight of them, caused those murderers to bury them at the stair foot, meetly deep in the ground, under a great heap of stones'. His mission accomplished, Sir James rode back to the King 'in great haste' and reported all he had done. Richard was deeply grateful, and Tyrell was well rewarded. But the King regretted that the Princes had been buried in 'so vile a corner', and ordered that they should be reinterred as befitted 'a King's sons'. The bodies were therefore secretly moved by a priest of Sir Robert Brackenbury's, who died without telling anyone where their graves could be found. More concludes his account with the gratifying reflection that those responsible for the deaths of these 'two noble princes' suffered for their crime. Richard was 'slain in the field, hacked and hewed of his enemies' hands'. Tyrell was executed on Tower Hill for treason. Forest 'piecemeal rotted away' in Sanctuary, and Dighton, although still alive, was 'in good possibility to be hanged 'ere he die'.

More's version of the murder of the Princes was followed by almost all Tudor writers. Only when Buck argued that it was too full of contradictions to be credible was it challenged. Most modern scholars share his scepticism because they recognize that More's purpose in writing was to use the historical figure of Richard III to personify the evils of tyranny. In pursuit of this end, fidelity to fact was of secondary consequence.

It is difficult to believe that the mystery surrounding the Princes' disappearance was suddenly dispelled, some thirty years later, by Sir Thomas' enquiries. His account, so he tells us, was indebted to a confession made by Sir James Tyrell in 1502. Henry VII was desperately anxious to prove that the Princes were dead, to discourage Yorkist impostors, and his failure to publish this heaven-sent evidence throws doubts on its existence. The fact that Vergil, an official historian with access to State Papers, ignored the confession which More used so avidly, gives further pause for thought. Nor is it easy to understand why different versions of the Princes' fate continued to circulate long after Tyrell's alleged admission of guilt. Finally, men on the rack are liable to confess to whatever is required of them.

More's story contains so many contradictions that parts of it cannot be true. Sir James Tyrell, for example, is portrayed as a man of such little consequence that he needs to be introduced to the King. In reality, Richard had known him for many years, and in 1482 made him a Knight Banneret for his part in the Scottish campaign. Moreover, he was both Master of the Horse, in which capacity he played a leading part in the Coronation, and Master of the Henchmen. Brackenbury's role is even more incredible. First, he refuses to murder the Princes at great risk to himself, and then calmly surrenders the Tower to Tyrell to dispose of them as he pleases. Two years later, while others stayed at home, he died fighting by the King's side at Bosworth: remarkable loyalty to show to a man he knew to be guilty of regicide. Richard's attitude to Sir Robert is equally perplexing. So far from punishing him for disobedience, he confirms him in office, and grants him an allowance of six pence per day, per head, to buy meat for the lions in the Tower. Furthermore, it is difficult to believe that the King, whom More describes as 'close and secret', would have been so rash as to write letters to Brackenbury providing devastating proof of his guilt. Besides, if the murder was carried out as Sir Thomas describes, at least nine people knew about it: the King, Green, the Page, Tyrell, Forest, Dighton, Brackenbury, the Priest, and Will Slaughter, the Princes' one remaining servant. Experience does not suggest that this bunch of ruffians could ever have kept so startling a secret.

In 1674, during demolition work at the Tower, a chest was discovered buried ten foot in the ground under stairs leading from the King's Lodgings. It was found to contain skeletons 'of two striplings'. Charles II gave orders that these bones should be preserved in a marble urn designed by Sir Christopher Wren. In the belief that the remains were those of the Princes, they were placed in Henry VII's chapel at Westminster Abbey.

In 1933, the urn was opened, and its contents examined by Professor William Wright, and George Northcroft, a dental surgeon with long experience of children. They came to the conclusion that the remains belonged to two youths of roughly the age of the Princes in 1483. The discovery has often been cited as confirming More's statement that the boys were buried at the 'stairfoot'. By the same token, it must also be seen as contradicting his story of their subsequent re-interment. Moreover, the bones could well date from Roman or Tudor times, and it cannot even be proved they belong to males. The margin of error in assessing the age of the youths when they died, given the techniques available to Wright and Northcroft, was at least two years. It would not therefore be inconsistent with their evidence to say that Charles II gave royal burial to an eight-year-old Saxon girl. The discovery is undeniably suggestive, but does not justify the conclusion that this heap of bones authenticates More's story.

It has often been suggested that Richard had no motive for murdering his nephews, particularly after Parliament proclaimed them illegitimate. 'Their lives', wrote Sir George Buck, 'could not hurt him nor their deaths advantage him'. But Warwick was not discouraged from restoring Henry VI because Parliament had called him an usurper, nor was Edward IV prevented from recovering his Throne in 1471 by the

Act of Attainder passed the year before. The judicial murders of Yorkists by the early Tudors shows little confidence in acts disinheriting them. That a 'feigned boy' like Lambert Simnel, posturing as Richard, Duke of York, could seriously challenge Henry VII, shows that even death was powerless to dispose of the threat of Edward's sons. No usurper, says Machiavelli, can hope to 'be safe so long as those live whom they have deprived of their possessions'.

Not only did Richard have a compelling motive for wanting the Princes dead, but an unique opportunity for making his wish come true. Had he taken his duties as Protector seriously, they could hardly have been safer than in the Tower. 'No living being, except by his express injunctions, would have dared to lift a finger against them. No living being, apparently, had any interest in destroying them but himself'. There can seldom have been a crime which so few people were in a position to commit. Indeed, it is arguable, that the suspects may be narrowed down to one. Richard's defenders have eagerly pointed out that he could not have murdered Henry VI except on the King's orders, but have shown themselves strangely reluctant to apply this reasoning to the fate of Edward V.

The ingenuity expended on finding reasons for believing Richard innocent derives in large measure from that very attribute. One must not speak ill of the charity and compassion of the King's apologists, but one may perhaps question their perspicacity. There are three traditional lines of defence: to implicate other suspects, to point out that the Princes could have died naturally, and to suggest they might have escaped. It has also been argued that to have disposed of them secretly would have been self-defeating. But, in fact, Vergil reports that King Richard 'kept the slaughter not long secret', permitting 'the rumour of their death to go abroad, to the intent (as we may well believe) that after the people understood no issue male of King Edward to be now left alive, they might with better mind and good will bear and sustain his government.'

The three most favoured candidates, apart from Richard, for murdering the Princes, are Henry VII, Buckingham and

Norfolk. Naturally Henry can only be held responsible if the Princes were still alive when he came to the throne in August 1485. Sir Clements Markham cites two warrants in support of this contention, dated 23 July 1484 and 9 March 1485. One mentions 'the children', and the other, the 'Lord Bastard', a title elsewhere applied to Edward V. In fact, it is almost certain that these documents refer to the young Earl of Warwick, and Richard's own natural son, John of Gloucester.

Buckingham is an even more improbable suspect, who neither possessed a plausible motive for contemplating regicide, nor would have taken upon himself so grave an initiative without the King's approval. At least the Duke of Norfolk had a compelling reason for wishing Prince Richard dead. The fact that the boy was officially illegitimate did not dispose of his claim to the Mowbray inheritance, invested in him by Act of Parliament. Nevertheless, Norfolk would no more have dared murder the Princes than would Buckingham: except as Richard's accomplice.

It has often been suggested that the Princes died naturally. Plague was prevalent in the fifteenth century, and the drinking water at the Tower was almost as lethal as the executioner's axe. Their irregular burial could also be explained had they perished in some epidemic. If the bones discovered in 1674 were indeed those of the Princes, the skull of the older child showed evidence of osteomyelitis, which can prove fatal. On 16 June, Queen Elizabeth told Archbishop Bourchier that Prince Richard was 'so sore diseased with sickness' that she dared not trust him to another's care. The Princes' Neville inheritance could explain their ill health. Their aunts, Isabel and Anne, both died young, and both produced sickly children. Yet, despite these considerations, it would have been something of a coincidence for both Princes to have died during their uncle's brief reign. Nor, had they done so, would it have been like him to give them furtive burial, thus throwing away a chance to display his grief to the world.

The one absolute certainty about the death of the Princes is that nobody knows how, when, or where they died. But the balance of probability strongly suggests that they met violent ends on Richard's orders. They disappeared while he was their 'Protector'. Nobody had a better opportunity to have them killed, nor a more powerful motive for wishing them dead. If an innocent solution to the mystery existed, it was self-evidently in his interest to proclaim it. His failure to do so implies there was no such explanation.

Historians have sometimes become so intrigued by the problems surrounding the Princes' disappearance, that they have lost sight of its historical importance: the damage done to Richard's reputation by the belief that he had murdered them. It has often been suggested that he was no more culpable than Henry IV or Edward IV in removing rival claimants, but, in fact, he was singled out because his supposed victims were children.

In the late Middle Ages, Holy Innocents' Day, 28 December, was observed with great solemnity, and the 'shedding of infants' blood', to quote the words of the Act of Attainder of 1485, was 'an odious offence and abomination against God and Man'. Edward Hall summed up the prevailing view when he wrote, 'To murder a man is much odious, to kill a woman is in manner unnatural, but to slay and destroy innocent babes and young infants, the whole world abhorreth, and the blood from the earth crieth for vengeance to almighty God. Alas what will he do to other that thus shamefully murdereth his own blood without cause or desert? Whom will he save when he slayeth the poor lambs committed to him in trust?' Even judged by the tarnished standards of the fifteenth century, the Princes' murder seemed so atrocious as to goad men to rebel.

When the Queen Dowager heard of her sons' fate, 'she fell into a swoon, and lay lifeless a good while; after coming to herself, she weepeth, she cried out aloud, and with lamentable shrieks made all the house ring, she struck her breast, tore and cut her hair, and overcome in fine with dolour, prayeth also her own death, calling by name now and then among her most dear children, and condemning herself for a mad woman for that, being deceived by false promises, she had delivered her younger son out of Sanctuary, to be murdered of his enemy.'

The news which reached Richard at Warwick about unrest over the Princes, was not so alarming as to prevent him from continuing his Progress northwards. During the second half of August, he stayed at Coventry, Leicester, Nottingham, Doncaster and Pontefract. Bishop Langton, who accompanied him on his travels, told the Prior of Christ Church, Canterbury, that the King 'contents the people wherever he goes better than ever did any prince; for many a poor man that has suffered wrong many days has been relieved and helped by him and his commands in his Progress. Upon my word I never liked the qualities of any prince so well as his; God has sent him to us for the welfare of us all'. Richard's secretary, John Kendall, wrote with equal enthusiasm. 'Thanked be Jesus, the King's grace is in good health, and in like wise the Queen's grace, and in all their Progress have been worshipfully received with pageants, and others; and his lords and judges sitting in every place, judging the complaints of poor folk with due punishment of offenders against his laws'. Nevertheless, Vergil was not being unduly cynical in pointing out that self-interest obliged the King to assume the 'countenance of a good man', so as to 'merit pardon for his offences at God's hands', and 'to procure himself good will'.

Richard's visit to York in September provided a magnificent climax to his tour. From Leicester, he wrote letters commanding some seventy knights and gentlemen, 'as ye entende to please us and wolle advoide the contrarie at youre perille', to meet him at Pontefract so as to escort him on the last stage of his journey. It was also arranged that his son, Prince Edward, should join the royal party. A week before Richard reached York, Kendall wrote to the Mayor urging him to organize a reception of suitable splendour, assuring him of 'the entire affection that his grace bears towards you and your worshipful city, for your many kind and loving deservings shown to his grace heretofore, which his grace will never forget'. It was consequently his intention 'to do unto you that all the Kings that ever reigned upon you did never so much'. Kendall went on to advise the Mayor to receive the royal party 'as honourably as your wisdoms can imagine', with pageants, and 'with such good speeches as can well be devised, in view of the shortness of the warning'. Master Lancaster, the bearer of the letter, would acquaint him with Kendall's ideas about 'hanging the streets through which the King's grace shall come with cloth of arras, tapestry work, and others, for there come many southern lords and men of worship with them which will mark greatly how you receive their graces'.

The King, Queen, and Prince Edward, made their state entry into York at the end of August, accompanied by an imposing retinue of bishops, judges and nobles. They were met outside the city walls by the Mayor and Aldermen robed in scarlet. They then passed through Micklegate, where the head of Richard's father, the Duke of York, had been exhibited after the Battle of Wakefield. Enthusiastic crowds lined the streets to greet the King and Queen. The Mayor officially welcomed them to the City and presented them with considerable sums of money, towards which he personally contributed twenty pounds: two hundred times a labourer's weekly wage. Richard's 'good will at all times shown to the city' was not neglected, and the Mayor was rewarded by being offered the choice of 'a gown of cloth or a nambling horse'. There followed a round of 'tilts, tournaments, masques, revels and stage-plays, with other triumphant sports', and 'feasting to the utmost prodigality'. So costly was the royal visit that the Mayor was given a special allowance for entertaining four bishops, three barons, the Chief Justice, and an assortment of 'knights, learned men, esquires, and other of the King's Council'.

On Sunday, 7 September, the King and Queen attended a performance of York's *Creed Play*, the cost of which was defrayed 'by the most honest men of every parish in the city'. The following day, the Feast of the Nativity of the Blessed Virgin, witnessed the most impressive ceremony of all: the investiture of the Prince of Wales. The decision to hold it was taken surprisingly late. Not until 31 August did the King send orders to Piers Curteys, Keeper of the King's Wardrobe, to dispatch the necessary finery, including gowns, doublets, spurs, banners, 'three coats of arms beaten with fine gold, for our own person', and thirteen thousand badges bearing Richard's device of the White Boar.

The day began with a mass celebrated in York Minster by the Bishop of Durham. Why Rotherham did not officiate remains a mystery. Possibly the Archbishop was still in disgrace, or perhaps he preferred to remain aloof from proceedings he found distasteful. On his way to the Minster the King wore 'a notable rich diadem' and carried the royal sceptre. Both the Queen and her son, whom she led by the hand, also wore crowns. On returning to the Royal Palace, the King formally created Prince Edward 'Prince of Wales and Earl of Chester', to the 'great honour, joy and congratulation of the inhabitants', who were so delighted by the favours shown their city that they 'extolled King Richard above the skies'.

Throughout Richard's stay in York, 'he gave most gorgeous and sumptuous feasts and banquets for the purpose of gaining the affections of the people'. Before he left, he relieved the city of part of its burden of tax, as Kendall had promised he would. On 7 September, he addressed the Mayor, Aldermen and leading citizens in the Chapter House of the Minster, and told them he had not forgotten 'the good service' that they had done him for many years past. Nor was he unaware of 'the decay and great poverty of the City'. Consequently, he proposed to remit half the annual toll paid by York to the Exchequer. Moreover, he appointed the Mayor his chief Serjeant-at-Arms, with a fee of eighteen pounds, in token of his gratitude.

On leaving York, the King returned to Pontefract on his way back to London, while the Queen and Prince of Wales set out for Middleham. At Lincoln, on 11 October, Richard heard that the Duke of Buckingham intended to rebel, and at once took counter measures 'in no drowsy manner, but with the greatest activity and vigilance'. In particular, he sent John Otyr to York with a letter 'To our trusty and well-beloved the Mayor, Aldermen, Sheriffs and Commonalty', informing them 'that the Duke of Buckingham traitorously has turned upon us, contrary to the duty of his allegiance, and intendeth

the utter destruction of us, you, and all other our true subjects'. He concluded by begging them to send 'as many men
defensibly arrayed on horseback as ye may goodly make to our
town of Leicester the twenty first day of this present month
without fail.'

Buckingham's so-called 'rebellion' is most ineptly named.
Not only was the Duke one of the last people to join it, but his
failure to lend it effective support demoralized the movement.
Soon after the Coronation, 'the people of the Southern and
Western parts of the Kingdom began to murmer greatly, and
to form meetings and confederacies' to release the Princes
from the Tower. But after 'a rumour was spread that the sons
of King Edward had died a violent death', the rebels began to
turn their thoughts to deposing Richard in favour of Henry
Tudor.

The leaders of the revolt were mostly supporters of Henry
VI, Edward IV, Edward V, the Duke of Clarence, or the
Woodvilles. Sir Thomas Arundel, the Cornish rebel, was a
former Lancastrian. Sir John Fogge had been Edward IV's
Treasurer of the Household. Dorset was Edward V's half-
brother. The leaders of the rebellion in the south-east were Sir
William Haute, brother of the Sir Richard who was executed
on 25 June at Pontefract, and Sir Richard Guildford. The
southern leaders were John Cheyney, formerly Edward IV's
Master of Horse, Sir William Stonor, and Queen Elizabeth's
brother, Lionel, Bishop of Salisbury. Among the most prominent rebels of the south-west, were Sir Thomas St Leger,
Piers Courtenay, Bishop of Exeter, and Sir Thomas Arundel.
Some time about mid-September, the rebel confederacies
learned that the Duke of Buckingham proposed to support
them.

Buckingham's motives for turning against Richard have
never been wholly explained. The Croyland Chronicler
speaks of the Duke coming to regret his part in the Usurpation, and Vergil portrays him as deploring his failure to resist
'King Richard's evil enterprise'. Above all, he was supposed to
have been mortified by the murder of the Princes. According
to Richard Grafton, writing towards the end of the reign of

Henry VIII, the Duke told Morton, 'when I was credibly informed of the death of the two young innocents, to the which God be my judge I never agreed or condescended, O Lord, how my veins panted, how my body trembled, and my heart inwardly grudged', so that 'I abhorred the sight and much more the company' of the King. On his way home from Gloucester to Brecknock, the Duke considered how best 'to deprive this unnatural uncle, and bloody butcher, from his royal seat and princely dignity', and eventually resolved to invite Henry Tudor, 'the very heir of the House of Lancaster', to claim 'the Crown of this noble realm'.

More was inclined to explain Buckingham's conduct as proceeding from envy and ambition. The Duke, he wrote, could not 'bear the glory of another, so that I have heard of some that said that the Duke, at such time as the Crown was first set upon the Protector's head, his eye could not abide the sight thereof, but wried his head another way'. The Act of Attainder passed against the rebels in January 1484, described Buckingham as 'replete with rancour and insatiable covetise'. It was also rumoured that the Duke believed that he should have been better rewarded. As Shakespeare makes Richard II say to Northumberland about the future Henry IV:

> Thou shalt think,
> Though he divide the realm and give thee half,
> It is too little, helping him to all.

It has generally been agreed that Morton, 'a man of great natural wit', and lacking 'no wise ways to win favour', was partly responsible for Buckingham's change of heart. It has also been said that the King and Duke quarrelled over his claim to the Bohun estates. This story, however, appears to be refuted by a grant dated 13 July, 'To our right trusty and entirely beloved Cousin Henry, Duke of Buckingham', which proclaimed that the Duke was the rightful inheritor of the late Earl of Hereford, and bestowed on him the revenues of the Bohun estates 'from the Feast of Easter last past unto the time he be thereto restored by authority of Parliament'. It was commonly believed in his lifetime that Buckingham aspired to

THE TUDOR CLAIM TO THE THRONE

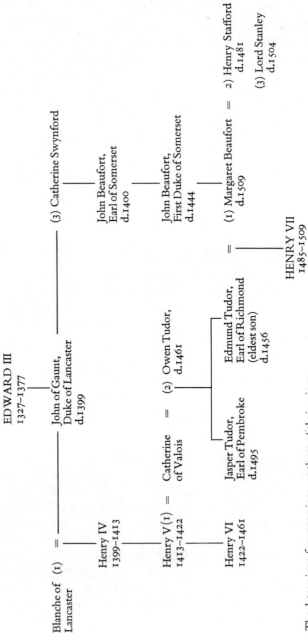

The dates given for sovereigns are those of their reigns.

the Throne himself, being descended from John of Gaunt and Thomas of Woodstock. If this was indeed so, presumably Morton persuaded him to support the superior claim of Henry Tudor instead.

Henry had no claim whatever to the Throne from his father's family, unless his alleged descent from Cadwallader, who defended Wales against the Saxons in the seventh century, is taken seriously. His grandfather, Owen Tudor, founded the fortune of the dynasty by marrying Henry V's widow, Queen Catherine of Valois: an auspicious match for the son of a brewer from Beaumaris. Owen was captured by Edward, Earl of March, after the Battle of Mortimer's Cross, and, much to his astonishment, executed in the Market Place at Hereford. His eldest son, Edmund Tudor, Earl of Richmond, married Lady Margaret Beaufort, but died before their son Henry was born in 1457. Margaret was the daughter and heiress of the first Duke of Somerset, John of Gaunt's grandson by Catherine Swynford. Although Henry IV passed an act in 1407 debarring Catherine's descendants from the succession to the Crown, its validity was questioned, and Margaret, in fact, became the progenitrix of all English Sovereigns from the accession of Henry VII. After the death of the Earl of Richmond, she married Buckingham's uncle, Henry Stafford, who died in 1481, and finally took Lord Stanley as her third husband. Lady Margaret was distinguished for piety and learning. She patronized Caxton, and founded professorships of Divinity at Oxford and Cambridge.

After the Battle of Tewkesbury in 1471, Jasper Tudor, Earl of Pembroke, escaped with his nephew, Henry, to Brittany, where they remained for many years. Both Edward IV and Richard III vainly tried to secure the return of the fugitives to England. When Buckingham invited Henry to invade, he did so on the condition that he swore 'a solemn oath that after he had once obtained his kingdom he would take to wife Elizabeth, King Edward's eldest daughter'. Some time in September, the Duke sent Henry a letter encouraging him to land on Saturday, 18 October, the day the rebels intended to raise their standard. The Dowager Queen, Dorset, Sir Edward

Woodville, and St Leger, in a word the most prominent supporters of Edward V, would never have endorsed this proposal had they thought that the Princes were still alive.

For several weeks, secret negotiations were conducted between the Queen Dowager, Lady Margaret, her son, and Buckingham. Lady Margaret appointed Reginald Bray as 'the chief dealer in this conspiracy', and instructed him to 'draw unto her party such noble or worshipful men' as would help the cause. She also sent 'a good, great sum of money' to Henry in Brittany, and advised him to land in Wales. Meanwhile, Lady Margaret negotiated with the Queen in Sanctuary, through the intermediary of a Welsh physician, Dr Lewis. The Queen willingly consented to the projected marriage between her daughter and Henry Tudor, and promised 'to procure all her husband King Edward's friends' to aid the Earl. Henry, after receiving assurances of help from Brittany, sent messages to England 'to give notice of his coming'.

When Richard learned of Buckingham's perfidy, he wrote to the Lord Chancellor from Lincoln, requiring him to bring or send the Great Seal. The letter concluded with a postscript in his own hand. 'Here, loved be God, is all well and truly determined for to resist the malice of him that had best cause to be true, the Duke of Buckingham, the most untrue creature living'. The Seal was handed over to the King on 19 October at the Angel, Grantham, an ancient hostelry opposite the Market Place, still open to travellers after seven hundred and fifty years as an inn. Richard, a King 'much to be feared for circumspection and celerity', sent proclamations to sheriffs in the south and west of England putting prices on the heads of leading traitors. A reward of a thousand pounds was offered for the capture of Buckingham. Other named rebels included the Bishop of Ely, and the Marquis of Dorset. Richard's proclamations appeared to imply that the profligacy of some of the leading conspirators was as odious as their treason. Dorset was more vigorously denounced for dishonouring 'sundry maids, widows and wives' than for raising the people against his Sovereign and disturbing the peace of the realm.

The Rebellion began with a precipitate rising in Kent. On 10

October, the Duke of Norfolk wrote to his 'right well-beloved friend, John Paston' to tell him 'that the Kentish men be up in the Weald, and say that they will come and rob the city'. He therefore begged Paston to join him as soon as possible with 'six tall fellows in harness'. With such hastily raised levies, the Duke seized the Thames crossing at Gravesend and saved London from attack. This premature outbreak gave the Government timely warning of the danger threatening it.

On St Luke's Day, Saturday, 18 October, the south and south-west of England took up arms, and Buckingham raised his standard. His plan was to cross the Severn and join forces with the rebels in Wiltshire and Somerset. No sooner had he started on his campaign, than his neighbour, Sir Thomas Vaughan, a namesake and relation of Edward V's late Chamberlain, besieged and captured Brecknock. But worse was to follow. On 15 October, three days before the uprising, 'the greatest wind that ever was at Bristol' began to blow. Ten days of torrential rain followed this gale and made the Severn impassable. So severe was the flood that houses and bridges were swept away, men were drowned in their beds, and the corpses of cattle and children floated across the fields. As for Buckingham, his forces were cooped up in Wales, demoralized, starved and unpaid. Because most of his levies has been 'brought to the field against their wills and without any lust to fight' they drifted back home in their hundreds. The Staffords had an evil reputation for being 'sore and hard dealing men', and it was not therefore surprising that the loyalty of the Duke's reluctant conscripts broke under the stress of adversity. When Buckingham found himself foresaken by his followers, he sought refuge at Lacon, near Shrewsbury, with Ralph Banaster, an old retainer of his family. Tempted by the thousand pounds promised by the King, or fearful of the penalties for harbouring rebels, Banaster betrayed the Duke to Thomas Mytton, one of the Sheriffs of Shropshire. Later, he received the Manor and Lordship of Yalding in Kent, previously belonging to the Staffords, in recognition of his 'loyalty'.

Buckingham was taken to Salisbury, where the King rejected his plea for an interview and ordered his summary execution. The third Duke later admitted that his father intended to plunge a dagger into Richard's heart. On All Souls' Day, Sunday, 2 November, the thirteenth birthday of Edward V, 'the most untrue creature living' was executed in the Market Place at Salisbury. A plaque in Blue Boar Row marks the site. All three Stafford dukes died violently. The first fell on the battlefield of Northampton, and the last was beheaded by Henry VIII for proclaiming that if the King died without issue he should succeed to the Throne. The Buckingham dukedom was later revived by James I for George Villiers. He too met an untimely end at the hands of an assassin.

On Monday, 3 November, Richard set off westwards, and a week later took up residence in the Bishop's Palace at Exeter, which Courtenay had abandoned a few hours before. The King's brother-in-law, Sir Thomas St Leger, his sister Anne's second husband, was the only rebel of consequence to fall into his hands. Large sums of money were offered in vain to save his life. Other leaders decided on flight when they saw their cause was lost. Three things, in particular, showed them the game was up: the execution of Buckingham, the King's arrival in the south-west, and the failure of Henry Tudor to invade. Many of the rebels, such as Dorset, Piers Courtenay, Sir Edward Woodville, Sir Thomas Arundel, and Sir John Cheyney, 'repaired to the sea-side; and those among them who could find ships in readinesss, embarked, and at length arrived at the wished-for shores of Brittany'. One of the earliest refugees was Bishop Morton, who made his escape by night from Brecknock Castle.

The storm which prevented Buckingham crossing the Severn, scattered Henry's fleet. The Earl set out on 12 October, but after a couple of days encountered 'a cruel gale of wind' which caused thirteen of his ships to run for shelter. His own and one other, after being 'tossed all the night long with waves', eventually anchored off the south coast of England, probably near Plymouth. The shore was 'beset with soldiers', and Henry sent a small boat to investigate. The troops encour-

Portrait of Richard III in the Royal Collection.

Northward view of Market Bosworth from Ambien Hill.

aged the expedition to land, claiming that Buckingham had sent them to escort the Earl to his camp. But Henry rightly suspected a trap, and when none of his other ships appeared, set sail for France. Soon after returning, he learned that the Duke had been beheaded and that a considerable number of noblemen intended to join him in exile. At least he could console himself for the loss of a Kingdom by blaming the English weather.

Richard returned to London on 25 November, and the following day handed back the Great Seal to Russell in a ceremony in the Star Chamber at Westminster, having 'triumphed over his enemies without fighting a battle'. Apart from a skirmish at Bodiam Castle in Sussex, the campaign was virtually bloodless, and the King's enemies had been scattered before the wind. When Parliament met in January 1484, about a hundred people were attainted, many of whom were later pardoned, and only some dozen rebels lost their heads. The royal clemency was remarkable, particularly if measured by the standard set two hundred years later by Judge Jeffrey's Western Assize. It even extended to Margaret Beaufort, 'mother to the King's great rebel and traitor'. Such magnanimity, says Vergil, owed much to the fact that 'the working of a woman's wit was considered of small account'. A special Act of Parliament proclaimed her guilty of 'sending messages, writings and tokens to Henry, stirring him to come into the realm to make war'. However, the King 'of his especial grace', and 'remembering the good and faithful services that Thomas Lord Stanley had done and intends to do him', consented not to invoke 'the great punishment of attainder of the said Countess that she deserves', but to transfer her property to her husband with eventual reversion to the Crown, provided he made himself responsible for ensuring that she ceased to conspire with the King's enemies. Buckingham's widow was less generously treated, but she was a Woodville. Happily for her, within two years the Wheel of Fortune turned once more when she married Jasper Tudor, who shortly before his nephew's Coronation was created Duke of Bedford.

Richard's rapid triumph proved very costly. It is true his

campaign was won without a battle, but that did nothing to lessen its expense. On the contrary, dead men need no pay, so to spill blood can save money. The Croyland Chronicler dated 'the waste in a short time' of Edward IV's 'most ample treasures' from the King's proclamation in October summoning levies to Leicester. Just before Christmas, the King was so impoverished that he was obliged to sell Sir Edmund Shaa silver plate worth over five hundred pounds. If Richard paid a high price for victory, his rival's defeat was not without compensation. By the end of the year many eminent refugees had joined Henry's Court in Brittany, including the Bishops of Ely, Salisbury, and Exeter, and a number of influential nobles and gentlemen who remained in contact with friends and relations in England. Self-interest committed such exiles to risk all on behalf of Henry Tudor, for they had little hope for the future unless he became King. Within two years, some of these refugees were prominent members of Henry's government.

Richard's distribution of lands and offices forfeited by the rebels was on a scale unrivalled since 1398, when Richard II disinherited his opponents and thereby provoked his overthrow. The October rising of 1483 showed how little support the King commanded in the south and south-west of England. Consequently, Richard resolved to replace the disaffected gentry of those parts with his own followers, mostly men from the north. Naturally, the dispossessed and their dependents saw such plantations as an intolerable affront. Nowhere was the process more widespread or resented than in Somerset, Dorset, Devon and Cornwall. Local feeling in the south-west was outraged by the authority and estates granted to Lord Scrope of Bolton, a Neville cousin of the King. Sir Richard Ratcliffe was another alien intruder. Before Buckingham's rebellion he owned a few acres at Sadbury-in-Gilling in the North Riding. By Easter 1484, he was one of the greatest landowners in England, possessing estates from Bournemouth to Lands End, many of which had belonged to the Earl of Devon. Sir James Tyrell was a further beneficiary of the King's selective patronage. In a grant of 9 November, Richard commanded his 'well-beloved servant Piers St Aubyn' to ensure that Sir James received the rents due to him from the estates of 'our rebel and traitor, Sir Thomas Arundel'. It was obvious policy for Richard to plant members of his personal affinity in the most disaffected parts of his kingdom, but it was only to be expected that their presence would be resented. By confining his patronage to so narrow a circle of associates, Richard strengthened their loyalty and influence, but did nothing to broaden the base of his support. 'The result became apparent at Bosworth', when he faced a second Tudor invasion 'with much the same group of men who had brought him to power two years earlier'.

Richard's sequestration of rebel property crucially threatened the landowning class, who passionately believed 'that not even treason should extinguish the rights of an heir'. It was consequently exceptionally rash of him to flout the law by distributing rebel estates before their forfeiture had been authorized by acts of attainder. No King had ever before anticipated Parliament's sanction in so high-handed a manner, and his transactions were seen as betraying a 'flagrant indifference to the established rules of law and rights of property'. In the short term, he may have acquired the 'unsteadfast friendship' of men like Sir William Stanley, who played a principal part, in betraying him at Bosworth, but the price he paid to secure their dubious allegiance was the hatred of most landowners.

The gentry in fifteenth century England were intensely parochial and looked upon local affairs as their strict preserve. Richard's planting of northerners in the south and south-west of his Kingdom, transgressed this sacred principle, and hence provoked the furious resentment of an élite united by blood, marriage, and common interests. Many concluded that the best way to restore their ancient privileges, and to end the domination of strangers with no roots in the community, was to change the régime. The Croyland Chronicler caught the prevailing mood when he complained of 'the immense estates and patrimonies' which the King 'distributed among his northern adherents, whom he planted in every spot throughout his dominions, to the disgrace and lasting and loudly expressed sorrow of all the people in the south, who daily longed more and more for the hoped-for return of their ancient rulers'. Naturally, what Sir Robert Brackenbury, Sir James Tyrell, Sir Robert Percy, and Lord Scrope regarded as gratifying examples of Richard's 'good lordship', seemed to his southern subjects proof of tyranny.

The year 1483 concluded with a momentous ceremony held at Rennes, the Capital of the Dukedom of Brittany. After Mass had been celebrated in the Cathedral on Christmas Day, Henry Tudor swore an oath 'that so soon as he should be King he would marry Elizabeth, King Edward's daughter'. His future subjects then paid him homage, and assured him 'that they would lose not only their lands and possessions, but their lives, before ever they would suffer, bear, or permit, that Richard should rule over them and theirs'. The Duke of Brittany promised to furnish the Earl with men, money and ships to help him invade England. In a sense, he was committed to the cause by the knowledge that the ten thousand crowns he had aready lent would never be repaid unless Henry became King. Richard's foreign policy for the rest of his reign was largely concerned with attempts to secure his rival's extradition. It is a measure of the uneasiness with which usurpers wear their crowns that an obscure Welsh rebel should seem so menacing.

CHAPTER NINE

'*A Scum of Bretons*'
1484–1485

King Richard: *Remember whom you are to cope withall –*
A sort of vagabonds, rascals and runaways,
A Scum of Bretons, and base lackey peasants . . .

Shakespeare *Richard III* V.3

The only Parliament of Richard's reign met on Friday, 23 January 1484 and sat for less than a month. Its main tasks were to ratify his title, to legalize his attainders, and to demonstrate his benevolence. Few Parliaments have ever proved so obsequious, unless packed or terrorized. The Commons even agreed to elect William Catesby as Speaker to please the King, although he had never sat in the House and was ignorant of its procedures.

In January 1484 Parliament passed the Royal Title Act to remove uncertainties about the Petition presented to Richard inviting him to be King. Its preamble acknowledged that 'diverse doubts, questions and ambiguities' had arisen over the fact that those who had met in June 1483 had not been 'assembled in form of Parliament'. It accordingly recapitulated the tenor of its predecessor's Petition and ratified it anew. Some members, however, were very reluctant to question Edward's marriage, because they believed that matters of Canon Law should be tried in Church Courts. A number of acts of attainder were then passed against those who had taken part in the recent rising. In fact, Parliament thereby sanctioned some very high-handed proceedings, as rebel lands had already been given to Richard's supporters 'without the normal delaying safeguards of legal inquisition as laid down in several statutes'. The three bishops Morton of Ely, Woodville of Salisbury, and Courtenay of Exeter, were dealt with in separate acts, as was Margaret, Countess of Richmond.

During their brief session, the Lords and Commons made a number of legal reforms concerning the qualifications of jurors, conditions of bail, land conveyancing, and the authority of the Court of Piepowder, whose duty it was to resolve disputes which arose at fairs and markets. Their most popular measure was the abolition of 'benevolences', a detested form of compulsory gift demanded by Edward IV. Finally, it passed two laws regulating trade. The first controlled the quality of cloth, and the second imposed a selective ban on imports to protect home manufactures. The latter's exemption of 'bokes wrytten or imprynted' constituted the earliest mention made by Parliament of the invention of movable type.

It has sometimes been claimed that these reforms show that Richard was 'a singularly thoughtful and enlightened legislator', whose sole concern was the welfare of his subjects. Nevertheless, the suspicion arises that the laws of 1484 were intended to 'win favour of the commonalty' and that the King 'was in no position to enact oppressive measures'. Francis Bacon, a distinguished Lord Chancellor, while commending Richard's 'politic and wholesome laws', remarks on the fact that 'they were interpreted to be but the brocage (trickery) of an Usurper', and 'rather feigned and affected things to serve his ambition than true qualities'. Although Buck complained of the 'malicious alchemy' which transmuted Richard's virtues into vices, the view persists that he was primarily a scheming politician, and that the legislative programme of 1484 reflected his need to win support. The efforts he made to portray himself as upholding the law of the land would have carried greater weight had he broken it less often. The fates of Edward V, Prince Richard, Hastings, Rivers and others, testify more eloquently than words to his true concern for justice.

The two most enduring achievements of Richard's reign were the establishment of the College of Heralds, and the Council of the North. The College was incorporated by a Royal Charter of 2 March 1484, and the King provided it with a residence on the Thames called Cold Harbour. The Council of the North was established in July 1484 and lasted until the Long Parliament abolished it in 1641. During the last years of Edward IV's reign Richard governed the region with semi-regal authority. But as King he dared not delegate to a subject the power he had once enjoyed, having no wish to create a Buckingham of the North: hence his decision to set up a Council like that which his brother established at Ludlow to govern Wales and the Marches. Its President was his sister Elizabeth's son, John de la Pole, Earl of Lincoln, and its headquarters Sandal Castle, near Wakefield. The Council was required to meet once a quarter in York in order to keep the peace, punish riots, and settle disputes, and soon proved the most successful means of governing the North devised in the fifteenth century.

There is nothing in Richard's reforms to suggest that his reign was that of a despot, although it was so judged by his subjects and posterity. The fifteenth century saw a tyrant as one who seized the throne unlawfully, and hence had no right to govern, or who ruled in defiance of constitutional custom. Few could doubt that Richard qualified on the first of these counts, or that his plantation of northerners in the southern part of his kingdom flouted the principle that the government of the Counties should be left to the local gentry. The favours shown to the King's northern affinity – seven out of nine churchmen in the Council came from Yorkshire or neigh-bouring parts – were totally unacceptable to all but their beneficiaries. It was because the majority of Englishmen believed that Richard had ridden roughshod over their interests, by seizing the Throne and imposing an alien rule on those who dared to resist, that they regarded him as a despot.

Since the moment the Queen and her five daughters sought refuge with the Church on the night of 30 April 1483, attempts to persuade her to leave had proved unavailing. The events of 16 June, when she reluctantly surrendered Prince Richard to his Uncle's safe-keeping did not encourage her to take such risks again. Nevertheless, she soon tired of the restricted life of Westminster, and her daughters yearned for a glimpse of a handsome young courtier. The King was equally eager to put an end to their sanctuary, partly to clear himself of a damaging reproach, and partly to stop the Princesses being smuggled abroad. It was even said that he hoped to arrange a match between his own son, the Prince of Wales, and Elizabeth of York. But anxious as both sides were to reach agreement the obstacles were daunting. Richard could hardly ignore the part the Queen Dowager had played in supporting the late rebellion, or the fact that Dorset and two of her brothers had joined Henry in Brittany. Nor was the Queen likely to forget that her brother-in-law was thought to have murdered her sons.

The Croyland Chronicler describes negotiations as being conducted with 'frequent entreaties as well as threats': familiar ingredients in Richard's diplomacy. It was only after being promised 'Mountains' that the Queen finally succumbed, 'so mutable is that sex'. Her decision to do so, like that of 16 June, was no doubt influenced by the belief that she would be dragged out by force if she failed to come to terms. According to Hall, the King's emissaries were men of 'wit and learning', who persuaded her to relent 'with great and pregnant reasons', including promises of 'innumerable benefits, not only to her but also to her son Lord Thomas Marquis Dorset'. In the end, 'putting into oblivion the murder of her innocent children', the slanders about her bigamous marriage, 'the bastardizing of her daughters', and ignoring her promises 'to the Countess of Richmond, mother to the Earl Henry', she submitted to 'the King's will and pleasure'.

The terms to which the Queen Dowager finally agreed show the depth of her distrust. On 1 March 1484, in the presence of a gathering of the Lords Spiritual and Temporal, and the Mayor and Aldermen of London, Richard was obliged to swear 'verbo regio', that 'if the daughters of Elizabeth Grey, late calling herself Queen of England', came out of Sanctuary, he would guarantee the 'surety of their lives', to protect them from 'ravishing and defiling contrary to their wills', and to find them 'suitable husbands'. He furthermore promised that 'Dame Elizabeth' should be provided with seven hundred marks a year to retire into private life. On the strength of these undertakings, the Princesses left Westminster to reside at Court under the care of their Uncle and Aunt.

Some time early in May 1484, the Prince of Wales died at Middleham Castle after a short illness. When the news reached his parents at Nottingham they were plunged into 'a state almost bordering on madness by reason of their sudden grief'. The blow to Richard was both political and personal. After thirty years of Civil War few Englishmen were likely to risk all to defend the rights of a childless King.

The young Earl of Warwick, if Rous is to be believed, 'was proclaimed Heir Apparent' soon after his cousin's death. But by August, Richard seems to have changed his mind, as he appointed his nephew Lincoln Lord Lieutenant of Ireland: a post customarily assigned by the Yorkists to their heirs. It is easy to understand such second thoughts. Warwick was only eight in 1484 and probably mentally retarded. Above all, if Clarence's attainder ceased to debar his son from the succession – not that in law it ever had – the boy's claim to the Throne was better than that of his Uncle.

Shortly after the Christmas festivities of 1484, during which 'far too much attention was given to dancing and gaiety', Queen Anne became ill. It is seldom wise to diagnose at a distance, but what little we know suggests tuberculosis, particularly as Richard 'shunned her bed' 'on the advice of his physicians'. She died at the Palace of Westminster on 16 March, aged thirty-one. A total eclipse of the sun which occurred that very day was widely construed as a heavenly exclamation mark. It was customary in the Middle Ages to attribute sudden deaths to the agency of poison. When the Queen's sister, Isabel, died at the age of twenty-four, her husband, the Duke of Clarence, sprang to that conclusion, and terrorized a jury into convicting her maid of murder. It was even alleged that Richard had poisoned Edward IV. Rous was the first writer to state categorically that Anne met her end in this manner, although 'The Great Chronicle' records that there was 'much whispering' to that effect. Even Richard's northern supporters, 'in whom he placed great reliance', seemed willing to 'impute to him the death of the Queen'.

His complaints to the Archbishop of York about the Queen's 'unfruitfulness', were seen as providing his motive for ridding himself of his wife. But strong as the evidence is that the King was suspected of murdering Queen Anne, there is not a shadow of proof to show that the charge was true.

Some time before the Queen died, it was rumoured that the King, either anticipating that event, or contemplating divorce, intended to marry his niece Elizabeth. The Croyland Chronicler describes a meeting of the Council at which Richard protested 'that such a thing had never once entered his mind'. Nevertheless, says the author, himself a Privy Councillor, some persons present 'very well knew the contrary to be true'. During the discussions, two of the King's closest supporters, Ratcliffe and Catesby, 'told him to his face that if he did not abandon his intended purpose' there might well be a rising in the North, where he was already suspected of killing the Queen to 'gratify an incestuous passion'. It was eventually agreed that the King should deny rumours about his intentions at a meeting of peers, aldermen and citizens, to be held on 30 March, exactly a fortnight after Anne's death, in the Great Hall of the Priory of the Knights Hospitallers of the Order of St John of Jerusalem. For a King of England to be obliged to proclaim publicly that he had neither murdered his wife nor intended to marry his niece, was an 'uniquely shameful spectacle'. A few days afterwards, Richard wrote to the Mayor of York to tell him that he had been the victim 'of false and abominable lies' spread by 'seditious and mischievous persons', and instructing him to punish anyone found guilty of spreading such slanders. In his effort to put an end to scandal, Princess Elizabeth was banished to Sheriff Hutton, where she remained until sent for by Henry VII the day after Bosworth. Richard, however, remained anxious to find a wife for himself and a husband for his niece, and sent an embassy to Lisbon to negotiate a double marriage with the Portuguese Royal Family.

The threat of a Tudor invasion was even more urgent than Richard's dynastic problems. Throughout 1484 rumours reached the government that Henry had set sail, and the army and navy were kept on constant alert, at great cost to the Exchequer. Even as late as December, not a propitious season to attack, orders were sent to Middlesex, Hertford and Surrey, to discover 'what number of people defensibly arrayed' could be collected 'upon half a day's warning' in the event of the arrival 'of our said Rebels and traitors'.

Richard came close to removing the threat by diplomacy rather than war. At first his pleas to the Duke of Brittany to hand over the rebels met with no success, but in the summer of 1484 Duke Francis suffered a mental breakdown, and his Treasurer, Pierre Landois, took over the government. Landois, hoping to win Richard's support in order to strengthen his own position in Brittany, agreed in June to seize the Earl of Richmond and send him back to England. Somehow Morton came to hear of this plan, possibly from Lord Stanley, and warned the Earl of his danger. Henry at once set out from Vannes with five attendants, allegedly to pay a visit in the neighbourhood. After travelling a few miles, he halted in a wood and changed clothes with one of his servants. The horsemen then rode as fast as they could to the frontier of Anjou, having earlier ensured that the young King of France, Charles VIII, would make them welcome.

The moment Landois realized that Henry had fled, he sent troops to seize him. Just an hour after the exiles crossed the border their Breton pursuers reached it. Had they spurred their horses more ferociously, Elizabeth II would not now be Queen of England. When Duke Francis recovered sufficiently to find out what had happened, he was so furious that he gave the English Court at Vannes a safe-conduct to France. Not long after, Henry was joined by the most loyal and illustrious of Lancastrians, John de Vere, thirteenth Earl of Oxford, who commanded the left wing of Henry VI's army at the Battle of Barnet. In 1473 he seized St Michael's Mount, but was forced to surrender it after a stubborn siege. For the rest of Edward's reign he was imprisoned in Hammes Castle, one of the fortresses guarding Calais, but eventually persuaded its Governor, Sir James Blount, to set him free, and the two men, much to Henry's delight, joined his Court at Montargis, south of Paris.

Throughout 1484 Richard felt threatened from all quarters, and the year ended with a treason trial which showed both his danger and his vigilance. The accused was William Colyngbourne, a gentleman from Lydiard in Wiltshire, whose family originated from the village of Collingbourne Abbas, a few miles south of Marlborough. William was educated at Winchester, twice served as Sheriff of Wiltshire, and acted for many years as the Duchess of York's Steward in the County. He held the post of Sergeant of the Pantry in Edward IV's Household, and took part in the French expedition of 1475. It seems likely that he supported Buckingham's rebellion, in which Wiltshire played so prominent a part. Whatever the precise nature of his offence, it was taken exceptionally seriously, as appears from the impressive commission appointed to investigate it, headed by the Dukes of Suffolk and Norfolk, assisted by thirteen peers, the Lord Mayor of London, and nine judges.

Colyngbourne was arraigned at the Guildhall on two charges. First, he was accused of having 'devised certain bills and writings in rhymes' calculated to 'stir the people to a commotion against the King', one of which was fastened to the door of St Paul's Cathedral. His scurrilous doggerel included the following couplet:

> The Rat, the Cat and Lovell our dog
> Rule all England under the Hog.

The 'Rat' was Richard's 'mischievous minion', Sir Richard Ratcliffe; the 'Cat' was Sir William Catesby, 'his secret seducer'; and the 'Hog' was 'the dreadful wild boar which was the King's cognizance'.

The second and graver indictment accused Colyngbourne and his associates of plotting 'the death of the King by provoking war, disturbances and dissension between the King and his liege-men within the realm of England', and conspiring to invite 'the so called Earl of Richmond to arrive in the land of England at Poole in the county of Dorset'. Most Tudor writers overlooked this part of the charge, probably because they were ignorant of it, but possibly from malice. Edward Hall, for example, describes the King as directing 'his bloody fury against a poor gentleman for making a small rhyme'. After Colyngbourne was found guilty, 'he was put to the most cruel death' on Tower Hill. A new gallows was constructed for the occasion, 'upon which, after he had hanged a short season, he was cut down, being alive, and his bowels ripped out of his belly, and cast into the fire there by him, and lived till the butcher put his hand in the bulk of his body; in so much that he said in the same instant, "O Lord Jesus, yet more trouble" and so died to the great compassion of much people'.

Throughout the early months of 1485 Richard waited anxiously for news of invasion, and in June his spies told him Henry would shortly put to sea. The King immediately made Nottingham Castle his headquarters from which to meet an attack from wherever it might come. Because of the town's central position in the kingdom, Charles I raised his standard there on 22 August 1642, the anniversary of Bosworth. The defence of South-eastern England was committed to the Howards. Brackenbury, as Constable of the Tower, was ordered to protect London, and Lovell was given command of a fleet based on Southampton to defend the South Coast. The Earl of Huntingdon kept watch in South Wales, while Lord Stanley's brother, Sir William, guarded the north of the Principality. On 22 June, instructions were sent to the Commissioners of Array 'in every shire in England' ordering them to prepare troops 'to do the King's service upon an hour's warning' at 'the peril of losing their lives, lands and goods'.

The very next day, a Proclamation was issued under the Great Seal calling upon Englishmen to resist Henry Tudor. It began by saying that the Bishop of Exeter, Sir Edward Woodville, Jasper Tudor, and the Earl of Oxford, 'with other divers rebels and traitors', of whom 'many be known for open murderers, adulterers, and extortioners', had 'chosen to be their captain one Henry Tudor', who was not only 'descended of bastard blood', but claimed 'the royal estate of this realm of

England where unto he hath no interest, right, or colour'. It went on to accuse Henry of having agreed with Charles VIII to surrender Calais and the English claim to the French Crown, of promising titles and offices to his followers at the expense of those holding them, and of proposing to disinherit and destroy 'all the noble and worshipful blood of this realm'. It furthermore prophesied that if Henry became King there would be 'the most cruel murders, slaughters and robberies, and disinherisons that ever was seen in any Christian realm'. These references to adulterers and disinheritance were a staple ingredient of Richard's propaganda. Indeed, he had made exactly the same charges about the Woodvilles in his letters to York in June 1483. The extravagance of his language was not well calculated to render his claims credible.

About the time it became known that Henry might soon land, Lord Stanley sought the King's permission for leave to visit his family. It was a reasonable enough request seeing that he had spent almost two years at Court as Steward of the Royal Household. But Richard was naturally suspicious, and only permitted him to go provided he handed over his son, George, Lord Strange, as an hostage. Admittedly Lord Stanley had been cleared of complicity in Buckingham's rebellion, but neither he nor the King had forgotten his arrest in June 1483, and his family were well known for adjusting their loyalty to suit their dynastic interests. It therefore seemed possible that the prospect of having his step-son on the Throne might tempt him to change his allegiance.

Henry's invasion was much indebted to the help of Charles VIII, who lent men, money and ships. In a sense, Richard provoked the French to support the rebel cause. Ever since his outspoken condemnation of the peace signed at Picquigny he was believed to be hostile to France. Consequently the government at Paris saw Richard as its enemy, and was attracted by the possibility of replacing him with a grateful protégé.

On 1 August 1485, Henry's fleet of some fifteen ships set sail from Harfleur. In all, there were almost three thousand troops aboard, including Scots and Bretons. Apart from Richmond himself, the military commanders accompanying the expedition were his Uncle, Jasper Tudor, the veteran Earl of Oxford, and Philibert de Chandée, later made Earl of Bath, in charge of the French contingent. After a week at sea, a favourable south wind brought them to Milford Haven on the evening of 7 August. On disembarking at Mill Bay, Henry knelt down and kissed the sand of his native Wales, while the Red Dragon of Cadwallader fluttered overhead. Despite the obvious advantages of a descent on the Welsh coast, the landing achieved a measure of surprise.

The simplest strategy for the rebels to follow was to march through South Wales, cross the Severn at Tewkesbury, and make for London. In fact, they took a northerly route by way of Cardigan, Welshpool and Shrewsbury, and then headed south eastwards through Newport, Stafford, Lichfield, Tamworth and Atherstone. As soon as it became clear that they intended to march down Watling Street, Richard moved south from Nottingham to intercept them. The force with which Henry landed was too small to engage the King's army, and the route he took through central Wales to the Midlands was chosen to meet the needs of recruiting. Moreover, he knew he would face stiff resistance if he ventured into Gwent, whereas he had little to fear from Sir William Stanley, Justiciar of North Wales. In so far as the rebels reached Bosworth without the loss of a man the strategy was justified.

At first, only a few stalwarts were willing to offer support, remembering, no doubt, the disastrous collapse of Buckingham's rebellion. People waited to see what chance of success there was before risking all on what could prove a lost cause. Rhys ap Thomas, an eminent Welshman, was the first to commit substantial forces to Henry when he joined him near Welshpool on 12 August. Four days later, Sir Gilbert Talbot, who was the Uncle of the Earl of Shrewsbury, rode into the Tudor camp at Newport with five hundred men. Soon after, Sir John Savage, Lord Stanley's nephew, offered his services, as did Sir Walter Hungerford, Sir Thomas Bourchier, and Sir Simon Digby.

Between them, Lord Stanley and Sir William commanded

forces of sufficient strength to decide the issue either way. It was consequently crucial to both sides to win the brothers' support. Even before he set sail from Harfleur, Henry was given to understand that he could rely upon help from his step-father. He was therefore disturbed to learn on reaching Shrewsbury 'that his friends would be ready to do their duty *in time convenient*'. The fact that Lord Strange was the King's hostage in part explains this equivocal offer. On 17 August, Sir William secretly met Henry at Stafford, and presumably explained the problem facing his family. A second conference followed three days later at Atherstone to discuss a joint strategy should battle be joined, but the Stanleys still refused to commit themselves openly. The next day, Sunday, Henry marched south, and pitched camp that night a mile from the village of Shenton, at a place called 'White Moors', which in May was ablaze with flowering hawthorns.

Richard first heard of Henry's landing during a visit to Beskwood, a hunting lodge on the edge of Sherwood Forest, and at once summoned Norfolk, Northumberland, Stanley and Brackenbury to join him with the largest force they could muster. Stanley, however, sent back a message to say that he was far too ill to move having caught 'sweating sickness'. This terrible plague, which carried away two Lord Mayors of London in the course of a few days, raged throughout England for most of the summer of 1485. Some said it had been brought from Europe by Henry's mercenaries, while others attributed it to over-indulgence in ale. It was highly infectious, generally fatal, and struck its victims with such rapidity that they often died within three hours of its onset. Happily, Lord Stanley made an astounding recovery, and only a few days later he was well enough to join his troops at Bosworth. Meanwhile, Lord Strange attempted to escape, but was caught in the act, and confessed to intending to join the Earl of Richmond, his Uncle Sir William, and his cousin Sir John Savage. His father, he claimed, knew nothing of this conspiracy. Strange was placed under close guard pending his attainder, and the rebel knights were denounced as traitors.

As soon as it became clear that Henry intended to march on

London, Richard moved his headquarters from Nottingham Castle to the White Boar inn at Leicester. Two days later, on Sunday 21 August, he rode out of the city 'amidst the greatest pomp', mounted on a white charger, 'wearing the crown on his head', and clad in the steel armour in which he had fought at Tewkesbury. The royal army crossed the river Soar by Bow Bridge, marched through the villages of Peckleton and Kirkby Mallory, and pitched camp for the night near Sutton Cheyney, a short distance south of Market Bosworth, and some two miles from the rebels at White Moors.

Considering the decisive nature of the battle of Bosworth, information about it is disappointingly sparse. The first account of it which can be dated with precision, is a letter written on 1 March 1486 by a retired diplomat, Diego de Valera, to Ferdinand, King of Aragon. His news was partly derived from English wool merchants, and partly from Juan de Salazar, a soldier of fortune, who fought for Richard at Bosworth. This so-called 'Spanish letter' contains palpably false or confused information, but the fact that it was written within six months of the battle lends it unique importance. The Croyland Chronicler, writing at much the same time, only devotes a few lines to the fighting, probably because his military knowledge was scant. The fullest surviving account is provided by Vergil, who derived much of his information from such eye-witnesses as Henry Tudor, the Earl of Oxford, Lord Stanley, and Norfolk's son, Surrey. Unfortunately, his narrative is at times confused and contradictory, as is often the way with descriptions of campaigns.

The night before the battle, Richard had 'a terrible dream' in which he 'imagined himself surrounded by a multitude of demons'. Vergil attributes the King's disturbed sleep to a troubled conscience, but treachery could equally account for his restlessness. What later became known as the 'Battle of Bosworth' was first described as taking place at 'Redmoor', a local name for the ground over which the armies fought. At daybreak, on Monday 22 August, Richard occupied the crest of Ambien Hill, overlooking Henry's camp. The ridge of the hill, which runs from East to West, commands views for miles

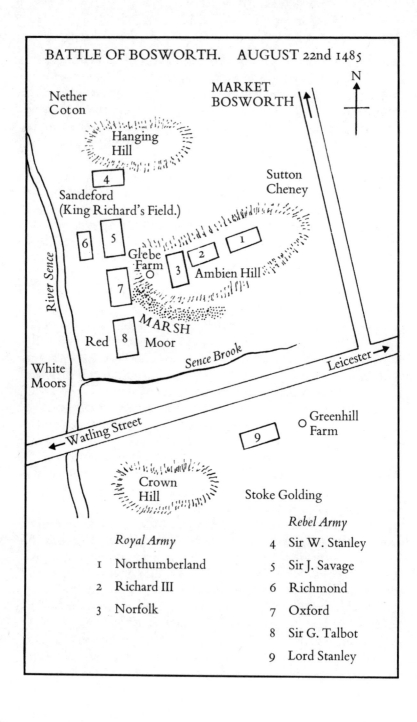

BATTLE OF BOSWORTH.   AUGUST 22nd 1485

N

Nether
Coton

MARKET
BOSWORTH

Hanging
Hill

4

Sutton
Cheney

Sandeford
(King Richard's Field.)

6   5

Glebe
Farm

2

1

River Sence

3

Ambien Hill

7

MARSH

Red   8   Moor

Sence Brook

Leicester

White
Moors

Watling Street

Greenhill
Farm

9

Crown
Hill

Stoke Golding

Royal Army

1   Northumberland

2   Richard III

3   Norfolk

Rebel Army

4   Sir W. Stanley

5   Sir J. Savage

6   Richmond

7   Oxford

8   Sir G. Talbot

9   Lord Stanley

around. It is not particularly high or steep, indeed its western tip, where the fighting took place, is little more than a gentle slope. Throughout the battle, Richard wore a crown over his helmet to raise morale and to emphasise Henry's pretension. It is said he was urged not to make himself so conspicuous, just as Nelson was warned at Trafalgar to cover his decorations for fear of attracting snipers. 'In honour I gained them,' the admiral replied, 'and in honour I will die with them'.

The Duke of Norfolk, who commanded the vanguard of the royal army, ordered his archers, pikemen, and gunners to spread out in a thin line across the western escarpment of Ambien Hill. Richard had no alternative but to keep his rear and centre battles (divisions) in column, because the ridge he occupied was too narrow to permit any other manoeuvre. The King commanded the centre, which was mainly composed of cavalry, although the speed with which his entire force mobilized suggests that most of his troops were originally mounted. Northumberland, whose intentions were as suspect as those of the Stanleys, took up position in the rear towards Sutton Cheyney. On Richard's right, a mile or so to the north, Sir William Stanley's redcoats were visible in the vicinity of 'Hanging Hill', near Nether Coton, an eminence from which many a felon had taken leave of the world. On the King's left was a considerable swamp behind which Lord Stanley's troops were mustered. Richard's position had the tactical advantage that it gave him a commanding view of the enemy, who were forced to attack uphill. On the other hand, his chosen terrain was so confined as to prevent him deploying a considerable part of his army. Northumberland never saw the rebels, let alone engaged them. Richard's 'master-stroke' in seizing Ambien Hill had the effect of confining almost all the fighting to Norfolk and Oxford's battles, thus preventing him from exploiting his larger force.

Henry's army was slower than Richard's to take the field, and manoeuvred with some difficulty round the bog guarding the King's left. Henry wisely left strategy to Oxford, as no man on either side had more experience of command. One problem which added to his difficulties was the number of languages spoken by his troops, many of whom, so Shakespeare claimed, were little more than

> A sort of vagabonds, rascals and runaways,
> A scum of Bretons, and base lackey peasants. . . .

Sir John Savage commanded the Tudor left, Oxford the centre vanguard, and Sir Gilbert Talbot the right. Henry himself took up position with a small band of followers somewhere behind his left wing, about a mile south of Sir William Stanley's men. There are no reliable figures for the sizes of the contending forces at Bosworth, but, such evidence as there is suggests that the King commanded some ten thousand troops, Henry half that number, Sir William about three thousand and his brother one thousand. Unless the Stanleys supported their cause, the rebels faced odds of two to one against them.

Before fighting broke out, Richard ordered Lord Stanley to join him on Ambien Hill, threatening to put Lord Strange to death should his message be disobeyed. It is said that Stanley replied he had more sons and declined to make any move. The King immediately arranged for Strange's execution, but those 'to whom the order was entrusted', decided 'to delay the performance of this cruel' instruction until the battle was over. Henry also sent urgent appeals to both Stanley brothers, and was 'no little vexed' to receive equivocal answers. In fact, Lord Stanley only finally committed himself when he saw that the rebels had won.

Most of the campaigns of the Wars of the Roses lasted for days not weeks. Between 1455 and 1485 there were less than three months of active fighting. Battles rarely continued for more than a couple of hours. Towton was exceptional in beginning at dawn and ending at dusk. Much of the fighting consisted of hand-to-hand mêlées, or, to use the technical language of medieval chivalry, besognes or rencounters. Apart from swords and daggers, the weapons employed were battle axes, maces, and flails, designed to crush rather than penetrate armour. Fighting on foot could be hot work for men encased in steel from head to toe, particularly in summer. Indeed, because knights suffered from heat exhaustion, battles tended to be brief; and because flight was difficult in armour, casualties were heavy. Mêlées, by definition, were confused and made elaborate strategy impossible. Generals were usually to be seen in the thick of the fight, their standards flying overhead as a rallying point for their men. But what identified them to their troops, equally attracted the notice of the enemy, and made them prime targets for attack: particularly as the outcome of a struggle could be decided by a single prominent death. At Barnet, for example, as soon as it became known that Warwick had been killed, his followers fled.

The battle on 22 August began with an exchange of fire between Norfolk's troops, spread across Ambien Hill, and Oxford's men below. When arrows and cannon balls ran out, the two vanguards closed and engaged in a series of mêlées. The fiercest fighting raged around Glebe Farm, on the western slope of the hill. During the engagement, Norfolk was killed, and his son, Surrey, took over command. Although Oxford was forced to attack up hill, he slowly gained ground, and after almost two hours of hand-to-hand combat was more than holding his own.

At this stage in the battle, Richard's scourers (mounted scouts) reported that Henry Tudor with a small bodyguard had detached himself from the left wing of his army, probably intending to ride to Nether Coton to urge Sir William Stanley to engage. The King instantly resolved to seize the opportunity thus presented and lead a cavalry attack against Richmond and his escort. Although this was characteristic of those impulsive decisions for which the Yorkists were famous, there were strong arguments for the strategy. Above all, had Henry been killed the rebel cause could hardly have survived him. The moment was one when the morale of the royal army threatened to disintegrate, particularly after it learned of Norfolk's death. On all sides, there were rumours of treachery and desertion, and Richard's worst fears may have been confirmed by some movement of Sir William Stanley's troops, or by Northumberland's refusal to come to his aid.

The fact that Northumberland played no part in the fighting suggests a number of possibilities. It is conceivable that he was obeying instructions to remain in reserve while keeping watch on the Stanleys. If so, he may subsequently have hoped to placate Henry VII by representing his inactivity as a refusal to offer support, although his imprisonment hardly suggests the acceptance of such a story. It could be that his position on the east of Ambien ridge prevented him from fighting, at least without undertaking a risky flanking manoeuvre. But whatever his reason for not engaging, it appears that Richard feared treachery, and no-one was better placed than the Earl to stab him in the back.

It has recently been argued that the King's attack aimed at a double indemnity: to win all, if possible, by killing Henry Tudor; but, should this fail, to escape from the field to fight another day. Were circumstances to require a strategic withdrawal, the direction of Richard's charge offered the best chance of effecting it. To retreat to Sutton Cheyney was unthinkable if Northumberland was false. Nor would it have been wise to head to the north or south, seeing that both flanks of the royal army were covered by Stanley forces, not to mention the marsh at the foot of Ambien Hill. But the way lay open to the west, should it be deemed necessary to take it, at precisely the point where Richard led his attack.

The King, with some hundred members of his Household, manoeuvred round the right wing of his army under Sir William Stanley's gaze. Soon this small but loyal fellowship of Richard's most ardent supporters began thundering down the slope of Ambien Hill towards Henry's retinue. During fierce hand-to-hand fighting, Henry's banner-bearer, Sir William Brandon, was cut down, reputedly by the King himself, who was also said to have unhorsed Sir John Cheyney, a veritable giant of a man. When the Tudor cause seemed all but lost, Stanley at last decided to intervene, and his redcoats bore down on Richard's escort, shouting 'A Stanley! A Stanley!' At this desperate moment, the King's mount was killed. 'Swift horses' were brought and he was 'exhorted to fly', but he could not be persuaded to turn his back on the rebels. 'That very day', he protested, 'he would make either end of war or life'. De Valera claimed that it was Salazar who urged him to retreat. 'Sir,' he said, 'seek safety. You cannot hope to win this battle, for your followers have openly betrayed you.' But Richard replied, 'God forbid that I yield one foot. This day I will perish as a King or have the victory'. Eventually, surrounded by enemies and 'pierced with numerous deadly wounds', he 'fell in the field like a brave and most valiant prince'. Even Rous, who abused Richard more viciously than any other contemporary, conceded 'that he bore himself like a noble soldier, and despite his little body and feeble strength, honourably defended himself to his last breath, shouting again and again: "Treason! Treason! Treason!"' As Malcolm said of Cawdor in Shakespeare's *Macbeth*, 'Nothing in his life became him like the leaving it.' Richard III was the last King to die in battle on English soil, and the first since Harold fell at Senlac in 1066; the only other year of three Kings until Edward VIII's abdication.

It is just possible that Sir William Stanley intended to secure a royal victory, not to rescue the rebels. At Bosworth, both Richard and Henry used the royal arms on their banners and tabards (a cloth surcoat worn over armour in order to display identifying heraldic devices). Nothing would have been easier than to confuse the two men, particularly when observed through the narrow slit of a helmet. Indeed, just such a possibility may have persuaded Richard to wear the crown which he lost during the battle. The theory that Stanley's troops mistook the King for Henry, and hence attacked and killed him, is not without support. An old tradition asserts that Richard died at the hands of his own men and there are other examples of such heraldic confusion. Oxford's 'star' was mistaken at Barnet for Edward IV's 'sun in splendour'. De Valera's account maintained that Lord Tamorlant – a confused figure combining characteristics of Northumberland and the Stanleys – 'had not really intended Henry to be King'. Finally, Shakespeare may have relied on a tradition of mistaken identity when he made Richard exclaim:

> I think there be six Richmonds in the field,
> Five have I slain today instead of him.

Just how near the King came to success is shown by the fact that Brandon was killed only a few feet away from Henry, whose troops were 'almost out of hope of victory'. Richard's death, however, ensured the downfall of his cause, and enabled his successor to claim divine endorsement of his title, there being no clearer evidence of right than trial by battle. In the first proclamation of his reign, Henry VII announced that 'Richard, Duke of Gloucester, late called King Richard, was slain at a place called Sandeford within the shire of Leicester'. A stone memorial in 'King Richard's Field' now marks the spot where he supposedly fell fighting. Ratcliffe and Brackenbury were among those killed in the final mêlée, Catesby was captured and executed, Northumberland and Surrey were sent to the Tower, and Lincoln and Lovell escaped.

Bosworth, the only battle which Richard fought as Commander in Chief, ended in disaster. Admittedly, his problems were aggravated by treachery, but the rebel force was inferior to his own. The cavalry charge in which he fell was a desperate gamble: magnificent, but not war. His courage is not in dispute, but his military skill has often been exaggerated.

The victorious rebels displayed scant regard for the late King's remains. His hair was contemptuously 'torn and tugged' like that of 'a cur dog', and his corpse was thrown over the back of a horse, his arms and legs dangling down on both sides, with a halter strung round his neck. In this manner, 'nought being left about him so much as would cover his privy member', and besmeared with blood and mud, he was trussed behind a Pursuivant-at-arms called 'Blanc Sanglier', or 'White Boar', and 'as shamefully carried to the town of Leicester as he gorgeously the day before' left it.

For two days, Richard's corpse was exposed at the House of the Grey Friars so that all might satisfy themselves that he was indeed dead. The Franciscans then buried him in their Collegiate Church of St Mary's. After some years, Henry commissioned a coloured marble monument for his erstwhile rival, adorned with an alabaster effigy and a grudging inscription in Latin. Not long after, the tomb was destroyed at the dissolution of the monasteries, and Richard's bones were thrown into the river Soar. He, and his nephew Edward V, are the only two English Kings since the Norman Conquest to have no known resting place.

After Richard was struck down at Sandeford, the rebels pursued the remnants of his army in the direction of Stoke Golding. On a nearby eminence, subsequently known as 'Crown Hill', Lord Stanley set the crown on Richmond's head, while his troops shouted 'God Save King Henry!' This precious emblem of majesty had been discovered under a hawthorn bush, presumably concealed by a marauder who hoped to recover it after the battle was over. The device of a crown on a hawthorn bush was later incorporated into the design of the East Window of Henry VII's Chapel at Westminster Abbey.

However unpopular Richard may have been, he was, in fact, overthrown by 'a few well aimed sword thrusts in a bog', not a national uprising. Although most Englishmen stood aloof from these dangerous proceedings, they rejoiced to learn of the victory won by the rebels at Bosworth.

CHAPTER TEN

'*The Throne Majestical*'

Know then it is your fault that you resign
The supreme seat, the throne majestical,
The scept'red office of your ancestors . . .

Shakespeare   *Richard III* III.7

The history of Richard's usurpation poses two intriguing questions: why did he aspire to the Crown, and by what means did he attain it? Contemporary writers were agreed that he was driven to act as he did by inordinate ambition. Mancini had no hesitation in representing him as obsessed by an 'insane lust for power'. Shakespeare may have exaggerated, but he did not invent the single-minded villain whose heaven it was 'to dream upon the Crown'. The whole history of the Plantagenets shows that they were destructively self-seeking, and nowhere was this more clearly seen than in the Duchess of York's children. Her daughter Margaret, Duchess of Burgundy, earned the nickname 'Juno' so vigorously did she support the House of York; two of her sons deposed reigning Kings and took their places; and the third, the Duke of Clarence, was found guilty of having attempted 'to exalt himself and his heirs to the regality of the Crown of England'.

In 1579, Thomas Legge, Master of Caius College, Cambridge, wrote a Latin play, *Richardus Tertius*. His history came from More and his philosophy from Seneca. The King, as portrayed by Legge, was consumed by 'the lust to rule pure and simple'. Shakespeare, who seems to have known Legge's play, shared his belief that Richard was hungry for power, and both men drew on a tradition with deep roots in history.

Richard was so courageous that it seems incongruous to

suggest that he was driven to usurp by fear as well as ambition. But to be brave is not to be blind to danger, and he was well aware that his nephews were more Woodvilles than Plantagenets. From the first, the Queen and Lord Rivers showed that they had no intention of surrendering control of Edward V and the sovereign power which went with him. Once they succeeded in monopolizing the royal authority, Richard's fate was sealed. As he saw it, to survive, let alone to flourish, he had to seize the King.

The principal blame for the power struggle which ensued belongs to Edward IV, not to Richard's intrigues. When Edward entrusted the Prince of Wales to the care of his wife's family, they were placed in so strongly entrenched a position that force alone could dislodge them.

The events of 30 April irrevocably alienated the Protector from his nephew, as the boy's courageous defence of Rivers and Vaughan showed. In the letter which Richard wrote to Sir Edmund Shaa, explaining his reasons for seizing the King, he described the decision as 'necessary for his own safety'. As the day of the Coronation approached, it looked increasingly improbable that he would lay down his office and brave the King's resentment. In a sense he had no alternative but to seize the Throne to save himself from the hostility his strategy had inspired. Such considerations in no way vindicate his conduct, but they show the vicious spiral of events which his illicit acts engendered.

A further factor which is said to have played a part in encouraging Richard to make his bid for the Throne, was his need to recompense his supporters as lavishly as they expected, and this he could never do unless he became King. Hence, the need to dispose of honours, offices and crown lands, was a powerful incentive to usurp. It has also been suggested that he was genuinely concerned to avoid the evils of Civil War and minority rule. Finally, it seems likely, to say the least, that Richard shared those feelings of jealousy towards the Woodvilles which were so common at the time; and envy, as J. M. Barrie once remarked, 'is not merely the most corroding of vices, it is the greatest power in the land'.

It is difficult enough to decide what persuaded Richard to choose the course he followed, but harder still to ascertain when he finally made up his mind to depose the King. The death of Edward IV necessarily compelled Richard to contemplate his future, and it is barely conceivable that it did not occur to him to supplant his nephew as soon as he learned of his succession. He was not so unworldly as to fail to perceive the promising possibilities which a royal minority offered. But there is no hard evidence to support More's view that Richard's ambition reached maturity before 1483.

A number of nineteenth century writers were so impressed by Darwin's theories that they tried to interpret history in terms of them. It did not demand much ingenuity to apply the notion of 'the struggle for survival' to Richard III's career, or to show that his policy may have evolved in response to changing circumstances. John Jesse, whose *Memoirs of Richard III* were published in 1862, three years after *The Origin of Species*, acquitted Richard of any serious crime during his brother's reign, arguing that Edward IV would never have risked giving him custody of his sons had he thought him guilty of the atrocities with which Tudor writers charged him. At first, Richard merely sought to be recognized as Protector, an office to which his brother's will entitled him. 'But as he advanced, step by step, towards the accomplishment of this legitimate end', he decided 'to consult his own safety by the destruction of others', and overpowered by 'the dazzling temptation of a crown' finally grasped 'the glittering prize which was placed within his reach'.

All accounts of the events of 30 April were written in the knowledge that the Duke of Gloucester deposed his nephew only a few weeks later. It is hardly surprising therefore that the events at Stony Stratford have generally been seen as the first sign of Richard's plan to usurp. But, in fact, the Coup was directed against the Woodvilles, not Edward V. Unfortunately, far from diminishing the dangers confronting the Duke, it greatly increased his peril. It is true it reduced the immediate threat from the Queen's family, but only by making the King an implacable enemy. Thereafter Richard's hope of safety lay in 'removing, or at least undermining, everything that might stand in his way of his mastering the Throne'. Nothing, however, he did during his first month as Protector betrayed an intention to act unconstitutionally.

During the course of the week beginning 10 June, the Protector summoned troops from the north, executed Lord Hastings, seized Prince Richard from Sanctuary, and cancelled the Coronation. By 17 June it was plain for all to see that the die was cast. Indeed, he no longer bothered to keep his intentions secret, and 'no-one now doubted at what he was aiming'. Several factors converged to precipitate action. As the Coronation drew closer, Richard's position became daily more dangerous, and the need to take counter-measures more insistent. Both Richard's mother and wife joined him in London earlier in the month, and no doubt helped him to make up his mind. Finally, the various soundings he made to find out who was dependable, seem to have convinced him of the urgent need to crush growing opposition. So, while it is possible that he resolved to usurp the moment he heard of his nephew's accession, his decision to do so was only divulged in the second week of June.

Most fifteenth and sixteenth century historians credited Richard with unswerving foresight, sagacity and cunning. They questioned neither the malevolence of his designs nor the genius with which he pursued them. Such opinions were not confined to Richard's contemporaries. Bishop Stubbs, in the nineteenth century, wrote of him as being 'brave, cunning, resolute and clear-sighted'. Yet by no means all writers subscribe to such opinions. Legge, for example, in *Richardus Tertius*, acknowledged that Gloucester's ruling passion was ambition, but saw no reason for crediting him with exceptional resource. 'The craft of More's Richard he does to a certain extent retain', with his brash professions of loyalty that disguise purposed treachery, and 'open friendliness that covers secret emnity'; but nowhere in his play is to be found 'that devilish ingenuity' with which Shakespeare's Richard turns all occasions to his purpose, or 'that masterly certainty with which every stroke of his superb mind always hits its mark'.

Nor does Legge's hero show any sign 'of intellectual influence over those about him'. In so far as he wins supporters, it is 'because their plans and aims coincide with a part of his'. *Richardus Tertius* blunders from crisis to crisis until in the final scene he 'can find nothing better to do than pour out his terror and despair'. Shakespeare is more faithful to history when he shows the King at Bosworth hurling himself into the thick of battle as one possessed.

That two plays, written within a few years of each other, should present such contrasting interpretations, is a measure of the complexity of Richard's character. Shakespeare portrays him as courageous and resourceful; but Legge shows him as hesitant, helpless and dependent, as much the luckless plaything of fate as a feather in a whirlwind. For one playwright Fortune ruled Richard, for the other Richard ruled Fortune. Shakespeare's version is dramatically more dazzling but Legge's may come nearer the truth.

The historian's task is to make sense of the past. In so doing, he may be tempted to impose a rationality on events they do not possess, and to imagine that the pattern he discerns originates from the evidence. The belief that the Usurpation involved a calculated strategy, in which every step was meticulously planned in advance, may well proceed from ill-judged efforts to find explanations for what is unreasonable, or without reason. Chaos is chaos and to make sense of it is nonsense. That is why the view that Richard acted impulsively deserves to be taken seriously. As Oliver Cromwell remarked: 'No man climbs higher than he who knows not whither he is going.'

The history of the House of York shows that the family were wilful yet indecisive. Edmund, Duke of York, the founder of the dynasty, was a helpless waverer. His bewildered handling of Hereford's rebellion against Richard II in 1399 was highly characteristic. Richard's father was equally irresolute, yet prone to sudden, rash decisions. Throughout his career he bungled opportunities, and he finally died in a precipitate assault on Queen Margaret's forces at Wakefield. James Gairdner, the most learned of Richard's nineteenth century biographers, rejected the notion that he was a 'cold, deeply politic, and calculating villain', preferring to portray him as 'headstrong and reckless' like other members of his family.

It is easy to understand why Tudor Chroniclers came to the conclusion that Gloucester meticulously planned every phase of the Usurpation in advance. Reading history backwards, they saw a 'clockwork sequence' of incidents, starting with the seizure of Edward V and ending with his Uncle's Coronation. Recently, this view of events has fallen out of favour and it has become fashionable to represent Richard as an impulsive man of action, disposed to take short cuts to his 'immediate objective without pausing to work out the long-term effects'. It has even been suggested that his portraits betray a nervous and anxious look. Vergil describes the uneasy way in which he 'was wont to be ever with his right hand pulling out of the sheath and putting in again the dagger which he did always wear'.

Those who believe that Richard was politically inept, see evidence of his clumsiness from the moment his brother died: shown, for example, by his total failure to gain the Queen's confidence. Once he became King, matters went from bad to worse, and his reign 'seems little more than the story of one ill-considered action after another'. At several crucial moments, such as the coup at Stony Stratford, the execution of Hastings, the seizure of the Duke of York, and 'that last mad and lonely charge against Henry Tudor at Bosworth', he revealed his instinctive preference for headstrong, brutal solutions. Most of the mistakes he made, and much of the harm he did, took him by surprise, as if he neither intended nor foresaw the sequel of his decisions. Whether this portrait of a bewildered ditherer, struggling to solve problems by haphazard resort to violence, is true or false, it bears no resemblance whatever to the mastermind depicted by Tudor writers.

The execution of Hastings was characteristic of the Yorkist approach to politics. After a period of uncertainty, shown, for example, by the plan to prolong the Protectorate, Richard suddenly took 'irrevocable action, compounded of mistrust, fear, ambition and a sense of betrayal'. There is little to suggest that he gave much thought to the long-term consequences of this coup. The haste and savagery with which he acted hardly implies calculation. Before taking a step which could easily have led to armed resistance, it must have been wiser to have waited a few more days for his northern troops to arrive. The fact that he did not do so has even been cited as proof that he faced a genuine conspiracy.

It was essential for Richard to demonstrate convincingly that Edward V was a bastard, yet the charge was made in a most incompetent manner. At first, it was claimed that Edward IV was not his father's son. Next, it was said that his Woodville marriage was bigamous because of his prior betrothal. Then three different ladies were named as his pre-contracted wife. Such clumsy improvisations show every sign of being hasty and ill-considered. When Dr Shaa in his sermon claimed that Richard was the only one of the Duke's sons to look like his father, the Protector, according to More, was supposed to appear in the gallery overlooking Paul's Cross so that all could see for themselves how strong was the similarity. But, in fact, he missed his cue and arrived late, so that Shaa was obliged to abandon the matter in hand to remind his listeners once more how closely Richard resembled the Duke.

It cannot be wise to be too dogmatic about Richard's personality in view of the broad spectrum of opinion on the subject. It is clear, however, that fifteenth and sixteenth century writers exaggerated his depravity, and credited him with a greater consistency of purpose than he actually seems to have possessed. Despite the tendency of modern historians to question his skill and foresight, contemporary testimony cannot be ignored. The Croyland Chronicler, for example, represents Richard as an artful villain, whose stratagems were no less brilliantly conceived than they were faultlessly accomplished. It may also be argued that Richard's very success must be seen as confirming this view.

Opinion has long been divided over the means which Richard employed to make himself King. Some writers have attributed his Usurpation to the support of those who were tired of Civil War and minority rule. Others have seen his seizure of the Throne as the triumph of force and fraud. Be that as it may, it would be difficult to deny that brutal intimidation played some part in the proceedings. Probably the great majority of Edward's subjects deplored his deposition but dared not lift a finger on his behalf.

The force actually used, as distinct from that which was threatened, was deployed in the arrest and execution of Rivers, Hastings, Grey, Vaughan and Haute; and in the imprisonment also of Rotherham, Stanley, and Morton. From the moment that Edward V succeeded his father, hardly a day went by without some threat of violence. The principal subject of debate at the first council meeting of the new reign was the size of the escort which should accompany the King to London.

The Coup of 30 April was mainly achieved by force, with a sprinkling of fraud to add savour. Mancini insists on the part played by duress throughout that day. He says that Richard 'seized' Rivers and his companions and threw them in prison. He speaks of the 'large body of soldiers' with which the Dukes confronted the King at Stony Stratford. He refers to Edward V 'surrendering' himself to his uncle's care, and maintains that Richard throughout was 'demanding rather than supplicating'. More vividly recreates the tension which started at dawn when the inn where Lord Rivers was sleeping was surrounded by armed men, and troops were despatched to guard the road to Stony Stratford to 'compel' travellers to turn back. Rivers was placed 'in ward' and the Dukes set out to meet the King 'in a goodly array'. Before long, Edward's household servants were arrested in his presence and his escort from Ludlow was dismissed. That evening he was a virtual prisoner at Northampton, and his followers were ordered to leave Stony Stratford 'under penalty of death'. It is true Hastings later boasted that not so much blood had been shed 'as would be produced by a cut finger'. But this fortunate outcome does not dispose of the fact that the Dukes rode to Stony Stratford accompanied by a menacing escort, that the King's retinue were threatened with execution, and that he himself was taken into custody.

It should hardly be necessary to argue that the beheading of Hastings, and the seizure of his associates, were acts of violence. No other episode during the Usurpation so manifestly involved a crude resort to force. On 30 April Richard rattled his sabre but kept it in its scabbard, but on 13 June it was drawn and blood was shed. At one stroke, he rid himself of the King's most powerful protagonist, and gave notice to all potential opponents of the risk they ran. Contemporary sources show that the message was not lost on them. According to Vergil, when the full significance of the coup was 'understood', people began 'to look for nothing else but cruel slaughter', in the belief 'that Duke Richard would spare no man so that he might obtain the Kingdom'.

Most of those in the best position to resist Richard showed more prudence than chivalry, while many supported him 'rather for fear than any hope of benefit'. Mancini speaks of a general reluctance to risk the hazards of antagonizing the Protector and his 'multitude of troops'. Those who had been foremost in expressing the wish that 'the Prince should succeed his father in all his glory', cravenly watched his deposition without venturing to protest. It cannot, however, be denied that to have denounced the Usurpation would have been a hazardous undertaking, and in the late fifteenth century people were more concerned with survival than heroics.

Richard naturally claimed that the Queen released the Duke of York from Sanctuary of her own free will. In fact, she capitulated to blatant threats bolstered by false promises. The Council, on 16 June, held a lengthy discussion about violating Sanctuary. In the end, a majority agreed that if the Queen remained obdurate force should be used as a last resort. To that end, the Abbot's lodgings were surrounded by troops. It was only when the Queen 'saw herself besieged and preparation for violence' that she at last agreed to surrender her son, 'trusting in the word of the Cardinal of Canterbury that the boy should be restored after the Coronation'. Vergil describes the 'innocent child' as being 'pulled out of his mother's arms', and the Croyland Chronicle speaks of Bourchier as 'compelled' to intercede. Considering how obstinately the Queen had resisted previous attempts to persuade her to hand over her son, her sudden change of heart suggests the deployment of a new and powerful argument.

Horace Walpole, following Sir George Buck, claimed that the Church and Nobility signified their assent to Richard's Usurpation by supporting him at Westminster Abbey on 6 July, and by petitioning him to become King in the first place. Walpole, however, ignored the simple fact that they acted under duress. In late June and early July, London was one armed camp. Richard's troops were everywhere, Martial law had been proclaimed, and the events of the last month left no one in any doubt that he had the power and resolve to destroy his opponents. The appropriate inference to be drawn from the conduct of those who hailed him as King, is not that they sanctioned his Usurpation but that they were too terrified to oppose it. After a quarter of a century of dynastic warfare, they had learned 'that these matters be Kings' games and they that be wise will meddle no farther'.

Duplicity and fraud played almost as great a part in Richard's strategy as the exploitation of terror. Sir Thomas More portrays him as an instinctive actor, who hoped to disguise the treachery in his heart by brazen professions of loyalty. This 'deep dissembler' never hesitated to show friendship to those 'he inwardly hated', or to 'kiss whom he thought to kill'. Shakespeare, enlarging on the theme, makes Richard proclaim:

> Why, I can smile, and murder while I smile,
> And cry 'content' to that which grieves my heart,
> And wet my cheeks with artificial tears . . .
> I can add colours to the Chameleon,
> Change shapes with Proteus for advantages . . .

The dutiful and reassuring letters which Richard sent the Council and the Queen soon after hearing of Edward IV's death were obviously designed to disarm suspicion. Richard's ostentatious professions of loyalty to his nephew proved equally insincere. It is inconceivable that Rivers would have agreed to meet the Duke at Northampton except under false pretences. The fact that he walked straight into the trap shows how cunningly it was baited. As for the convivial evening he spent with Gloucester and Buckingham, that too was plainly intended to catch him off guard. The parade of Woodville arms through the streets of London was nothing more than a disreputable masquerade, while the stories told about Hastings were widely seen to be 'feigned'.

The Queen from the first showed a profound distrust of her brother-in-law: hence her reluctance to surrender her son on 16 June. 'The Great Chronicle' says that she was eventually persuaded by 'dissembling fair promises'. It seems unlikely that the Archbishop would have given her his assurances unless he too had been duped. Vergil speaks of the 'crafty and subtle manner' in which Richard insisted that 'he did not seek the sovereignty', but was only concerned with 'the profit of the realm'. By this means, he so 'inveigled the minds of the nobility', that the more gullible of them failed to perceive 'to what end his practices would fall out'.

The technical grounds on which Richard claimed the throne were mostly counterfeit and were seen to be so at the time. 'There was no man so dull', says More, describing Buckingham's reception at the Guildhall on 24 June, 'but he perceived well enough that all the matter was made between them'. The Coronation was the last spurious act of the drama in which Gloucester was crowned 'with lies on his lips and blood on his hands'.

There is no contemporary account of the deposition of Edward V which does not stress the duplicity of his Uncle. The Croyland Chronicler was particularly outraged by Richard's double-dealing, and indignantly contrasted the outward respect he showed his nephew at Stony Stratford, with the way he dismissed his attendants, arrested his relations, and took him into custody, all the while paying him 'every mark of respect', by 'uncovering the head, bending the knee, or other posture of the body required in a subject'.

Had Richard been guilty of nothing more than occasional subterfuge, he would merely have been following the example of most medieval Kings. The fifteenth century was an age of sophisticated intrigue in which honest politicians were as common as candid horse-dealers. But Richard's duplicity was deeply ingrained. Furthermore, the shrill note of moral indignation which rings through his proclamations came ill from one who was commonly supposed to have butchered his own flesh and blood. Throughout his reign he rebuked vice with a zeal which approached obsession. To hear him denounce the adultery of 'the unshameful and mischievous woman called Shore's wife', one would not have supposed that he himself was the father of natural children. In so far as he seemed ill qualified to cast the first stone, he acquired a reputation for hypocrisy. On 10 March 1484, he circulated a letter to his bishops expressing his 'fervent desire' to see 'virtue and cleanness of living to be advanced, increased and multiplied, and vices and all other things repugnant to virtue, provoking the high indignation and fearful displeasure of God, to be repressed and annulled'. Some writers have exhibited this document as telling proof of Richard's high principles, but others have questioned the sincerity of his concern for the moral welfare of his Kingdom. His sentiments were plainly unimpeachable but the propriety of his voicing them has been challenged.

There are strong reasons for suspecting that Richard's Court was not beyond reproach. During its Christmas festivities in 1484, the Croyland Chronicler complained that 'too much attention' was given 'to dancing and gaiety and frivolous changes of apparel'. But what concerned him more deeply was the King's 'incestuous passion' for Princess Elizabeth. Langton, who owed the See of St David's to Richard's favour, wrote to the Prior of Christ Church, Canterbury, in September 1483, singing the praises of a patron whose wisdom had been so conspicuously displayed in his appointment of Welsh bishops. His letter concludes with a sentence in Latin. Like Gibbon, his English text was chaste and 'licentious passages' were consigned to 'the decent obscurity of a learned tongue'. Unfortunately, Langton's manuscript is almost impossible to decipher because of the ravages of damp. The Latin appears to read: 'Neque exceptionem do voluptas aliqualiter regnat in augmentatia.' So even Langton, it seems, felt bound to admit that sensual pleasures increasingly ruled at Court.

Among the magnificent collection of books and manu-scripts which Lord Harley presented to the British Museum in 1753, was a folio volume of grants of the reigns of Edward V and Richard III, catalogued as Harleian Manuscript 433. This remarkable Register, which is only now being published in full, provides an unrivalled insight into the way in which Richard rewarded loyalty and won friends. It is seldom poss-ible, however, to draw a sharp distinction between the legit-imate exercise of royal patronage and corrupt practice. Whether a particular grant is a gift, reward, or bribe, is something the documents naturally do not make clear. Most contemporary writers, however, agreed with Vergil that Richard hoped 'to mollify the multitude with largesse and liberality' and 'to win the hearts of his adversaries with rewards and promises'. More and Fabyan were of the same opinion. In return for 'large gifts', wrote Sir Thomas, the Protector secured 'unsteadfast friendship.' 'Few or none favoured his party', says Fabyan, 'except it were for dread, or for the great gifts that they received of him'. Men like Buck-ingham, Northumberland, Howard and Catesby, would have required a degree of unworldliness they showed few signs of possessing, had hope of reward played no part in their think-ing.

All the bishops, including three Lord Chancellors, Bour-chier, Rotherham, and Russell, took part in the Coronation, the most magnificent of the century. Consequently it has been argued that the Usurpation could not have been 'so utterly unauthorized, so flagrant, so abhorrent to the feelings' of Richard's fellow-countrymen as is often represented. Only three Bishops ever openly defied him: John Morton, Lionel Woodville, and Piers Courtenay. Others showed some evidence of uneasiness, including Bourchier, Rotherham, and Russell. Mancini says that the Archbishop crowned Richard 'unwillingly'. Later the same year, for reasons no longer known, he was briefly disgraced. During the thirty-two years of his Archbishopric he swore allegiance to five Kings and broke his oath to two of them: Henry VI and Edward V. Nor could he have flourished under Henry Tudor had his loyalty to his late master proved provocatively stubborn. From the first, Russell showed misgivings, as well he might. Rous says that he only accepted the office of Lord Chancellor 'much against his will', and Stallworth told Stonor 'My lord has much business and more than he is content withal'. Richard in the last month of his reign is thought to have dismissed him for some real or imagined infidelity. But like Bourchier he soon reappeared as a trusted adviser of Henry VII.

The Wars of the Roses taught Englishmen that the simplest way to prosper was to yield to the victor. The Church consequently aimed to co-operate with those most likely to prevail, believing it wiser to drift with the tide of events than to battle against it. Late fifteenth century bishops were royal nominees selected for secular reasons. During the last twelve years of his reign, Edward IV filled some twenty vacant sees with politicians and administrators, most of whom remained ministers of the Crown despite their spiritual duties. Three of his bishops had formerly been his secretary, and almost half had legal training. The feebleness of their opposition to Richard, and the fickleness of their allegiance to Edward V, alike derived from the very qualities to which they owed their appointments.

The support the Church gave Richard was mostly passive. Recognizing that acquiescence was the better part of valour, they connived at the fiction that Edward V was a bastard. Possibly some bishops actually believed that Richard was rightfully King, while others prudently gave him the benefit of the doubt. For those whose consciences were troubled, the legend of the 'Pre-Contract' offered consolation. Moreover, the judgment of God might be seen in Richard's success and it could not be wise to resist the divine will. The Clergy's 'support' at the Coronation was offered to a King in possession. The choice which confronted them was not should they help him win the Throne but could they refuse to crown him. Their role was to endorse a *fait accompli* not to bring it about.

231

The success of the Usurpation was one of those 'stubborn and irresistible facts' which brook no denial. One is reminded of Carlyle's rejoinder to the Lady who said she 'accepted' the Universe: 'By God, she'd better!'

It is possible for bishops as a body to resist their sovereign. Seven of them did just that in 1688. But Richard's bishops were more worldly than those of James II, and their first instinct was to support the authority to which they owed their sees. Bourchier was partly to blame for the conduct of his brethren, and was anyway too old and bewildered to give a resolute lead. He yearned to be left to die in peace at Knole, not to become a leader of revolt. Under such guidance, it is not surprising that a bishop like Alcock of Worcester saw no dishonour in acting as tutor to Edward V, Councillor to Richard III, and Lord Chancellor to Henry VII. His triumphant survival in five reigns was barely surpassed by the Vicar of Bray.

The fickle allegiance of the clergy in 1483 was discreditable to their order, and shows how urgently the Church in England needed reformation. Richard owed his throne to his own exertions, not the support of the bishops, but by hallowing his Usurpation they helped him to retain it.

The great majority of the House of Lords in 1483 showed no disposition to risk their lives or possessions on behalf of any dynasty. After thirty years of Civil War, few nobles were anxious to meddle in royal government. Men like Northumberland preferred to stand aloof – even on the battlefield. Two thirds of the Peerage in Richard's reign were of recent creation, and little resembled the feudal patriarchs of the earlier years of the century. Indeed, most English nobles had become little more than titled landowners, virtually incapable of defying the King. During his reign, Edward IV made five dukes, two marquises, fourteen earls, two viscounts, and sixteen barons. It was hardly to be expected that these Yorkist peers would rush headlong into conflict with the crown. Moreover, most of them had so alienated their retainers by avaricious practices that they dared not risk an appeal to their loyalty.

Only a small number of the most politically active nobles

played any part in supporting the Usurpation. Some helped Richard because they were old associates like Francis Lovell, who had been brought up with him at Middleham, and served him loyally thenceforth. Others, like Buckingham, Hastings, and Stanley, were prepared to assist him provided he undertook to protect the interests of the old nobility against 'upstarts' like the Woodvilles. Others again resented Edward IV's arbitrary disregard for the laws of inheritance, and looked to him to redress their grievances. Because the principal beneficiaries of such depredations were the late King's sons, several important nobles had an interest in their downfall, and supported the Usurpation to recover their estates. Chief among them, were Buckingham, Westmorland, Howard, and Huntingdon. This small but powerful faction gave Richard the active help he required to depose the young King. But they would never have prevailed unless most of their fellow peers had proved willing to acquiesce.

The dynastic struggles of the fifteenth and sixteenth centuries left Englishmen with a horror of rebellion, and the thought of deposing a King held few attractions, except for men like Warwick. Moreover, the punishment for treason provided a powerful argument for not committing it. Convicted traitors were hanged, cut down, castrated, and disembowelled, while still alive. Nor did the penalty end there. The wives and children of rebels were deemed to be tainted, and their lands and titles were forfeited to the Crown. Such ferocious procedures ensured that rebellion was never 'taken in hand, unadvisedly, lightly, or wantonly'. Nevertheless, the surprising fidelity shown to Henry VI owed much to the long-suffering loyalty of his subjects. What finally drove the Yorkists to set up a King of their own was the wholesale confiscation of their property by the 'Parliament of Devils'. If there was one political principle which united the landowning class, it was an heartfelt belief in the sanctity of inheritance.

The great majority of English nobles attended Richard at his Coronation because they dared not do otherwise. Two years later, when their presence was even more vital, only nine nobles supported him at Bosworth. If the reluctance of peers to resort to arms helped Richard win the Throne, it equally helped him to lose it.

Once the Usurpation proved successful, many who hoped it would fail felt obliged to obey Richard. Morton told Buckingham that he did not intend to dispute the title of the 'King in possession'. Even usurpers evoke a measure of loyalty, and it was common enough to regret the deposition of Edward V while swearing allegiance to Richard III. Indeed, there was no other course a prudent man could steer.

> Treason doth never prosper: What's the reason?
> For if it prosper, none dare call it treason.

Norfok's son, the Earl of Surrey, was wounded and taken prisoner after Bosworth. In 1488, Henry VII visited him in the Tower and reproached him for fighting for Richard III. 'Sire,' replied the Earl, 'I beseech your Grace to consider that the prince whom I followed was solemnly and lawfully crowned King, with universal applause. And I did never hold it my part or duty to dispute or sift or question the title of the king his liege lord to the crown, but contrariwise to defend him and his crown. And I was then and ever shall be of the mind to serve and to love him with my heart who shall upon so good and honourable terms attain to the crown and wear it as he did. And I will live and die with him and in the defence of that crown wherever I shall find it, yea if it were set upon a stake.' Henry was so impressed by this loyal and courageous reply that it apparently persuaded him to set Surrey free.

The most powerful single group of Richard's supporters came from the north of England. After Warwick was killed at Barnet in 1471, Richard stepped into his shoes, partly as a result of his marriage to Anne Neville, and partly because he acquired a large share of the Earl's northern estates. By the time he became Protector, his authority in Cumberland, Westmorland, Yorkshire and Northumberland was unrivalled. Edward created this vast concentration of power to meet the threat of border raids from Scotland and to subjugate a notoriously lawless region. But, in doing so, he failed to recognise that the military resources he put at his brother's disposal might also be used to snatch the Crown from his son.

The Duke of Gloucester was 'well beloved and honoured of all the northern people', and nowhere more than in York, then the second city in the Kingdom. Yorkshire was virtually his native county. His father was Duke of York, and his mother and wife were Nevilles. Moreover, as a boy, he had learned the arts of chivalry in Warwick's Household at Middleham. When Edward IV became King in 1461, Yorkshire was still Lancastrian at heart, but Richard won over the North by restoring relative peace to its peoples. On learning of his death, the Mayor and Aldermen of York spoke of him as having been 'piteously slain and murdered to the great heaviness of this City'. Two years later, when everywhere else he was held in execration, they still spoke of him as 'the most famous prince of blessed memory'. Indeed, as Sir Francis Bacon wrote in his *History of Henry VII*, recollections of Richard 'laid like lees at the bottom of mens' hearts, and if the vessel was once stirred it would rise'. This was no mere rhetoric. As late as the reign of Henry VIII, Lord Dacre complained to Wolsey that he could not be expected to rival the Duke of Gloucester's achievements in governing the North. Even today, after five hundred years, Richard's memory is cherished in Yorkshire. In the Parish Church of St Helen, Sheriff Hutton, flowers are still placed on what many believe to be the tomb of his son.

Richard's popularity in the North owed much to liberal patronage. The Clergy, for example, had good cause to be grateful for his generous gifts to Churches. Early in 1483 he persuaded his brother to relieve York from paying a tax to meet the cost of the war against James III. Naturally this favour was greatly appreciated and earned him much good will. On 5 June, 1483, he assured the Mayor of York, John Newton, that he could never forget the City's 'kind and loving disposition' towards him, and that he remained its 'especial good and loving lord'. It may not be entirely fortuitous that only five days later he wrote asking for troops. In September 1483, he released the city from 'murage' and other tolls: a gesture more profitable to his reputation than his exchequer.

Some historians have argued that Richard's popularity in the North has been exaggerated, and that evidence drawn from the City records of York reflects the views of a ruling clique. Allowance must also be made for the florid phrases thought proper when writing of princes. The Mayor and aldermen had reason to be grateful for many royal favours, but their own archives show that by no means all their fellow citizens were equally well disposed. 'There are strong hints that less respectable factors in Richard's exercise of lordship may account for his popularity'. In the short term, prodigal patronage might win a specious acclaim, but in the long run it was liable to undermine government and wreak financial havoc.

In 1939 Angelo Raine published a two-volume collection of documents from the City archives of York. His research led him to conclude that Richard was 'distrusted and disliked by many of the commons' and that even the City Council did not regard him with unqualified devotion. It saw him as a man with whom it was rash to trifle, and consequently obeyed his orders, complied with his requests, and gave him presents: in return, of course, for substantial concessions. The relationship was a marriage of convenience not true love.

Part of the City Council's business was to resolve disputes. In February 1483, a quarrel broke out at the Eden Berrys, a tavern in Goodramgate near the Minster. It began when Stevyn Hoghson proclaimed that Thomas Wrangwysh ought to become Lord Mayor, because the Duke of Gloucester would 'do things for him'. This so incensed one Robert Rede that he proclaimed: 'If the Duke of Gloucester is for Wrangwysh then we don't want him'. The Mayor should be chosen by the commons 'and not by no lord'. On another occasion, somebody asked: 'What might the Duke of Gloucester do for our city?' 'Nothing but grin at us' was the disdainful reply. One has only to look at Richard's surviving portraits to see that people might easily think he was mocking them. In 1485, when Richard called on the City for troops to crush Henry Tudor's rebellion, it was suspiciously slow to raise them. It is true that a plague raged there that summer, but there are also signs that the Council dragged its feet because it was disenchanted.

Whatever Northerners may have thought of Richard, there can be no question of his preference for them when it came to government appointments. Indeed, the favours he showed them caused bitter complaints in other parts of England, to which the Chronicles testify with some emotion. The majority of Clerical members of the Council, men such as Rotherham, Stillington and Alcock, came from the north, as did peers like Northumberland, Viscount Lovell, Lord Dacre of Gillesland, and Lord Scrope of Bolton. Sir Robert Brackenbury, Sir Richard Ratcliffe, Sir James Tyrell, and the King's secretary, John Kendall, also had roots in Yorkshire or neighbouring counties. To this compact, inter-related group of loyal supporters, must be added a number of other Northerners upon whom Richard relied for a variety of services, foremost among whom were Ralph, Lord Neville, Sir Robert Percy, Sir Marmaduke Constable, Sir John Saville, and Sir Ralph Assheton. Part of the opposition to the Usurpation was regional in character. Those who lived in the south and west of the Kingdom deeply resented the preeminence of such 'riffraff' from the North. It was Richard's misfortune that all his early historians happened to live in the South.

Between 4 May and 6 July 1483, the political history of England was concentrated on the capital. Apart from the executions at Pontefract, and the movements of the army of the North, everything of importance took place within a couple of miles of Crosby Hall. Richard's military domination of London was so overwhelming as to make resistance unthinkable. The Lord Mayor was a fervent partisan and consequently there was nothing to fear from the City trainband. The nobles had sent their retinues home and were virtually disarmed. It was widely known that reinforcements were heading south. Recollections of Queen Margaret's army in 1461 inspired harrowing visions of murder, pillage, and rape. So such support as Londoners offered Richard owed more to 'fear than love'. Their mood was one of sceptical hostility, and when the Protector exhibited himself in the streets in the hope of winning applause, he was 'scarcely watched by anybody'. There would have been no need for a curfew in the capital had he felt confident of its approval.

Many people feared that the reign of Edward V would involve further Civil War and consequently accepted the Protector's claims in the interest of peace and prosperity. Between 1461 and 1483 the Throne changed hands five times, and the deposition of Edward V was not at first 'so repugnant to the feelings of Englishmen as it afterwards appeared when the sequel was divulged'. The experience of the early weeks of the new reign, during which London seethed with plots and counter-plots, may have made the Usurpation seem preferable to the growing threat of anarchy.

Richard relied, of course, on the support of relations, friends and retainers. As far as his family was concerned, he principally looked to his mother, his wife, and his sister Elizabeth's eldest son, Lord Lincoln. Francis, Lord Lovell, probably served him more disinterestedly than any other friend. He also depended on a number of men who thought that their talents had been neglected by the late King. Prominent among such place-seekers were Stillington, Ratcliffe, Catesby, and Tyrell.

It has often been argued that to understand Richard, let alone to judge him, he has to be seen as the creature of his age. 'We ought to recall', says Horace Walpole, 'the temper and manners of the times we read of. It is shocking to eat our enemies; but it is not so shocking in an Iroquois as it would be in the King of Prussia. And this is all I contend for, that the crimes of Richard, which he really committed, were more the crimes of the age than of the man'. From his earliest youth, Richard was brought up amidst bloodshed, proscriptions and treachery, at a time when life was held cheap, and fraud was admired. The ideas to which Machiavelli gave expression in *The Prince* were very much in the air in the late fifteenth century. But even when every allowance is made for the degraded standards of his age, the fact remains that Richard fell far below them.

CHAPTER ELEVEN

History and Myth

Let Truth and Falsehood grapple: who ever knew
Truth put to the worse in a free and open encounter?

Milton *Areopagitica.*

Throughout the sixteenth century historians increasingly tended to portray Richard III as a 'bloody tyrant and a homicide; one raised in blood, and one in blood established'. For over a century after his death not a single voice was raised on his behalf by the chroniclers of his reign: partly because there were few surviving Yorkists to come to his defence, and partly because to incriminate the dynasty which deposed him verged on treason. Moreover, Henry VII's title to the throne was so dubious 'that he needed all the justification for his accession that he could find; and the blacker his predecessor's character could be made to appear' the easier it became to vindicate his overthrow.

Sixteenth century writers regarded history as a living source of instruction for the present. They saw the historians' task as essentially didactic: to proclaim the lessons of the past, and to demonstrate their relevance. 'He who would foresee what is to happen', says Machiavelli, 'should look to what has happened: for all that is is has its counterpart in time past.'

The Tudors lived through a period of rebellions which threatened the very survival of government. At times in Elizabeth I's reign it seemed as if her life alone preserved the realm from anarchy. Consequently most of her subjects lived in mortal terror of Civil War, and regarded the deposition of an anointed King – to say nothing of regicide – as an atrocious crime. The Tudors were obsessed by the warning signals they deciphered in fifteenth century precedents. As they saw it, what was sown in 1399, when Henry IV usurped the throne, was reaped in the Wars of the Roses: the bloody harvest of that first disobedience. Because 'the powers that be are ordained of God', to depose a sovereign was to incur divine displeasure. Nowhere was the work of an almighty hand more evidently proclaimed than in 'the disorder, horror, fear and mutiny' which plagued the late Middle Ages.

Shakespeare devotes eight plays to warning his audiences of the evils of Civil War and holds up a glass before them in which they may see the bitter fruits of rebellion. Nobody in their senses he concludes would revive 'these bloody days again, and make poor England weep in streams of blood'. Tudor governments were equally anxious that the lessons of the fifteenth century should be marked, learned and digested. Accordingly, 'for the better understanding of simple people', a number of homilies were written to be read out in churches on Sundays and Holy Days. The 'Exhortation concerning good Order', published in 1547, began with the reminder that 'it is written of God in the Book of Proverbs "Through me Kings do reign; through me counsellors make just laws; through me do princes bear rule and all judges of the earth execute judgment." ' Satan was the author of dissension, and God's first command to Adam was obedience. It was consequently the supreme duty of Christians to submit to the divinely constituted authority of their Sovereign, to 'render unto Caesar the things that were Caesar's.' Not content with mere exhortation, the Homilies dwelt on the penalties for sedition, including as they did the most gruesome death which human ferocity could devise, everlasting damnation, and a return to 'the calamities, miseries and mischiefs' of the Wars of the Roses.

Shakespeare's fifteenth century plays have two main political themes: the 'divinity' that 'doth hedge a King', and the havoc wrought by rebellion. His treatment of both concepts reflects the accepted wisdom of his age, just as his historical framework derives from Hall and Vergil. The very title of Hall's work anticipates its message: 'The Union of the Noble and Illustrious Families of Lancaster and York'. Hall shows how Henry IV's seizure of the Throne in 1399 'was the beginning and root of the great discord and division' which made the fifteenth century so 'troublous' a season, until finally brought to a 'triumphant' conclusion in 'the reign of the high and prudent prince King Henry the Eighth, the indubitable flower and very heir of the said lineages'. Shakespeare foreshadows this historical pattern in *Richard II* by representing the deposition of the King, the 'figure of God's Majesty, His Captain, Steward, deputy-elect', as 'so heinous, black, obscene a deed', as to provoke divine retribution. No sooner does Henry 'ascend the regal throne' than the Bishop of Carlisle prophesies in a virtuoso display of dramatic irony:

> The blood of English shall manure the ground,
> And future ages groan for this foul act,
> Peace shall go sleep with Turks and infidels,
> And, in this seat of peace, tumultuous wars
> Shall kin with kin, and kind with kind confound . . .

The Bishop's predictions are fulfilled to the letter in seven subsequent plays. For example, during the battle of Towton in part three of *Henry VI*, a son enters 'that hath killed his father', and 'a father that hath killed his son'. It seems likely that this particular scene was suggested by the 1569 'Homily against Rebellion', which lists amongst the calamities of Civil War that it encourages 'the brother to seek and often to work the death of his brother, the son of the father; the father to seek or procure the death of his sons'. Carlisle's warnings may have fallen on deaf ears as far as Henry IV was concerned, but Shakespeare would have failed in his purpose had it been lost on his fellow countrymen.

There was one question which few dared ask but none the less needed answering. If it was such an atrocious crime to rebel, what was the Earl of Richmond doing at Bosworth? To concede his right to revolt was to undermine absolutism, to deny it was to challenge his claim to the throne. Somehow a way had to be found to escape this awkward dilemma. It was consequently argued that Richard was so unprecedented a villain that the ordinary rules of obedience ceased to apply. On a few rare occasions rebellion could be justified, for example to reinstate a lawful sovereign, or to rid the realm of a regicide. Hence the necessity to portray Richard III as an usurper and a tyrant. Hall's masterly special pleading goes a long way to resolve the inconsistency of Tudor propaganda. In his pages, Richard is shown as such a monster of iniquity as to justify his overthrow. Indeed, Henry is represented as sent by God to put an end to tyranny. This view of events was precisely that of the Act of Attainder of November 1485, which accused the 'late Duke of Gloucester' of 'unnatural, mischievous and great Perjuries, Treasons, Homicides and Murders, in shedding of infants' blood', and many other 'abominations against God and Man'.

In preliterate ages oral traditions were preserved with a fidelity we should now find astonishing. Even towards the end of Elizabeth's reign, stories about Richard were still handed down by word of mouth. John Stow, an indefatigable anti-quarian, told Sir George Buck 'that he had spoken with old and grave men who had often seen King Richard, and that they had affirmed he was not deformed, but of person and bodily shape comely enough'. It is always possible therefore that where Tudor Chroniclers, like Grafton, Hall, or Holinshed, mention events to which nobody else refers, they are drawing on folk memories.

Chronicles covering Richard's reign continued to appear throughout the sixteenth century, although they rarely had much to add to More or Vergil. Because they were drawn from the same original sources, their narratives naturally bear a marked resemblance. Sometimes historians have appealed to such literary inter-dependence as proof of authenticity, but to repeat facts is not to corroborate them. Towards the end of the century, authors increasingly tended to represent rumours and hints as if they were verified facts.

Shakespeare's historical plays were deeply indebted to *The Chronicles of Raphael Holinshed*, a composite work beginning with Noah and ending in 1576. Its account of the years 1483 to 1485 came from Vergil, More and Hall, but painted Richard even blacker than they did. It was left to Shakespeare to scale the peak of calumny with his dazzling portrait of 'hell's black intelligencer' who snarls and bites and plays the dog. Understandably enough, he seldom hesitates to sacrifice historical fidelity to the needs of his drama. The exuberant villainy of *Richard III* was only partly a work of imagination. Nevertheless, the hunch-backed tyrant who fretted and strutted his hour upon the stage of the Globe Theatre, was a travesty not a portrait.

Sir George Buck was the first author to occupy the ground on which all subsequent apologists for Richard have pitched their tents. His great-grandfather, John Buck, was beheaded after the Battle of Bosworth. Sir George served in the fleet which scattered the Armada, was knighted by James I, and made 'Master of the Revels'. In 1619, two years before he went mad, he wrote *The History of King Richard the Third*, a rambling, erudite work. It was partly based on early manuscripts preserved in the Tower of London, Sir Robert Cotton's Library, the College of Arms, and the Library of Thomas Howard, Earl of Arundel, to whom he dedicated his book. Buck made extensive use of a manuscript version of the Croyland Chronicle he found in Cotton's collection. He was, moreover, the first writer to recognize the importance of fifteenth century documents, and to appreciate the extent to which slanders against Richard proceeded from Tudor partisanship, the source of which he traced back to More's *History*. This, in its turn, he believed was based on a Latin work composed by Bishop Morton, 'the chief instigator and prime submover of all these treasonable detractions'. Morton, inspired by rancour and malice, charged Richard 'with many foul crimes', and More then 'translated and interpreted and glossed and altered his Master's book at his pleasure'. So great was his reputation that later writers treated his *History* as 'canonical', and became mere 'trumpeters and echoes' of his views. In his attempt to discredit Sir Thomas' authority, Buck disparaged his piety and learning, and accused him of seeking 'preferment and advancement'.

Buck's *History* consists of five books. The first two are

devoted to Richard's career and reign, and the remaining three examine the accusations of previous writers, all of which are dismissed. In particular, he shows that many charges are not to be found in contemporary documents but first appear in the pages of Tudor Chronicles. After a painstaking survey of early manuscripts, he reached the conclusion that there was not enough evidence to prove that Richard was deformed, or responsible for killing Prince Edward of Lancaster, Henry VI, or Clarence. He went on to claim that More's account of the murder of the Princes in the Tower was too contradictory to be credible, but he was on less sure ground in arguing that Richard had no reasons for wishing his nephews dead, or that Perkin Warbeck was Edward's younger son. At times, Sir George wrote every bit as recklessly as the authors he condemned.

Naturally Buck denied that Richard III was either a tyrant or an usurper. Since Edward V had no right to the Throne, it was no crime to seize it. Sir George accepted the truth of the pre-contract, and was the first writer to name Lady Eleanor Butler as the lady betrothed to the King. Following the arguments of the Royal Title Act of 1484, he claimed that both Houses of Parliament invited Richard to reign, and that the legality of his succession was endorsed at his Coronation. Richard, according to Buck, was a loyal brother, devoted husband and affectionate father, who only accepted the Crown with great reluctance. Having done so, he showed himself to be upright, generous, and humane; winning renown for wise laws and charitable works. Sir George justly complained of the double standards of many of Richard's critics, who bitterly denounced him for the judicial murder of Hastings, while averting their eyes from a long line of kings every bit as guilty of similar 'acts of empire'.

Buck was right to insist on the tendency of Tudor historians to exaggerate the extent of Richard's depravity. However, the reasons he gave for their employing 'their wits and their pens to make King Richard odious' were wholly inadequate. Their 'libels and railings' he attributed to malice 'towards the princely family of York', mortal hatred of Richard, and their desire to 'insinuate themselves into the favour of great ones'. But he never explained the persistence of animosity to a long dead King, whom he described as 'wise', 'magnificent', 'valiant', 'magnanimous and pious'. His picture of John Morton, Cardinal Archbishop of Canterbury and Lord Chancellor of England, busily writing scurrilous pamphlets in the hope of winning preferment, can hardly be taken seriously. Nor is it more probable that Sir Thomas More, 'who scorned to save his life' by submitting to Henry VIII, would have 'prostituted his pen' in the supposed interest of the Court.

Buck refused to face the fact that most of the accusations he found in Tudor histories had already been made in Richard's own lifetime. The belief that he murdered his nephews, to take only one example, was not the least of the reasons for Buckingham's rebellion. If Richard was really as innocent as Buck suggests, it is hard to believe that a handful of chroniclers could have inveigled their fellow countrymen into regarding him as a tyrant. Not all the obloquy which Yorkist propaganda heaped on Henry VI discouraged attempts to have him proclaimed a saint. In fact, of course, the Tudor view of Richard proceeded less from 'mindless partisanship' than from recollections of his reign. It is consequently 'a gross distortion' of the available evidence to contend that sixteenth century writers '*invented* the wickedness of Richard III'.

The eighteenth century, the so-called Age of Reason, subjected the traditional portrait of Richard to fastidious scrutiny. Curiously enough, David Hume, for all his reputation as a sceptical philosopher, never questioned the Tudor view in his *History of England*, which remained a standard work as late as the eighteen-eighties when Winston Churchill read it at Harrow. Hume wrote as if Buck had never been born, and his ready acceptance of Richard's infamy reflected his view that the Middle Ages were a dark night of barbarism. Other historians, however, were disposed to discount some parts of the tradition. In 1736, Francis Drake, a surgeon turned antiquarian, published a history of his native city of York based on municipal archives. His portrait of Richard was far from favourable, but, nevertheless, showed that the King, who was generally 'represented as a monster of mankind', was 'not so esteemed in his lifetime' in the North.

The most challenging apology for Richard to appear in the eighteenth century was Horace Walpole's *Historic Doubts of the Life of Richard the Third*. For all its display of forensic skill, it added little to Buck's arguments, apart from brevity. Its two main concerns were to expose the inconsistencies which impaired the traditional portrait, and to argue that nobody possessing the high reputation which Richard enjoyed at the time of his brother's death, would so soon have turned into the bloody tyrant of Shakespeare's Tragedy. Walpole's role was that of a defending counsel who discredits hostile witnesses but fails to present evidence of his own to confound the prosecution. In his admiration for the Middle Ages, so intriguingly exhibited at Strawberry Hill, he anticipated the Gothic Revival of the nineteenth century; but in his confident faith in the natural goodness of Man he was true to his own time.

In 1793 Walpole, now Lord Orford, published a 'Postscript' to his *Historic Doubts* retracting one of its most important assertions. Originally, he had argued that no man could be so malevolent as Richard was generally painted. He reached this conclusion because of his faith in human perfectibility, a characteristic doctrine of his age sustained in despite of millennia of experience. What led him to change his mind was the French Revolution. Few who lived through the Reign of Terror preserved their faith in political benevolence. Walpole's 'Postscript' was 'more than the despairing cry of a disillusioned old man', it was 'the death rattle of the Age of Reason'. He still insisted that Richard was not as black as some would have us believe, but no longer presumed to set limits to Man's depravity. 'I must now believe', he wrote, 'that any atrocity may have been attempted or practised by an ambitious prince of the blood aiming at the crown'. The very crimes which Walpole had earlier 'supposed to have been too manifold and too absurd to have been perpetrated even in a very dark age', had since 'been exhibited in the compass of five years' by Philip Egalité, Duke of Orleans. It had consequently become impossible to argue that no one would wade 'so deeply into wickedness'.

Reactions to Richard in the nineteenth century were profoundly affected by a revolution in thinking about the nature of history itself. Like many movements of thought the impetus came from external pressures. The Romantic Movement created a new concern for the past, as the sales of Scott's novels showed. In particular, it encouraged a more sympathetic approach to the Middle Ages and an effort to understand them in terms of their own world-picture. Previously historians had tended to regard the peoples of earlier centuries as precisely like themselves, although few things can be less historical than to superimpose the present on the past. But romanticism insisted on the importance of the spirit of the age. Hence its tendency to represent Richard as the creature of his times.

A further movement in thought which influenced attitudes to history may broadly be called Positivist: that is a belief in the primacy of scientific method for arriving at truth. As Positivism grew fashionable, historians became increasingly concerned to develop a more critical approach to research. But apart from this fresh emphasis on the need for objective techniques, there was also a new interest in gathering historical data, and a vast number of publications devoted to early manuscripts helped extend and disseminate knowledge. The impressive labours of the Historical Manuscript Commission, and the work of a new breed of professional scholars, revealed a mass of documents which had hitherto 'blushed unseen' in the Public Record Office, the British Museum, and other archives. John Nichols, for instance, printer, antiquary, and a founder member of the Camden Society, printed and often edited its earlier publications, including a volume of *Grants of King Edward V*. Sir Henry Ellis, Principal Librarian of the British Museum, was another assiduous editor, as the bibliography of the present work illustrates.

Both a cause and consequence of the growing awareness of the importance of history to human understanding, was the development of critical historical techniques in Bible Studies.

Many of the problems confronting New Testament scholars resembled those facing students of Richard III. Both shared a common concern to discover beneath obscuring layers of legend the person who gave rise to them. The same techniques were required to isolate the 'Jesus of History' from the 'Christ of Faith', as to distinguish between the Richard of tradition and the flesh and blood prince who was killed in the Battle of Bosworth.

Until Gairdner published his *Richard the Third* in 1878, almost all earlier nineteenth century histories were in some degree revisionist. One of the most judicious accounts of the Usurpation ever written appeared in Sharon Turner's *The History of England in the Middle Ages*. His book was published in 1825 after thirty years research. As a young lawyer, Turner spent his summer holiday in 1792 on a tour of the South of England. One evening, as he travelled towards Weymouth, where the King and the Court were residing, he spent a night at an inn in Cerne Abbas. Struck by the profound contrast between George III's secure and placid existence and Richard III's tumultuous career, he resolved to try to discover what Richard was really like before he became 'disfigured by passion, prejudice and injustice'. In his effort to find the truth, Turner immersed himself in fifteenth century documents. After years of careful investigation, he came to the conclusion that Richard was probably innocent, and certainly not proved guilty, of most of the crimes with which he was commonly charged. But he did not acquit him of the judicial murders of Rivers, Hastings and others, nor of putting the Princes to death. Turner wrote with rare restraint, and was the first historian to paint a recognizable portrait of a credible human-being. His measured response was a welcome change from excited attempts to condemn or vindicate Richard.

In 1844 Miss Caroline Halsted published the first true biography of Richard. So eager was she to defend his reputation that she sometimes protested too much. The heroic Prince who figured in her pages was no less a caricature than Shakespeare's devious miscreant. Her research was commendably painstaking, and she rested her case on a mass of

248

unpublished material. But at times her handling of this evidence appeared to owe more to wishful thinking than deference to logic. In the course of her labours, Miss Halsted paid numerous visits to Middleham, where the Rector, William Athill, proved so obliging that the pair became man and wife. She now lies buried close to the altar of the parish church which Richard endowed so handsomely. Indeed, one of the principal arguments of her book is that his generosity to religion is inconsistent with villainy. Experience, however, lends as little support to this theory as does modern research into schizoid disorders. It should not be forgotten that the guards at Belsen religiously put out breadcrumbs to prevent sparrows from starving. Besides, the conflicting elements of Richard's tormented nature are too well documented to be dismissed. Miss Halsted's *Richard III* is a pioneering work, mellifluous in style, romantic in tone, and charitable to a fault.

The tide in Richard's favour began to ebb in 1878 with the publication of Gairdner's *History of the Life and Reign of Richard III*. Gairdner's lifetime of research in the Public Record Office won him so formidable a reputation for scholarship that his views were instantly accepted by other leading historians of the day, such as Green, Stubbs and Oman. In 1862, he fell under the spell of the Tractarian Movement which disposed him to treat tradition with too much respect. It was probably this, and not as he claimed 'a minute study of the facts', which convinced him of 'the general fidelity of the portrait with which we have been made familiar by Shakespeare and Sir Thomas More', and persuaded him to liken attempts to set aside tradition, to learning 'an unknown language without a teacher'. It would be hard to deny he was right to stop Miss Halsted in her tracks, for she was heading towards absurdity. But, for so scrupulous a scholar, he was too credulous when handling Tudor historians, and too conservative to recognize just how powerful were the arguments in favour of sober revision.

In 1906 Sir Clements Markham published the most passionate defence of Richard so far written: *Richard III: His Life and Character reviewed in the light of Modern Research*. The defiant tone of the book is set by the claim in its Preface that 'Richard III must be acquitted on all the counts of the indictment'. During the course of his distinguished career as a naval officer, explorer, and civil servant, Sir Clements contrived to produce some eighty books. This prodigious output was hardly conducive to meticulous scholarship, and his fifteen biographies betray the haste with which they were rushed into print.

Markham's first campaign on Richard's behalf was fought in 1891, when he attacked Gairdner in the pages of the English Historical Review, from which encounter he emerged bloody but belligerent. It was his contention that Richard's evil reputation was the consequence of a sustained conspiracy to revile him, master-minded by the ubiquitous Cardinal Morton. Indeed, he seems to have supposed that the principal occupation of the Archbishop of Canterbury was to falsify the records of the previous reign. Markham misjudged the extent and misconceived the purpose of Tudor 'propaganda'. In fact, it was only necessary to tell the truth to blacken Richard's name.

Having promised to acquit Richard on 'all counts', Markham claimed that the Princes were still alive in 1485, and were put to death on the orders of Henry VII. His principal reason for so saying, was a strained interpretation of a Household Regulation of 1484 which mentions some unnamed children of high rank. The mass of evidence showing that the boys disappeared from sight before Richard's Coronation, he conveniently overlooked. As Gairdner was quick to point out, Markham refused to 'believe writers who say that Richard did the deed', but was ready to blame Henry 'without any testimony at all'. Sometimes Sir Clements seemed incapable of distinguishing between supposition and fact. At one moment, he dismisses an author as hopelessly unreliable – suborned, no doubt, by Morton – and in the next, happily cites him as an authority to buttress his argument.

Markham suffered acutely from what Macaulay described as ' "Lues Boswelliana", or disease of admiration'. His biographies of Thomas Fairfax and Edward VI show the same symptoms of indiscriminate hero-worship as his life of

Richard III. Moreover, his portrait of Richard is too straightforward to capture so complex a character, and too improbable to command assent. Nowhere does he pose, let alone resolve, the problems arising from so contradictory a nature. He presents a pious Prince, the son of a pious mother, whom the clergy praised in 1484 for his 'noble and blessed disposition', but refuses to show the other face of the coin: the vicious politician whose ruthless seizure of power dismayed his own supporters. It is one of the minor wonders of the world that so many of Markham's readers have been willing to believe that the last Plantagenet king was a compound of Sir Galahad, Baden Powell and Mrs Grundy. The tone of his book was so intemperate and his conclusions were so incredible, that professional historians refused to take him seriously. But the general public were less severe, and found his eccentric conjectures intriguing. In recent years, the rehabilitation of 'a long dead king' has become a growth industry, exercising 'a strange and unexplained fascination' for women writers. No book on Richard III has been more widely read than Josephine Tey's *The Daughter of Time*, a novel based on Markham's speculations. One consequence of her success has been to persuade the public to accept Sir Clement's views.

So industrious were nineteenth century scholars that no-one can hope to discover again such treasures as they unearthed. But it still remains possible to make important finds, as Armstrong showed when he published Mancini's manuscript. Moreover, in recent years, the fifteenth century has been radically reassessed. Previously it was neglected by historians because it seemed a desolate era given to senseless violence. But since the Second World War, scholars have looked at the late Middle Ages anew, inspired by the pioneer work of Bruce McFarlane.

'The Richard III Society', founded in 1924, has strenuously encouraged research by publishing specialized articles in its quarterly journal *The Ricardian*, by sponsoring publications such as its four volume edition of Harleian Manuscript 433, and by providing its members with a valuable lending library. In its early days, it was somewhat intolerant of those who challenged its preconceptions. But recently, more objective views have prevailed, without prejudice to its conviction that the traditional portrait of Richard needs re-examining. Nevertheless, the Society's activities have not always been furthered by its lunatic fringe, who appear to believe that only the perversity of the Vatican stands in the way of Richard's canonization.

There have been two major biographies of Richard in the last quarter of a century. The first, by Professor Kendall, was published in 1955. It was praised at the time, with unintended irony, as an 'imaginative' account of Richard's reign and career. The book belongs to the same genre as Markham's, but is more restrained and scholarly. There are times, however, when Kendall appears to assume that the verdict 'not proven' is the same as 'not guilty'. The Professor's literary style evokes the work of historical novelists, providing a rich pot-pourri of drama, romance and surmise. It is arguably too severe to describe his work as 'fiction', but there is no doubt that it is disturbingly unreal. One has to take one's leave of the fifteenth century, if not one's senses, to accept Kendall's portrait of Richard as an 'upright and loyal young prince of the Renaissance'.

Professor Ross's *Richard III*, published in 1981, seems likely to achieve the pre-eminence which Gairdner's work enjoyed for half a century. The sure-footed way with which he picks his steps through a minefield makes him a safe guide. Ross is rare among Richard's biographers in remaining calm, detached, and rational, preferring the role of judge to that of advocate. While fully acknowledging the tendency of Tudor historians to elaborate, he sees their enrichments as growing out of reality. However much sixteenth century chronicles may distort the truth, they never sever their roots with Richard's own age. Hence Ross inclines to the view, expressed by every author from Mancini to Shakespeare, that Richard seized the Throne by force and fraud, that he shed innocent blood in the process, and thenceforward reigned as a tyrant. While Kendall was anxious to whittle away this hard core of tradition, Ross feels obliged to retain it.

The dialectical process, conceived by Hegel and turned upside down by Marx, would seem to explain the endless fluctuations which characterize the study of Richard III. Gairdner's reaction against the revisionism of Buck, Walpole and Miss Halsted, led to a temporary revival of more hostile attitudes. But he, in turn, provoked Markham's furious onslaught and Kendall's more measured dissent. Now Ross believes that the time has come to submit revisionists to the same critical scrutiny as they have directed towards traditional histories.

Without venturing to predict the pattern of future research, it seems reasonable to assume that most of the cards have already been dealt and that little remains except to reshuffle the pack. Improbable as it may be that after five hundred years new documents will be found requiring a total revision of all that is known about Richard, the flood of literature devoted to his career shows no signs of diminishing.

It was not so much the positive support of Richard's followers which helped him to win the Throne, as the acquiescence of those who decided not to oppose him. As Burke once observed, 'when bad men combine, the good must associate; else they will fall, one by one'. Seductive reasons can always be found to underwrite appeasement, although few which can look to history for justification. It is no longer fashionable to adorn tales with a moral, but two New Testament texts are so apt that to quote them is irresistible. The first comes from St Matthew. 'All they that take the sword shall perish by the sword'. The second is found in St Paul. 'Whatsoever a man soweth that also shall he reap'.

SOURCE REFERENCES

The 'source references' listed below enable readers to trace quotations used in 'The Year of Three Kings'. Source references have also been supplied, whenever it has seemed helpful to do so, for matters mentioned in the text without direct quotation. For example, page 76 above refers to Lord Hastings spreading scurrilous stories about Lord Rivers, and page 256 below lists an article on the subject.

Source references are listed as follows:

50:28. Edition of Banns. Strachey. Rotuli, VI. 240.

The first figure refers to the page of *The Year of Three Kings* to which the source reference applies. The figure after the colon indicates the number of lines from the top of the page listed to the key phrase of a quotation. Such key phrases are followed by the names of authors or editors of works to which reference is made. Next, an abbreviated version is given of the titles of books or articles cited, as indicated by the use of italics in the 'Select Bibliography' beginning on page 269. Articles are often specified by reference to the Journal in which they appear. Where books are published in more than one volume, the appropriate volume is indicated in roman numerals after its shortened title. The final figure listed supplies the page or pages of the work to which reference should be made. When citation of an entire work is intended no page numbers are supplied.

When a number of consecutive quotations in a paragraph derive from a single source, page references are only given when the quotation first appears. Neither dates of publication nor page references are listed for works of general literature of which there are many editions.

CHAPTER I   *'This Sun of York'*

38: 7 Stupid offspring.   Riley. *Registra*. I. 415.
38:33 Courage like man.   Bullough. *Narrative*. 102. Quoting Hall.
44:28 Whirlwind from North.   Riley. *Croyland*. 423.
45:26 Be it known.   Maxwell Lyte. *Eton*. 59.
45:38 Henry VI offended.   Flenley. *Chronicles*. 161.
46:22 Evident proof.   Rymer. *Foedera*. XI. 709.
47: 3 All the water.   Shakespeare. *Richard II*. III, 2.
47:15 Good rule.   Williams. *Cambridge*. 442.
47:34 Sensual enjoyments.   Riley. *Croyland*. 484, 483.
48:31 Mean calling.   Ellis. *Vergil*. 117.
48:32 Humble origin.   Armstrong. *Usurpation*. 61.

49:19   Dart of Cupid.   Ellis. *Union*. 264. Quoting Hall.
49:21   Live unchastely.   Armstrong. *Usurpation*. 61.
49:24   Tribute of love.   Fahy. *Review*. 667–672.
50: 9   His honour.   Sylvester. *Richard III*. 63–65.
50:28   Edition of Banns.   Strachey. *Rotuli*. VI. 240–2.
50:31   The Spousesse.   Ellis. *New Chronicles*. 654.
52: 6   Merry guise.   Dupont. *Chroniques*. II. 326–8.
52: 9   Treuly Chafyd.   Ellis. *Vergil*. 117.
52:34   Principal promoters.   Armstrong. *Usurpation*. 67.
54: 2   Obscure family.   Armstrong. *Usurpation*. 63.
54: 3   Highly maligned.   Sylvester. *Richard III*. 8.
54:12   Great Lords.   Halliwell. *Chronicle*. 46.
54:17   Pleasant to King.   Bullough. *Narrative*. 187.
54:37   But a subject.   Halsted. *Richard III*. I. 436. Quoting Habington.
56: 1   Crouchback.   Davies. *York*. 221.
56: 2   Possible exception.   Hanham. *Historians*. 121. Quoting Rous.
56:31   Specially grudged.   Sylvester. *Richard III*. 11.
58: 3   Pure displeasure.   Bruce. *Arrivall*. 38.
58:27   Himself alone.   Riley. *Croyland*. 469–470.
59:18   Contemplated exhaltation.   Riley. *Croyland*. 478.
59:27   New treasons.   Strachey. *Rotuli*. VI. 193–4.
59:33   Made answer.   Riley. *Croyland*. 479–480.
61:25   Gain or loss.   Riley. *Croyland*. 481.
62: 4   Noble gests.   Strachey. *Rotuli*. VI. 197.
62: 6   Frivolous outlay.   Riley. *Croyland*. 481.

CHAPTER 2   *Richard's Early Historians*

65: 8   Seen men.   Armstrong. *Usurpation*. 93.
65:18   Date wrong.   Armstrong. *Usurpation*. 59.
65:26   Story runs.   Armstrong. *Usurpation*. 71, 61.
66:15   Ten days.   Riley. *Croyland*. 510.
66:17   Canon law.   Fulman. *Rerum*. 557.
66:18   Unnamed envoy.   Riley. *Croyland*. 469.
66:23   Disputed claims.   Riley. *Croyland*. 470.
66:28   Persons unknown.   Riley. *Croyland*. 496.
67: 9   Accurate recital.   Riley. *Croyland*. 505.
67:17   Thirteenth day.   Riley. *Croyland*. 488, 496.
67:36   Unequal shoulders.   Hanham. *Historians*. 121, 120.
68:23   Bald, uncouth.   Hay. *Anglica*. XXVIII.
68:35   Nether lip.   Ellis. *Vergil*. 227.
68:37   Paid historian.   Markham. *Richard III*. 171–2.
69:14   Cherished myths.   Hanham. *Historians*. 135.
69:15   Gullibility.   Hay. *Vergil*. 110.
69:27   Accusations linger.   Sylvester. *Richard III*. XII.
70: 6   Vice punished.   Churchill. *Shakespeare*, 236. Quoting *A Mirror for Magistrates*.

70:12 Personified vice. Crowder. *Fifteenth.* 119. Myers article.
70:17 Peculiar loathing. Sylvester. *Richard III.* xv. Quoting Erasmus.
70:24 End life. Chambers. *More.* 15, 332.
70:28 Nothing well spoken. Hanham. *Historians.* 159.
70:32 Wise men. Sylvester. *Richard III.* 9.
70:38 Discreditable lampoon. Markham. *Review.* 807.
71: 4 Lived fifty. Sylvester. *Richard III.* 3.
71:21 Narrative substantiated. Sylvester. *Richard III.* 77. Edwards. *Essays.* 235.
71:24 Melancholic work. Kincaid. *Buck.* 122, 125.
71:34 La magnanimité. Sheffield. *Gibbon.* III. 342.
72:14 His description. Thomas. *Chronicle.* 230.
72:16 Sharp eye. Ross. *Richard III.* xl.

CHAPTER 3   'The Young Prince'

74: 8 Damp cold. Armstrong. *Usurpation.* 59.
74:10 Appendicitis. Churchill. *History.* I. 377.
75:26 All haste. Ives. *Institute.* 228.
76:11 Beloved servant. Dugdale. *Baronage.* I. 580.
76:15 Principal accomplice. Armstrong. *Usurpation.* 69.
76:27 Best preferment. Nichols. *Grants.* 2.
76:32 Scurrilous stories. Ives. *Institute.* 221.
77:30 Rule parties. Sylvester. *Richard III.* 11.
77:38 Child's reign. Sylvester. *Richard III.* 14.
78:18 Original will. Nicolas. *Excerpta.* 366–379.
78:25 Deceased King. Hanham. *Historians.* 118.
78:30 Dearest Uncle. Nichols. *Grants.* xiii.
78:33 Uterine Uncle. *Calendar.* 352–3.
78:34 Bidding prayer. Nichols. *Grants.* xxxviii.
79: 3 Last will. Jacob. *Fifteenth.* 215.
79:10 Right to decide. Roskell. *Review.* 226.
79:14 Sincerely repentant. Riley. *Croyland.* 483–4.
79:23 One Mistlebrook. Sylvester. *Richard III.* 10.
79:31 All naked. *Archaeologia.* I. 349.
79:35 Lord Howard. Payne Collier. *Household.* 384.
79:38 This noble. Thomas. *Chronicle.* 230.
80: 6 Edward poisoned. Ellis. *Vergil.* 171–2.
80: 9 O land. *Ecclesiastes.* X. 16.
80:16 Now deceased. Riley. *Croyland.* 484.
80:29 Our city. *Commission.* XI. Appendix III. 170.
81: 3 Deliberation. Strachey. *Rotuli.* IV. 336–7.
81:22 State papers. Saltmarsh. *Henry VI.* 1.
82: 8 About the age. Kingsford. *London.* 189–190.
82:13 Lord Howard. Payne Collier. *Household.* 384.
83: 1 Good estate. Tudor-Craig. *Richard III.* 47.

83: 3   The souls. Melhuish. *Middleham.* 2.
83: 9   Messengers. Armstrong. *Usurpation.* 71, 73.
83:18   Most loving. Ellis. *Vergil.* 174.
83:22   Due obedience. Riley. *Croyland.* 486.
83:25   Home and abroad. Armstrong. *Usurpation.* 73.
83:35   Be kindled. Sylvester. *Richard III.* 15–16.
84: 9   Plenteous tears. Riley. *Croyland.* 486.
84:12   The first. Ellis. *Vergil.* 174.
84:16   Edward Prince. Strachey. *Rotuli.* VI. 232.
84:24   Have fettered. Turner. *History.* III. 406.
84:34   Through Slaughter. Gray. *Elegy.*
84:37   Natural affection. Ellis. *Vergil.* 174.
85: 9   Scorned to wed. Armstrong. *Usurpation.* 75.
85:11   Most secret. Sylvester. *Richard III.* 90.
85:17   What day. Armstrong. *Usurpation.* 75.
85:32   Gold and blue. *Archaeologia.* I. 350.
86: 5   Habit royal. *Archaeologia.* I. 351.
86:17   Needy boys. Maxwell Lyte. *Eton.* 499.
86:21   Well wrought. *Archaeologia.* I. 352.
86:32   Their staves. Gairdner. *Letters.* I. XVII.
86:36   Embroidered coats. *Archaeologia.* I. 353.
87:35   Duke of Gloucester. Armstrong. *Usurpation.* 71.
88:15   False progeny. Gairdner. *Chronicles.* 94.
88:25   Estranged Lords. Halliwell. *Chronicle.* 46.
88:37   All speed. Riley. *Croyland.* 485.
89: 4   The amity. Sylvester. *Richard III.* 17–18.
89:21   Only accede. Armstrong. *Usurpation.* 73,75.

CHAPTER 4   *'The Mighty Dukes'*

93: 1   Submit conduct. Riley. *Croyland.* 486.
93: 5   Joyous countenance. Sylvester. *Richard III.* 18.
95:38   Set distance. Sylvester. *Richard III.* 19.
96:11   Clad in black. Ellis. *New Chronicles.* 668.
96:18   Profound grief. Armstrong. *Usurpation.* 77.
96:35   For certain. Riley. *Croyland.* 487.
97: 2   Rule King. Sylvester. *Richard III.* 20.
97:14   Good and faithful. Armstrong. *Usurpation.* 77,79.
98:13   Not approach. Riley. *Croyland.* 487.
98:16   Picked men. Halsted. *Richard III.* II. 27.
98:24   Dissimulated countenance. Thomas. *Chronicle.* 230.
98:25   Welsh stupidity. Armstrong. *Usurpation.* 83.
99: 1   He wept. Sylvester. *Richard III.* 20.
99:38   Great falls. Addison. *Roads.* 91.
100: 5   Wonderously amazed. Ellis. *Vergil.* 175.
100: 9   Gathering power. Sylvester. *Richard III.* 21.
100:18   Said openly. Armstrong. *Usurpation.* 79.

100:24   Queen's name.   Riley. *Croyland*. 487.
100:27   Great commotion.   Sylvester. *Richard III*. 23.
101: 4   Rumble and business.   Sylvester. *Richard III*. 22.
101:13   Lords assembled.   Sylvester. *Richard III*. 23–4.
101:33   Be faithful.   Armstrong. *Usurpation*. 85.
101:34   Visited Queen.   Sylvester. *Richard III*. 23.
102: 6   Sinister rumour.   Armstrong. *Usurpation*. 81,83.
103:22   Behold Prince.   Ellis. *New Chronicles*. 668.
104:34   Encouraging pressage.   Riley. *Croyland*. 487.
105: 6   Arouse hatred.   Armstrong. *Usurpation*. 83.
105:13   Barrels of harness.   Sylvester. *Richard III*. 24–5.
105:26   Convenient spots.   Armstrong. *Usurpation*. 83.
106: 9   Rule King.   Sylvester. *Richard III*. 20.
106:29   Rivers innocent.   Riley. *Croyland*. 489.
106:31   Good men.   Sylvester. *Richard III*. 59.
106:33   Source of danger.   Armstrong. *Usurpation*. 91.
106:34   Thwart Duke.   Ellis. *Vergil*. 175.
106:35   Falsely charged.   Hanham. *Historians*. 120.
107:14   To wear crown.   Shakespeare. III. *Henry VI*.I. *2*.
107:20   Far off shore.   Shakespeare. III. *Henry VI*.III. *2*.
107:25   Rumour current.   Armstrong. *Usurpation*. 81.

CHAPTER 5   *'Kings' Games'*

109: 7   Having entered.   Armstrong. *Usurpation*. 83,85.
109:15   Usurp sovereignty.   Armstrong. *Usurpation*. 71.
109:17   Commissions of peace.   Nichols. *Grants*. XII.
109:20   By thadvise.   Horrox. *Manuscript* 433. I. *44*.
109:23   More intrigued.   Sylvester. *Richard III*. 25.
109:32   Against will.   Hanham. *Historians*. 119. Translating Rous.
109:34   Much business.   Kingsford. *Stonor*. II. 161.
110: 9   Wise man.   Sylvester. *Richard III*. 25.
110:22   Noble order.   Rymer. *Foedera*. 185.
110:27   Short gown.   *Archaeologia*. I. 361.
111: 2   Urgent business.   Nichols. *Wills*. 347.
111: 4   Howard writ.   Payne Collier. *Household*. 393.
111:12   Buckingham's suggestion.   Riley. *Croyland*. 487.
111:16   Grant at Tower.   Horrox. *Manuscript* 433. I. *42*.
111:36   The detention.   Riley. *Croyland*. 488.
112:18   Woodham Martin.   Horrox. *Manuscript* 433. I. XXIII, 40,42.
112:28   Buckingham grants.   Horrox. *Manuscript* 433.I. 9,13–15.
113:25   Ripeness of years.   Nichols. *Grants*. XLVII–XLIX.
114:17   Seas unsafe.   Armstrong. *Usurpation*. 81.
114:22   Sore longed.   Ellis. *Union*. 447.
114:35   Authority of Council.   Armstrong. *Usurpation*. 85.
115: 3   Edward alive.   Nichols. *Grants*. 2–3.
115: 4   Go to sea.   Nichols. *Grants*. 3.

115:25   Losing wares.   Armstrong. *Usurpation.* 87.
117: 9   In another place.   Sylvester. *Richard III.* 44.
117:10   Hastings' initiative.   Armstrong. *Usurpation.* 91.
117:16   Great resource.   Armstrong. *Usurpation.* 91.
117:27   Treacherous man.   Kincaid. *Buck.* 85.
117:30   Prudence and virtue.   Chambers. *More.* 56.
117:35   Much misliked.   Sylvester. *Richard III.* 44–6.
118:30   Terrible words.   Sylvester. *Richard III.* 46.
119: 1   Mollify the multitude.   Ellis. *Vergil.* 179.
119:13   Richard's letter.   Davies. *York.* 149–150.
120: 4   Lawless enterprises.   Sylvester. *Richard III.* 58.
120: 7   The credence.   Davies. *York.* 151.
120:23   My Lord Neville.   Gairdner. *Paston.* III. 306.
121: 2   Nothing to report.   Kingsford. *Stonor.* II. 159.
121: 4   Utterly destroy.   Davies. *York.* 149.
121: 9   Immediate action.   Wood. *Deposition.* 258.
121:16   Crown bereft.   Ellis. *Vergil.* 187.
121:19   Twenty thousand.   Kingsford. *Stonor.* II. 161.
121:26   Descent from North.   Riley. *Croyland.* 422–3, 489.
121:28   Fabyan estimate.   Ellis. *New Chronicles.* 669.
121:36   Ides of June.   Ellis. *Vergil.* 180.
122:11   Never doubted.   Armstrong. *Usurpation.* 91.
122:14   Favour cause.   Thomas. *Chronicle.* 230.
122:22   A mischief.   Ellis. *Vergil.* 180.
122:22   Lists Pilkington.   Hay. *Vergil.* 204–5.
122:25   Innermost quarters.   Armstrong. *Usurpation.* 91.
122:29   Angry countenance.   Sylvester. *Richard III.* 47–8.
122:35   Procured you all.   Ellis. *Vergil.* 180.
123: 8   Doublet sleeve.   Sylvester. *Richard III.* 48.
123:22   Gay apparel.   Sylvester. *Richard III.* 56.
123:27   Having offspring.   Barker. *Etoniana.* 388.
123:30   Bewitch him.   Sylvester. *Richard III.* 55.
124: 1   Mistress Shore.   Kingsford. *Stonor.* II. 161.
124:22   Necromancy.   Kelly. *Studies.* 223.
124:26   Very freely.   Ellis. *Vergil.* 181.
124:29   'Ifs' and 'ands'.   Sylvester. *Richard III.* 49.
125: 2   Soldiers stationed.   Armstrong. *Usurpation.* 91.
125:11   Squared timber.   Thomas. *Chronicle.* 230.
125:13   Without judgment.   Kingsford. *London.* 190.
125:17   Process of law.   Thomas. *Chronicle.* 230.
125:22   Grazed a little.   Thomas. *Chronicle.* 231.
125:25   To the teeth.   Sylvester. *Richard III.* 49.
126:23   Treason, treason.   Ellis. *Vergil.* 181.
126:32   Traitorous purpose.   Sylvester. *Richard III.* 54.
127:15   Every child.   Sylvester. *Richard III.* 55.
127:25   Eleven hours.   Shakespeare. *Richard III.* III. 6.
127:29   Much trouble.   Kingsford. *Stonor.* II. 161.
127:31   Ignorant crowd.   Armstrong. *Usurpation.* 91.

127:36   So gross.   Shakespeare. *Richard III*. III. *6*.
128: 1   Generally lamented.   Ellis. *Vergil*. 182.
128: 7   Murdered for truth.   Thomas. *Chronicle*. 230.
128: 9   Perceived well.   Ellis. *Vergil*. 182.
128:13   Good Knight.   Sylvester. *Richard III*. 53.
128:17   Smitten off.   Ellis. *New Chronicles*. 668.
128:20   True service.   Dunham. *Transactions*. 18.
129: 5   Gracious Sovereign.   Horrox. *Manuscript* 433. II. 4–5.
129:13   Body of patron.   Roskell. *Bulletin*. 147.
129:22   Tudor house.   Tudor-Craig. *Richard III*. 7.
129:24   Not June 13th.   Wolffe. *Review*. 1974. Thomson. *B.I.H.R.*
         Hanham. *Review*. 1975. Wolffe. *Review*. 1976 Coleman. *B.I.H.R.*
129:26   Building ceased.   Hamilton Thomson. *Transactions*. 193.
129:34   False pretext.   Armstrong. *Usurpation*. 91.
129:38   Absolute necessity.   Walpole. *Doubts*. 124.
130: 7   Guards distracted.   Stow. *Annales*. 762.
130:14   Great rumour.   Malden. *Cely*. I. 132.
130:22   Dangerous conspiracy.   Hanham. *Historians*. 41.
130:32   Of all folk.   Sylvester. *Richard III*. 49.
131:21   Without judgment.   Riley. *Croyland*. 488.

CHAPTER 6   *'This Palpable Device'*

132: 4   Busy search.   Kingsford. *London*. 191.
132: 6   Adjacent neighbourhood.   Armstrong. *Usurpation*. 91.
133: 4   Foresaw the Duke.   Armstrong. *Usurpation*. 89.
133: 8   Sore thirsted.   Sylvester. *Richard III*. 25–6.
133:20   Naughty persons.   Ellis. *Vergil*. 177.
133:25   Heinous deed.   Sylvester. *Richard III*. 26.
133:38   King crowned.   Armstrong. *Usurpation*. 89.
134: 4   What a sight.   Ellis. *Vergil*. 177.
134: 8   Held by mother.   Armstrong. *Usurpation*. 89.
134:10   Place of refuge.   Sylvester. *Richard III*. 26.
134:16   Not one.   Ellis. *Vergil*. 177.
134:19   No subtlety.   Ellis. *Vergil*. 178.
135:23   Mine advice.   Sylvester. *Richard III*. 27–28.
136: 6   Out of realm.   Sylvester. *Richard III*. 30–33.
136:21   Queen besieged.   Armstrong. *Usurpation*. 89.
136:23   Great multitude.   Riley. *Croyland*. 488.
136:26   Up and down.   Payne Collier. *Household*. 402.
136:28   Monday last.   Kingsford. *Stonor*. II. 161.
137: 6   Ancient observance.   Armstrong. *Usurpation*. 79, 81.
137:23   Prevent violation.   Armstrong. *Usurpation*. 89.
137:30   Sore diseased.   Sylvester. *Richard III*. 35–42.
138: 5   Trusting the Cardinal.   Armstrong. *Usurpation*. 89.
138: 9   Fair promises.   Thomas. *Chronicle*. 230.

138:10 Sleight. Ellis. *Vergil*. 176.
138:13 Good feelings. Riley. *Croyland*. 488.
138:15 None harm. Kingsford. *London*. 190.
139: 2 Loving words. Kingsford. *Stonor*. II. 161.
139: 2 Now welcome. Sylvester. *Richard III*. 42.
139: 5 Came abroad. Ellis. *Vergil*. 178.
139:20 All company. Halsted. *Richard III*. II. 328. Quoting Baker's Chronicle.
139:24 Entire progeny. Armstrong. *Usurpation*. 89.
139:28 Openly manifest. Riley. *Croyland*. 489.
139:33 Time to devise. Sylvester. *Richard III*. 59.
140: 8 Title and station. Armstrong. *Usurpation*. 95.
140:22 At this day. Davies. *York*. 154–5.
140:30 Queen's kinsfolks. Sylvester. *Richard III*. 42–43.
141: 3 Last document. Rymer. *Foedera*. XII. 187.
141: 5 Attendants debarred. Armstrong. *Usurpation*. 93.
141:26 Seen many. Armstrong. *Usurpation*. 93.
141:37 Own advancement. Sylvester. *Richard III*. 59.
142: 6 Duke Richard. Ellis. *Vergil*. 182.
142:13 Warned by example. Armstrong. *Usurpation*. 97.
142:20 Knew well. Ellis. *Vergil*. 183.
143: 5 Invention devised. Sylvester. *Richard III*. 60–61.
144:11 Falsely. Strachey. *Rotuli*. VI. 193.
144:26 Give colour. Riley. *Croyland*. 489.
144:29 That invention. Sylvester. *Richard III*. 67.
144:33 Divine word. Armstrong. *Usurpation*. 95.
145: 5 Fraudulent grounds. Hanham. *Historians*. 108.
145: 6 Feigned title. Hanham. *Historians*. 120.
145:35 Recognised instrument. Armstrong. *Transactions*. 57.
146:13 Multiplying brood. Sylvester. *Richard III*. 67–8.
147: 5 High of stature. Ellis. *Vergil*. 184.
147:13 Vehemently troubled. Ellis. *Vergil*. 184.
147:29 Charles V's ambassador. Brewer. *Henry VIII*. VIII. 281.
147:34 Falsely accused. Ellis. *Vergil*. 184–5.
148:22 Turned into stone. Sylvester. *Richard III*. 69.
148:23 Natural wit. Ellis. *New Chronicles*. 669.
148:27 For shame. Sylvester. *Richard III*. 69.

CHAPTER 7   *'A World of Cares'*

149:22 Divers Lords. Sylvester. *Richard III*. 70.
150:13 Legally contracted. Armstrong. *Usurpation*. 97.
150:33 Rendered ineligible. Armstrong. *Usurpation*. 97.
151:19 Abominable strumpet. Sylvester. *Richard III*. 72–3.
151:32 Filial reverence. Sylvester. *Richard III*. 75.
152: 3 Lawfully begotten. Sylvester. *Richard III*. 74–75.

152:14   Wanton wench.   Kincaid. *Buck*. 182.
152:19   Graciously incline.   Sylvester. *Richard III*. 76.
152:23   Citizens are mum.   Shakespeare. *Richard III*. III. 7.
152:27   All hushed.   Sylvester. *Richard III*. 76–8.
153: 1   Obstinate silence.   Sylvester. *Richard III*. 76–78.
153:17   Some followers.   Shakespeare. *Richard III*. III. 7.
153:26   Sugared words.   Ellis. *New Chronicles*. 669.
153:29   Marvelled and said.   Thomas. *Chronicle*. 230.
153:38   Some semblance.   Wood. *Deposition*. 279.
154:14   Divers doubts.   Strachey. *Rotuli*. VI. 240–2.
154:26   Constitutional authority.   Wood. *Deposition*. 279.
154:34   The address.   Riley. *Croyland*. 489.
155: 5   Prudent persons.   Strachey. *Rotuli*. VI. 240–2.
155:29   Noble lady.   Kincaid. *Buck*. 176, 183.
156:10   1484 Act repealed.   Strachey. *Rotuli*. VI. 289.
156:28   Very enamoured.   Jones. *Commynes*. 353–4.
157:10   Wicked bishop.   Jones. *Commynes*. 397.
157:24   Offering hereafter.   Strachey. *Rotuli*. VI. 240–2.
157:29   Fable exploded.   Lockyer. *History*. 41.
157:31   Fraudulent grounds.   Hanham. *Historians*. 108. Quoting Lluyd.
157:33   Convenient pretext.   Sylvester. *Richard III*. 60.
157:35   Own advancement.   Hanham. *Historians*. 120.
158: 1   The alliance.   Armstrong. *Usurpation*. 97.
158: 4   Laymen not qualified.   Riley. *Croyland*. 495–6.
158:34   Honour, estate.   Strachey. *Rotuli*. VI. 194.
159:15   Innocent of deed.   Hanham. *Historians*. 119–120.
159:23   No redress.   Hanham. *Historians*. 119–120.
160: 5   Inclined to pity.   Sylvester. *Richard III*. 58–9.
160:13   Richard's victims.   Gairdner. *Richard III*. 74.
160:16   Mayor and Aldermen.   Sylvester. *Richard III*. 79.
161: 3   Purposely betaken.   Armstrong. *Usurpation*. 97.
161:10   Distress and decay.   Sylvester. *Richard III*. 80.
161:15   Golden yoke.   Shakespeare. *Richard III*. III. 7.
161:16   Love he bore.   Sylvester. *Richard III*. 80.
161:19   Cousin of Buckingham.   Shakespeare. *Richard III*. III. 7.
161:30   King Edward's.   Sylvester. *Richard III*. 82.
162: 8   Mockish election.   Sylvester. *Richard III*. 82–4.
162:19   Notably assisted.   Halsted. *Richard III*. II. 520.
163: 5   King's chair.   Thomas. *Chronicle*. 232.
163:10   Obtruded himself.   Riley. *Croyland*. 489.
163:14   Long oration.   Ellis. *New Chronicles*. 669.
163:20   Straight manner.   Thomas. *Chronicle*. 203.
163:23   Out of mind.   Sylvester. *Richard III*. 84–5.
163:27   Conveyed to choir.   Thomas. *Chronicle*. 203.
163:31   Great congratulations.   Halsted. *Richard III*. II. 520–1.
163:34   Proclaimed King.   Ellis. *New Chronicles*. 669.
164:18   Divers places.   Halsted. *Richard III*. II. 520–1.
164:35   True title.   Halsted. *Richard III*. II. 520–521.

165: 6 Scarcely watched. Armstrong. *Usurpation.* 95.
165:20 Castles. Lordships. Horrox. *Manuscript.* 433. I. 66–83.
165:22 Norfolk dukedom. Crawford. *Ricardian.* 337.
165:34 Among provinces. Horrox. *Manuscript.* 433. I. 82–3.
166:12 Twenty thousand. Kingsford. *Stonor.* II. 161.
166:17 Best jacks. Ellis. *New Chronicles.* 669.
166:31 Proclamation forbidding. Halsted. *Richard III.* II. 520–2.
167:19 Greeted onlookers. Armstrong. *Usurpation.* 101.
168:12 Elysium. Shakespeare, III. *Henry VI.* I. *2.*
168:30 Feigning Sick. Sylvester. *Richard III.* 91–2.
169: 4 Holy hymns. Nicolas. *Excerpta.* 381–2.
169:11 Relic survived. Tudor-Craig. *Richard III.* 34.
169:13 Oil preserved. McKenna. *Review.* 102–3.
169:15 Buy oil. Wolffe. *Henry VI.* 49. Quoting Schramm.
169:37 Unwillingly. Armstrong. *Usurpation.* 101.
170: 2 Next cupboard. Kincaid. *Buck.* 49.
170:16 Not King. Nicolas. *Excerpta.* 383.

CHAPTER 8 *'Young Edward Lives'*

173:15 Great area. Hanham. *Historians.* 122. Quoting Rous.
173:17 Right reverent. Hanham. *Historians.* 49.
174:22 Affirming. Hanham. *Historians.* 121. Quoting Rous.
175: 5 Concerning snakes. Boswell. *Johnson.*
175:16 Shooting and playing. Thomas. *Chronicle.* 234.
175:18 Inner apartments. Armstrong. *Usurpation.* 93.
175:24 Sure keeping. Ellis. *New Chronicles.* 669.
175:27 Common fame. Ellis. *New Chronicles.* 670.
175:37 Princes killed. Bernier. *Journal.* 37.
176: 2 Extremely cruel. Jones. *Commynes.* 396.
176:11 Appearance of castle. Riley. *Croyland.* 491.
176:22 Notorious manner. Lockyer. *History.* 58.
176:24 Whispering. Thomas. *Chronicle.* 234.
176:28 Rid out. Thomas. *Chronicle.* 234.
176:33 Dolorous end. Sylvester. *Richard III.* 85–9.
178:35 Grants allowance. Horrox. *Manuscript* 433.I.166.
178:37 Close and secret. Sylvester. *Richard III,* 9.
179:10 Two striplings. Sanford. *Genealogical.* 402.
179:16 Wright and Northcroft. Tanner. *Archaeologia.*
179:34 Their Lives. Kincaid. *Buck.* 55.
180: 7 Be safe. Lerner. *Prince.* 407.
180:13 Living being. *Jesse Memoirs.* 173.
180:33 Rumour of death. Ellis. *Vergil.* 188–9.
181: 3 Markham cites. Markham. *Richard III.* 237–8.
181:27 Sore diseased. Sylvester. *Richard III.* 35.
182:17 Infant's blood. Strachey. *Rotuli.* VI. 275–8.

182:20   Much odious.   Ellis. *Union*. 379.
182:29   Fell into swoon.   Ellis. *Vergil*. 189.
183: 7   Contents people.   Sheppard. *Christ Church*. 45.
183:13   King's grace.   Raine. *York*. I. 78.
183:20   Countenance.   Ellis. *Vergil*. 192.
183:26   To please us.   Horrox. *Manuscript* 433. II. 10–11.
183:32   Entire affection.   Raine. *York*. I. 78.
184:19   Good will.   Davies. *York*. 165.
184:22   Tilts, tournaments.   Drake. *Eboracum*. 117.
184:27   Knights.   Davies. *York*. 176.
184:31   Honest men.   Davies. *York*. 172.
184:38   Three coats.   Horrox. *Manuscript* 433. II. 42.
185: 8   Rich diadem.   Ellis. *Vergil*. 190.
185:17   Sumptuous feasts.   Riley. *Croyland*. 490.
185:22   Good service.   Davies. *York*. 174–5.
185:33   Drowsy manner.   Riley. *Croyland*. 491.
185:37   traitorously turned.   Drake. *Eboracum*. 118.
186:10   Murmur greatly.   Riley. *Croyland*. 491.
186:34   Duke's regret.   Riley. *Croyland*. 491.
186:35   Deploring failure.   Ellis. *Vergil*. 194.
187: 1   Credibly informed.   Bullough. *Narrative*. 281.
187:14   Bear the glory.   Sylvester. *Richard III*. 92.
187:19   Insatiable covetise.   Strachey. *Rotuli*. VI. 244.
187:25   Too little.   Shakespeare. *Richard II*, V. 1.
187:28   Natural wit.   Sylvester. *Richard III*. 92.
187:33   Beloved cousin.   Horrox. *Manuscript* 433, II. 2–4.
189:33   Solemn oath.   Ellis. *Vergil*. 194.
190: 2   Woodville endorsement.   Sheffield. *Gibbon*. III. 345.
190: 7   Chief dealer.   Ellis. *Vergil*. 196–8.
190:21   All well.   Ellis. *Original letters. Series II*. I. 159.
190:27   To be feared.   Ellis. *Vergil*. 200.
190:36   Sundry maids.   Riley. *Croyland*. 534.
191: 2   Well-beloved friend.   Gairdner. *Paston*. III. 308.
191:18   Greatest wind.   Gairdner. *Richard III*. 138. Quoting Seyer.
191:25   Against wills.   Ellis. *Vergil*. 199.
191:36   Manor of Yalding.   Horrox. *Manuscript* 433. I. 118.
192:27   Find ships.   Riley. *Croyland*, 492.
192:33   Cruel gale.   Ellis. *Vergil*. 201–3.
192:35   Tossed all night.   Riley. *Croyland*. 495.
193:12   Without fighting.   Riley. *Croyland*. 495.
193:21   Great rebel.   Strachey. *Rotuli*. VI. 150–1.
193:23   Woman's wit.   Ellis. *Vergil*. 204.
193:24   Sending messages.   Strachey. *Rotuli*. VI. 150–1.
194: 4   Short time.   Riley. *Croyland*. 495.
194: 8   Silver plate.   Horrox. *Manuscript* 433. II. 66.
195: 1   Piers St Aubyn.   Horrox. *Manuscript* 433. II. 34.
195:10   Apparent at Bosworth.   Horrox. *Manuscript* 433. I. xxvi.

195:15 Not even treason. Lander. *Community*. 205.
195:20 Flagrant indifference. Ross. *Richard III*. 110.
195:22 Unsteadfast friendship. Sylvester. *Richard III*. 9.
195:36 Immense estates. Riley. *Croyland*. 496.
196:12 Marry Elizabeth. Ellis. *Vergil*. 203–4.

CHAPTER 9   *'A Scum of Bretons'*

197:12 Diverse doubts. Strachey. *Rotuli*. VI. 240.
197:23 Delaying safeguards. Wolffe. *Demesne*. 192.
198:12 Bokes wrytten. Ramsay. *Lancaster*. II. 519.
198:16 Singularly thoughtful. Hanbury. *American*. 113.
198:19 Win favour. Ellis. *Vergil*. 204.
198:20 No position. Hanham. *Historians*. 16.
198:22 Wholesome laws. Lockyer. *History*. 39, 38.
198:26 Malicious alchemy. Kincaid. *Buck*. 126.
200:13 Frequent entreaties. Riley. *Croyland*. 496.
200:15 Mountains. Ellis. *Vergil*. 210.
200:20 Pregnant reasons. Bullough. *Narrative*. 286–7.
200:32 Verbo regio. Ellis. *Original*. 149.
201: 6 Sudden grief. Ellis. *Croyland*. 497.
201:11 Heir Apparent. Hanham. *Historians*. 123.
201:21 Too much attention. Riley. *Croyland*. 498–9.
201:33 Poisoned Edward IV. Goodman. *Castilian*. 94. Quoting de Valera.
201:34 First writer. Hanham. *Historians*. 121.
201:36 Much whispering. Thomas. *Chronicle*. 234.
201:37 Great reliance. Riley. *Croyland*. 499.
202: 2 Unfruitfulness. Ellis. *Vergil*. 211.
202:11 Never once. Riley. *Croyland*. 499.
202:25 Uniquely shameful. Lander. *Conflict*. 94.
202:28 Abominable lies. Davies. *York*. 208–9.
203: 5 Defensibly arrayed. Horrox. *Manuscript* 433. II. 182.
204:21 Certain bills. Bellamy. *Treason*. 121. Quoting Holinshed.
204:26 The Rat. Bullough. *Narrative*. 286. Quoting Hall.
204:34 Death of King. Grimston. *Croke*. 122–3. (Translated from Latin)
205: 3 Bloody fury. Bullough. *Narrative*. 285.
205: 6 Cruel death. Ellis. *New Chronicles*. 672.
205:27 Every shire. Horrox. *Manuscript*. 433. II. 228–9.
205:35 Divers rebels. Gairdner. *Paston*. II. 319.
206:12 Letters to York. Davies. *York*. 149–150. Gairdner. *Paston* III. 306.
208: 6 Time convenient. Ellis. *Vergil*. 218. Author's italics.
209: 3 Greatest pomp. Riley. *Croyland*. 502.
209:13 de Valera's letter. Nokes. *Spanish*.
209:29 Terrible dream. Ellis. *Vergil*. 221.

209:30   Imagined himself.   Riley. *Croyland*. 503.
211: 7   In honour.   Southey. *Life of Nelson*. Chap. 9.
212: 3   Sort of vagabonds.   Shakespeare. *Richard III*. V. 3.
212:21   Order entrusted.   Riley. *Croyland*. 503.
212:24   No little vexed.   Ellis. *Vergil*. 222–3.
214:11   Recently argued.   Hammond. *Ricardian*. 22–3. Quoting Cane.
214:34   Swift horses.   Ellis. *Vergil*. 225.
215: 1   Seek safety.   Nokes. *Spanish*. 2.
215: 3   God forbid.   Riley. *Croyland*. 504.
215: 9   Noble soldier.   Hanham. *Historians*. 123.
215:12   Nothing in life.   Shakespeare. *Macbeth*. I. 4.
215:17   Stanley's intention.   Harris. *Ricardian*.
215:27   Old tradition. Hutton. *Bosworth*. 219.
215:33   Not intended. Nokes. *Spanish*. 3.
215:37   Six Richmonds.   Shakespeare. *Richard III*. V. 3.
216: 3   Out of hope.   Ellis. *Vergil*. 224.
216: 9   Richard slain.   Raine. *York*. I. 121.
216:23   Torn and tugged.   Sylvester. *Richard III*. 89.
216:27   Nought left.   Thomas. *Chronicle*. 238.
216:30   Shamefully carried.   Bullough. *Narrative*. 299–300. Quoting Hall.
216:37   Alabaster effigy.   Tudor-Craig. *Richard III*. 68–9.
217: 9   God save.   Ellis. *Vergil*. 226.
217:17   Sword thrusts.   Burne. *Battlefields*. 137.

CHAPTER 10   *'The Throne Majestical'*

218: 5   Insane lust.   Armstrong. *Usurpation*. 91.
218: 8   Dream upon.   Shakespeare. III. *Henry VI*. III. 2.
218:15   Exalt himself.   Strachey. *Rotuli*. VI. 193.
218:20   Lust to rule.   Churchill. *Shakespeare*. 376.
219:19   Own safety.   Armstrong. *Usurpation*. 81.
219:38   Corroding vices.   Barrie. Address. Edinburgh University.
220:24   Step by step.   Jesse. *Memoirs*. 96.
221: 1   Removing or undermining.   Armstrong. *Usurpation*. 85.
221:10   No-one doubted.   Armstrong. *Usurpation*. 95.
221:27   Brave, cunning.   Stubbs. *Constitutional*. III. 225.
221:32   More's Richard.   Churchill. *Shakespeare*. 377–9.
223: 2   Deeply politic.   Gairdner. *Richard III*. 124.
223: 8   Clockwork sequence.   Cheetham. *Richard III*. 124.
223:14   Nervous and anxious.   Crowder. *Society*. 131. Article by Myers.
223:16   Wont to be.   Ellis. *Vergil*. 227.
223:24   Ill-considered action.   Wood. *Addendum*. 9–10.
223:38   Irrevocable action.   Wolffe. *Review*. 89. 843.
224: 8   Genuine conspiracy.   Wood. *Addendum*. 4.
224:21   Richard's missed cue.   Sylvester. *Richard III*. 68–9.

225:18	Seized Rivers. Armstrong. *Usurpation*. 75, 89.
225:26	Compel travellers. Sylvester. *Richard III*. 19.
225:32	Under penalty. Riley. *Croyland*. 487.
225:34	Cut finger. Riley. *Croyland*. 488.
226:11	Cruel slaughter. Ellis. *Vergil*. 181–2.
226:16	Rather for fear. Ellis. *Vergil*. 182.
226:18	Multitude of troops. Armstrong. *Usurpation*. 97.
226:20	All his glory. Riley. *Croyland*. 485.
226:32	Queen besieged. Armstrong. *Usurpation*. 89.
226:36	Innocent child. Ellis. *Vergil*. 178.
226:37	Bourchier compelled. Riley. *Croyland*. 488.
227:17	Kings' games. Sylvester. *Richard III*. 83.
227:23	Deep dissembler. Sylvester. *Richard III*. 9.
227:27	I can smile. Shakespeare. III. *Henry VI*. III. 2.
228: 7	Stories feigned. Armstrong. *Usurpation*. 91.
228:11	Fair promises. Thomas. *Chronicle*. 231.
228:14	Subtle manner. Ellis. *Vergil*. 179.
228:21	No man. Sylvester. *Richard III*. 82.
228:25	Lies on lips. Dunham. *American*. 756.
228:33	Mark of respect. Riley. *Croyland*. 487.
229: 8	Mischievous women. Rymer. *Foedera*. XII. 204.
229:12	Reputation for hypocrisy. Davies. *York*. 221, 224.
229:13	Fervent desire. Steele. *Letters*. 263.
229:26	Frivolous changes. Riley. *Croyland*. 498.
229:28	Langton praises. Sheppard. *Christ Church*. 45.
229:34	Licentious passages. Gibbon. *Autobiography*.
229:38	Neque exceptionem. Hanham. *Historians*. 50.
230:16	Mollify multitude. Ellis. *Vergil*. 179.
230:19	Large gifts. Sylvester. *Richard III*. 9.
230:20	Few or none. Ellis. *New Chronicles*. 670.
230:31	So flagrant. Jesse. *Memoirs*. 509.
230:36	Crowned unwillingly. Armstrong. *Usurpation*. 101.
231: 6	Against will. Hanham. *Historians*. 119.
231: 8	Much business. Kingsford. *Stonor*. II. 161.
231:18	Edward IV's creations. Chrimes. *Fifteenth*. 116–7.
233:27	Taken in hand. Prayer book. Solemnization of Matrimony.
234: 5	King in possession. Sylvester. *Richard III*. 95.
234:10	Never prosper. Harrington. *Epigrams*. Bk. IV No. 5.
234:16	Prince I followed. Kincaid. *Buck*. 109.
235: 2	Well beloved. Kincaid. *Buck*. 20.
235:12	Piteously slain. Davies. *York*. 218.
235:15	Blessed memory. Raine. *York*. II. 24–5.
235:16	Like lees. Lockyer. *History*. 94.
235:33	Loving disposition. Davies. *York*. 147.
236: 8	Strong hints. Lander. *Community*. 327–8.
236:16	Richard distrusted. Raine. *York*. I. VI.
236:28	Do things. Raine. *York*. I. VII–VIII, 56.
237:37	Fear than love. Thomas. *Chronicle*. 230.

238: 1   Scarcely watched.   Armstrong. *Usurpation*. 95.
238: 8   Not so repugnant.   Gairdner. *Letters*. I. xx.
238:24   Temper and Manners.   Walpole. *Doubts*. 31.

CHAPTER 11   *History and Myth*

239: 2   Bloody tyrant.   Shakespeare. *Richard III*. V. *3*.
239: 9   Justification.   Myers. *Journal*. 182.
239:16   Foresee.   Campbell. *Shakespeare*. 28.
240: 5   Powers that be.   St Paul. *Romans*. XIII. *1*.
240: 8   Disorder.   Shakespeare. *Richard II*. IV. *1*.
240:13   Bloody days.   Shakespeare. *Richard III*. V. *5*.
240:17   Better understanding.   Tillyard. *Plays*. 65, 70.
240:34   Doth hedge.   Shakespeare. *Hamlet*. IV. *5*.
241: 3   Great discord.   Tillyard. *Plays*. 43.
241: 9   God's Majesty.   Shakespeare. *Richard II*. IV. *1*.
241:22   Killed father.   Shakespeare. III. *Henry VI*. II. *5*.
241:27   Death of brother.   Tillyard. *Plays*. 70.
242:10   Late duke.   Strachey. *Rotuli*. VI. 275.
242:20   Grave men.   Kincaid. *Buck*. 129.
243: 2   Black intelligencer.   Shakespeare. *Richard III*. IV. *4*.
243:28   Chief instigator.   Kincaid. *Buck*. 120–125.
244:32   Acts of empire.   Kincaid. *Buck*. 29.
244:35   Wits and pens.   Kincaid. *Buck*. 120, 125, 208.
245: 8   Scorned to save.   Walpole. *Doubts*. 19.
245:21   Mindless partisanship.   Pollard. *Medieval*. 150.
245:22   Gross distortion.   Ross. *Richard III*. XLVIII.
246: 1   Monster of mankind.   Drake. *Eboracum*. 124.
246:28   Despairing cry.   Myers. *Journal*. 194.
246:32   Now believe.   Walpole. *Complete*. II. 251–2.
248:21   Disfigured by passion.   Turner. *History*. III. 371.
249:25   Minute study.   Gairdner. *Richard III*. XI.
250: 2   All counts.   Markham. *Richard III*. v.
250:23   Strained interpretation.   Markham. *Richard III*. 236.
250:28   Believe writers.   Gairdner. *Review*. 456, 462.
250:36   Lues Boswelliana.   Macaulay. *Essays*. William Pitt.
251: 6   Blessed disposition.   Halsted. *Richard III*. II. 295.
251:17   Long dead.   Ross. *Richard III*. LI.
252:18   Fiction.   Hanham. *Historians*. 197.
252:21   Upright Prince. *Times Review*. 1955.
253:21   Bad men.   Burke. *Thoughts on the Cause of the Present Discontents*.
253:27   Take the sword. *St. Matthew*. XXVI. 52.
253:28   Man soweth.   St Paul. *Galations*. VI. 7.

SELECT BIBLIOGRAPHY

The following Select Bibliography is confined to works quoted or mentioned in the text of *The Year of Three Kings*. Readers requiring a comprehensive Bibliography should refer to Professor Ross' *Richard III*, or Guth's *Late Medieval England* in the Cambridge University Press series of 'Bibliographical Handbooks'. Italics are used in the list below to indicate the abbreviated book titles used in 'Source References'. The 'Barton Library', mentioned in the Select Bibliography, belongs to 'The Richard III Society', and contains unpublished material. Dates of publication are not generally supplied for works of which there are several editions.

Addison, W.   The Old *Roads* of England, 1980.

Archaeologia.   I. 1770.

Armstrong, C.   *Transactions* of the Royal Historical Society. 30. 1948. 'The Inauguration Ceremonies of the Yorkist Kings.'

Armstrong, C. (ed.)   The *Usurpation* of Richard III. (Mancini) 1969.

Arrivall.   Historie of the *Arrivall* of King Edward IV. (Fleetwood Chronicle) 1838.

Bacon, F.   See Lockyer. R. (ed.)

Barker, N. and Birley, R.   *Etoniana*. Nos. 125, 126. 1972. 'The Real Jane Shore.'

Bellamy, J.   The Law of *Treason* in England in the later Middle Ages. 1970.

Bernier, A.   *Journal* des État Généraux de France tenus à Tours en 1484. 1835.

Bindoff, S.   *Lecture*. (Unpublished). Barton Library 1973.

Boswell, J.   Life of *Johnson*.

Brewer, J. (ed.)   Letters and Papers of the Reign of *Henry VIII*. 1862.

Bruce, J. (ed.)   Historie of the *Arrivall* of King Edward IV (Fleetwood Chronicle) 1838.

Buck, G.   See Kincaid. A. (ed.)

Bullough, G.   *Narrative* and Dramatic Sources of Shakespeare. III. 1975.

Burke, E.   Thoughts on the Cause of the Present *Discontents*.

Burne, A.   The *Battlefields* of England. 1950.

Calendar.   *Calendar* of the Patent Rolls preserved in the Public Records Office. 1476–1485. 1901.

Campbell. L. (ed.)   A *Mirror* for Magistrates. 1938.

Campbell, L.   Shakespeare's '*Histories*'. 1964.

Cely Correspondence.   See Malden, H. (ed.)

Chambers, R.   Thomas *More*. 1935.

Cheetham, A.   *Richard III*. 1972.

Churchill, G.   Richard III up to *Shakespeare*. 1900.

Churchill, W.   *History* of the English Speaking Peoples. 1956.

Chrimes, S. (ed.)   *Fifteenth* Century England. 1972.

Chrimes, S.   *Lancastrians*, Yorkists and Henry VII. 1964.

Coleman, C.   British Institute of Historical Research. (*B.I.H.R.*) LIII. 1980. 'The Execution of Hastings.'

Commission.   See Historical Manuscripts *Commission*.

Commynes, P.   See Jones, M. (ed.)

Cornwallis, W.   See Kincaid, A. (ed.)

Crawford, A.   The *Ricardian*. June 1981. 'The Mowbray Inheritance'.

Croke, Sir G.   See Grimston, H. (ed.)

Crowder, C. (ed.)   English *Society* and Government in the Fifteenth Century. 1967.

Croyland Chronicle.   See Riley, H. (ed.)

Davies, R. (ed.)   Extracts from the Municipal Records of the City of *York*. 1843.

de Waurin, J.   See Dupont, L. (ed.)

Drake, F.   *Eboracum*. 1736.

Dugdale, W.   The *Baronage* of England. 1676.

Dunham, W.   *American* Historical Review. 81. 1976. 'The Right to Rule in England: Depositions and the Kingdom's Authority'.

Dunham, W.   *Transactions* of the Connecticut Academy. 39. 1955. 'Lord Hastings' indentured Retainers'.

Dupont, L. (ed.)   Anchiennes *Cronicques* d'Engleterre. (de Waurin. J.) 1858–1863.

Edwards, J. (ed.)   Historical *Essays* in Honour of James Tait. 1933. Pollard, A. 'The Making of Sir Thomas More's Richard III'.

Ellis, H. (ed.)   Chronicle of J. *Hardyng* with Continuation by R. Grafton. 1812.

Ellis, H. (ed.)   *Original* Letters Illustrative of English History. 3 series. 1825, 1827, 1846.

Ellis, H. (ed.)   The Chronicles of Richard *Holinshed* (1587). 1807.

Ellis, H. (ed.)   The *New Chronicles* of England and France. (Fabyan, R.) 1811.

Ellis, H. (ed.)   The *Union* of the Noble and Illustre Famelies of Lancastre and York. (Hall, E.) 1809.

Ellis, H. (ed.)   Three Books of Polydore *Vergil*. 1844.

Fabyan, R.   See Ellis, H. (ed.)

Fahy, C.   English Historical *Review*. 76. 1961. 'The Marriage of Edward IV and Elizabeth Woodville; a New Italian Source'.

Fleetwood Chronicle.   See Bruce, J. (ed.)

Flenley, R. (ed.)   Six Town *Chronicles* of England. 1911.

Fulman, W.   *Rerum* Anglicarum Scriptores Veterum. 1684.

Gairdner, J.   English Historical *Review*. VI. 1891. 'Did Henry VII Murder the Princes?'

Gairdner, J. (ed.)   *Letters* and Papers Illustrative of the Reigns of Richard III and Henry VII. 1861–3.

Gairdner, J. (ed.)   *Memorials* of King Henry the Seventh. 1858.

Gairdner, J. (ed.)   *Paston* letters. 1904.

Gairdner, J.   *Richard* III. 1898.

Gairdner, J. (ed.)   Three Fifteenth Century *Chronicles*. 1880.

Gibbon, E.   *Autobiography*.

Gibbon, E.   See Sheffield, Lord. (ed.)

Goodman, A.   English Historical Review. 88. 1973. 'A *Castilian* Report on English Affairs. 1486'.

Grafton, R. (ed.)   The *Chronicle* of J. Hardyng. 1543.

Grafton, R.   See Ellis. H. (ed.)

Grimston, H. (ed.)   The Third Part of the Report of Sir George *Croke*, 1683.

Guth, D.   Late Medieval England. 1377–1485.

Habington, W.   The *History* of Edward IV. 1460.

Hall, E.   See Ellis, H. (ed.)

Halliwell, J. (ed.)   A *Chronicle* of the First Thirteen years of the Reign of Edward IV. (Warkworth, J.) 1839.

Halsted, C.   *Richard III*. 1844.

Hamilton Thompson, A.   *Transactions* of Leicestershire Archaeological Society. XI. 1915. 'The Building Accounts of Kirby Muxloe Castle'.

Hammond, P.   *Ricardian*. March. 1975.

Hanbury, H.   The *American* Journal of Legal History. 6. 1962. 'The Legislation of Richard III'.

Hanham, A.   English Historical *Review*. 87. 1972. 'Richard III, Lord Hastings and the Historians'.

Hanham, A.   English Historical *Review*. 90. 1975. 'Hastings Redivivus'.

Hanham, A.   Richard III and His Early *Historians*. 1975.

Hardyng, J.   See Ellis, H. (ed.) Grafton, R. (ed.)

Harleian. MSS 433   See Horrox, C. (ed.)

Harrington, J.   Epigrams. 1618.

Harris, O.   The *Ricardian*. Dec. 1979. 'Tudor Heraldry at Bosworth'.

Hay, D.   Polydore *Vergil*: Renaissance Historian and Man of Letters. 1952.

Hay, D. (ed.)   The *Anglica* Historia of Polydore Vergil. 1485–1537. 1950.

Hearne, T. (ed.)   *Historia* Regum Angliae. (Rous, J.) 1716. The section on Richard III is translated by Hanham. See 'Richard III and his early Historians'. 118–124.

Historical Manuscripts *Commission*

Holinshed, R.   See Ellis, H. (ed.)

Horrox, C. and Hammond, P. (ed.)   British Library Harleian *Manuscript 433*. 1979, 1980.

Hume, D.   *History* of England.

Hutton, W.   The Battlefield of *Bosworth*. 1813.

Ives, E.   Bulletin of *Institute* of Historical Research. 41. 1968. 'Andrew Dymmock and the Papers of Antony, Earl Rivers, 1482–1483'.

Jacob, E.   The *Fifteenth* Century. 1978.

Jesse, J.   *Memoirs* of King Richard III. 1862.

Jones, M. (ed.)   Philippe de *Commynes*. Memoirs. 1972.

Kelly, H.   Medieval *Studies*. 39. 1977. 'English Kings and the Fear of Sorcery'.

Kendall, P.   *Richard III*. 1955.

Kincaid, A. (ed.)   The *Encomium* of Richard III. Sir W. Cornwallis. (1616). 1977.

Kincaid, A. (ed.)   The History of King Richard III. (*Buck*, G.) 1979.

Kingsford, C. (ed.)   Chronicles of *London*. 1905.

Kingsford, C.   English Historical *Literature* in the Fifteenth Century. 1913.

Kingsford, C. (ed.)   The *Stonor* Letters and Papers. 1919.

Lander, J.   *Conflict* and Stability in Fifteenth Century England. 1977.

Lander, J.   *Crown* and Nobility. 1976.

Lander, J.   Government and *Community*. 1980.

Lerner, M. (ed.)   The *Prince* and Discourse. (Machiavelli). 1950.

Levine, M.   *Speculum*. 34. 1959. 'Richard III. Usurper or Lawful King?'

Levine, M.   Tudor Dynastic *Problems*. 1973.

Lockyer, R. (ed.)   The *History* of the Reign of King Henry VII (Bacon) 1971.

Macaulay, T.   *Essays*. 'William Pitt'.

Machiavelli, N.   See Lerner, M. (ed.)

McKenna, J.   English Historical *Review*. Jan. 1967. 'The Coronation Oil of the Yorkist Kings'.

Malden, H. (ed.)   Selections from the Correspondence and Memoranda of the *Cely* Family. 1900.

Mancini, D.   See Armstrong, C. (ed.)

Markham, C.   English Historical Review. 6. 1891. 'Richard III: A *doubtful* verdict'.

Markham, C.   English Historical *Review*. 6. 1891. 'Richard III and Henry VII'.

Markham, C.   *Richard III*. His Life and Character. 1906.

Maxwell Lyte, H.   A History of *Eton* College. 1889.

Melhuish, J.   The College of King Richard III *Middleham*. 1962.

Mirror for Magistrates   See Campbell, L. (ed.)

More, T.   See Sylvester. R. (ed.)

Myers, A. (ed.)   English Historical *Documents*. 1969.

Myers, A.   History *Today*. 4. 1954. Reprinted in Crowder. *Society*. 'The Character of Richard III'.

Myers, A.   The *Journal* of the Historical Association. 53. 1968. 'Richard III and Historical Tradition'.

Nichols, J. (ed.)   *Grants* of Edward V. 1844.

Nichols, J. (ed.)   Collection of Royal *Wills*. 1780.

Nicolas, H. (ed.)   *Excerpta* Historica. 1831.

Nokes, E.   The Ricardian. March. 1972. 'A *Spanish* account of the Battle of Bosworth'.

Orford, Lord   See Walpole, H.

Paston letters   See Gairdner, J. (ed.)

Payne Collier, J.   *Household* Books of John Duke of Norfolk, 1844.

Peck, F.   *Desiderata* Curiosa. 1735.

Pollard, A.   See Edwards, J. (ed.)

Pollard, A.   Journal of *Medieval* History. 3. 1977. 'The Tyranny of Richard III'.

Pollard, A. (ed.)   The Reign of *Henry VII* from Contemporary Sources. 1914.

Raine, A. (ed.)   *York* Civic Records. 1939.

Ramsay, J.   *Lancaster* and York. 1399–1485. 1892.

Rastell, W.   English Works of Sir T. *More*. 1557.

Reese, M.   The *Cease* of Majesty. 1961.

Riley, H. (ed.)   Ingulph's Chronicle of the Abbey of *Croyland*. 1854.

Riley, H. (ed.)   *Registra* Quorundum Abbatum Monasterii Sancti Albani. 1872.

Roskell, J.   *Bulletin* of the John Rylands Library. 42. 1955. 'William Catesby, Counsellor to Richard III'.

Roskell, J.   English Historical *Review*. 68. 1953. 'The Office and Dignity of Protector of England'.

Ross, C.   *Edward IV*. 1974.

Ross, C.   *Richard III*, 1981.

Ross, C.   The *Rous* Roll. 1980.

Rous, J.   See Hearne, T. (ed.) Ross, C. (ed.)

Rowse, A.   *Bosworth* Field. 1966.

Rymer, T. (ed.)   *Foedera*, Conventiones et Litteras. 1704–1735.

Saccio, P.   Shakespeare's English *Kings*. 1977.

Saltmarsh, J.   King *Henry VI* and the Royal Foundations. 1972.

Sandford, F.   *Genealogical* History of the Kings of England. 1677.

Sheffield, Lord (ed.)   *Gibbon's* Miscellaneous Works. 1814.

Sheppard, J.   *Christ Church* letters. 1887.

Smith, M.   Henry VI's *Medical* Record. 1973. Barton Library.

Steele, R. (ed.)   Kings' *Letters*. 1903.

Stonor letters.   See Kingsford, C. (ed.)

Stow, J.   The *Annales* of England, 1592.

Strachey, J. (ed.)   *Rotuli* Parliamentorum. 1767–1777.

Stubbs, W.   The *Constitutional* History of England. 1874.

Sylvester, R. (ed.)   The History of King *Richard III*. (Sir T. More) 1976.

Tanner, L.   *Archaeologia*. LXXXIV. 1934. 'Recent Investigations Regarding the fate of the Princes in the Tower'.

Tey, J.   The Daughter of Time. 1951.

The *Great* Chronicle of London.   See Thomas, A. (ed.)

Thomas, A.   The *Great* Chronicle of London. 1938.

Thompson, J.   British Institute of Historical Research. (*B.I.H.R.*) 48. 1975. 'Richard III and Lord Hastings – a Problematical Case Reviewed'.

Tillyard, E.   Shakespeare's History *Plays*. 1956.

Tudor-Craig, P.   *Richard III*. 1973.

Turner, S.   *History* of England in the Middle Ages. 1825.

Vergil, P.   See Ellis, H. (ed.) Hay, D. (ed.)

Walpole, H. (Lord Orford)   *Complete* Works. II. 1798. 'Postscript to my Historic Doubts'.

Walpole, H.   Historic *Doubts* on the Life and Reign of King Richard III. 1768.

Warkworth, J.   See Halliwell, J. (ed.)

Williams, C.   *Cambridge* Medieval. History. VIII. 1936.

Wolffe, B.   English Historical *Review*. 89. 1974. 'When and Why did Hastings lose his head?'

Wolffe, B.   English Historical *Review*. 91. *1976*. 'Hastings Reinterred'.

Wolffe, B.   *Henry VI*. 1981.

Wolffe, B.   The Royal *Demesne* in English History. 1971.

Wood, C.   Traditio. 31. 1975. 'The *Deposition* of Edward V'.

Wood, C.   *Addendum*. (MSS in Barton Library)

INDEX

Characters listed under Dramatis Personae are indicated by an asterisk in the index. Uncertain dates are shown by a question mark. Where months are given without a year, the year omitted is 1483.

Act of Accord. 1460. 44, 46.
Albany. Alexander, Duke of. 1454–1485. 61.
Alcock. John. Bishop of Worcester. 89, 98, 232, 237.
Ambien Hill. 209, 211.
Angel. Grantham. 190.
Angers. Treaty of. 1470. 55, 57, 58.
"Anglica Historia". See Vergil, Polydore.
Anjou. See Margaret of.
Anne of York. See Exeter. Anne, Duchess of.
Anne. Queen. See Neville, Anne.
Argentine. John. 65, 141.
Armstrong. C. 64, 251.
Arundel. Sir Thomas. 186, 192, 195.
Atherstone. 209.
Attainder. Acts of. 1484. 187, 193, 197.
Attainder. Act of. 1485. 242.

Bacon. Sir Francis. 157, 198, 235.
Banaster. Ralph. 191.
Barnard's Castle. 116.
Barnet. Battle of. 1471. 57, 215.
Bath. Earl of. See de Chandée. Philibert.
Baynard's Castle. 46, 160–161, 162, 165.
Beaufort. See Somerset, Dukes of.
*Beaufort. Lady Margaret. 1443–1509; Marries Edmund Tudor. 1456. 189; Marries Henry Stafford. 189; Marries

Lord Stanley. 1482? 126, 189; In Queen Anne's Coronation procession. July 6. 168–169; Negotiates Son's Marriage to Elizabeth of York. 190; Compassionate treatment of. 193, 198.
*Bedford. Jacquetta. Duchess of. 1416?–1472. 48, 50.
Bedford. Jasper, Duke of. See Pembroke. Jasper, Earl of.
*Bedford. John, Duke of. 1389–1435. 38, 48.
Berwick. 44, 61.
Bohun, Eleanor. 94, 187–188.
Bohun, Mary. 94, 187–188.
Bona. Princess of Savoy. 52, 150, 156.
✗Bosworth. Battle of. August 22. 1485. 56, 209–216.
*Bourchier. Thomas. Archbishop of Canterbury. 1404?–1486; Career of. 134–135; Supports proclamation of Edward IV. 1461. 46; Swears fealty to the Prince of Wales. (Edward V). 1471. 84; A political trimmer. 87, 109, 230–231, 232; Opposes force in seizing Prince Richard. June. 135; Heads delegation to Queen Elizabeth. June 16. 134; Anxious to avoid violation of Sanctuary. 137; Promises to Queen

Elizabeth. 137; Acts under duress? 226; Innocence or senility of. 138; Crowns Richard III. July 6. 168–169, 230; Absent from Coronation banquet. 169; Disgraced. 230.
Brackenbury. Sir Robert. 165, 176–177, 178, 205, 208, 237.
Brampton. Sir Edward. 115.
Brandon. Sir William. 214.
Bray, Reginald. 190.
Brecknock Castle. 167, 191.
Brittany. Francis, Duke of. 1459–1488. 196, 203.
Buck. Sir George. 65, 117, 152, 155, 156, 177, 179, 198, 227, 242, 243–245.
Buckingham, Duchess of. See Woodville, Catherine.
*Buckingham. Henry, Second Duke of. 1453?–1483; Character of. 94–95; Royal descent. 92–93; Marries Catherine Woodville. 1466. 53, 94, 95; Disdain for Woodvilles. 53, 85, 93; Pronounces sentence of death on Clarence. 1478. 59; Grievances of. 94; Offers Gloucester help. April. 85, 93; Joins Gloucester at Northampton. April 29. 93; Conspires with Gloucester. 95; With Gloucester at Stony Stratford. April 30. 95–98; Supports Gloucester in Council. May. 108; Proposes

lodging King in Tower.
May. 110; Gloucester's
bounty towards. May.
112–113; Ordered to
attend Tower Council.
June 13. 122; Given
command of troops in
Tower? 125; Given
custody of Morton. 126,
167; Advocates seizing
Prince Richard by force.
June 16. 136; Agrees to
support Gloucester's
Usurpation. 140–141;
Guildhall address. June
24. 149–153; Organises
petition. June 25. 153;
Petitions Gloucester to
become King. June 26.
160–161; Rewards of.
June 28. 165; Welsh troops
in London. July. 166;
Splendid appearance of.
July 5. 167; Humiliated at
Coronation? July 6. 168;
Accompanies Richard's
Progress. July. 172;
Leaves Richard at
Gloucester. July. 174;
Murders Princes in
Tower? 180, 181; Joins
October rebellion.
185–186; Motives for
rebelling. 186–187; Offers
Crown to Henry Tudor.
187; Invites Henry to
land. 189; Reward offered
for capture of. 190, 191;
Raises Standard. October
18. 191; Held up by
storms. 191; Betrayed by
Banaster. 191; Executed.
November 2. 192.
Buckingham. Humphrey,
First Duke of. 1402–1460.
44, 85, 93.
*Burgundy, Charles "the
Bold". 1433–1477. 54, 57,
59.
*Burgundy. Margaret,
Duchess of. 1446–1503.
54, 59, 218.
*Burgundy. Mary, Duchess
of. 1457–1482. 59, 60–61.
*Butler. Lady Eleanor.
1435?–1466. 155–156,
158.

Calais. 43, 44, 54, 76, 89,
114, 164–165, 206.

Calais Manifesto. 1460. 44.
Cambridge. 172.
*Cambridge. Richard, Earl
of. 1375–1415. 42.
Carey. Sir Robert. 99.
Castillon. Battle of 1453. 39.
Catesby, William. d. 1485;
Career of. 118, 238;
Rewarded by Gloucester.
May. 113; Hastings'
trusted agent. 117; Sounds
Hastings for Gloucester?
June. 118; Drafts
Proclamation of Hastings'
treason? 127; Created
Chancellor of the
Exchequer. June 28. 165;
Elected Speaker. January
1484. 197; Warns Richard
against marrying niece.
1485. 202.
Catherine of Valois. 189.
Cely, George. 130.
Charles the "Bold". See
Burgundy, Duke of.
Charles II of England. 111,
179.
*Charles VI of France.
1368–1422. 38, 39.
Charles VIII of France.
1470–1498. 203, 206.
Cheyney. Sir John. 86, 186,
192, 214.
*Clarence. George, Duke
of. 1449–1478; Character
of. 54, 189; Denounces
Woodvilles. 53–54; Joins
Warwick's rebellion
against Edward IV. 1469.
54; Marries Isabel Neville.
1469. 54–55; Fights at
Edgecote. 1469. 55;
Denounced as traitor.
1470. 55; Signs Treaty of
Angers. 1470. 55, 57, 58;
Lands at Dartmouth.
1470. 55; Persuaded to
abandon Warwick. 1471.
57; Opposes Gloucester's
marriage to Anne Neville.
1472. 58; Death of
Duchess Isabel. 1476. 59;
Projected Burgundian
match. 1477. 59;
Browbeats Jury. 1477. 59;
Accuses Edward IV of
being bastard. 1478. 59,
144; Trial and execution
of. 1478. 59–60, 144, 162,
244; Buried at

Tewkesbury Abbey.
1478. 60.
Clarence. Isabel. Duchess
of. See Neville, Isabel.
*Clarence. Lionel, Duke of.
1338–1368. 39.
College of Heralds. 198.
Colyngbourne, William.
d. 1484. 86, 204–205.
Commynes. Philippe de.
156–157, 175–176.
Cordes, Lord. 114.
Cornazzano, Antonio. 49.
Coronation of Edward V.
1483; Date of decided by
Council. April. 80, 89;
Edward V tells Mayor of
Lynn fixed for May 4. 80;
Council discusses new
date of. May. 110;
Coronation robes made
for King. 110; Not
mentioned in Bishop
Russell's Sermon. 114;
Postponement of. June.
139–140.
Coronation of Richard III.
July 6. 1483. 164,
166–170, 230.
Council of the North.
198–199.
Courtenay, Piers. Bishop of
Exeter. 186, 192, 194,
198, 205.
Crosby's Place.
Bishopsgate. 104, 116,
117.
Croyland Chronicle.
Croyland Abbey's
"History of England". 66;
Second Continuator
covers years 1459 to 1486.
66; Continuator Russell,
Bishop of Lincoln? 66–67;
Continuator a reliable
eye-witness. 67; Council's
concern for Woodvilles.
111; On approach of
Northern Army. June.
121; On consequence of
Hastings' execution. 131;
Petition of June 25 got up
in north. 154; On cost of
suppressing
Buckingham's rebellion.
194; On alienation of
South by plantation of
Northerners. 195–196;
On Richard's intention to
marry his niece. 202; On

Croyland Chronicle – *cont.*
Battle of Bosworth. 1485.
210; On Richard's resolute
villainy. 224; On
Richard's double-dealing.
228; On licentious Court.
229.
Curteys, Piers. 110, 167,
184.

Dartmouth. 55.
de Chandée, Philibert. First
Earl of Bath. 207.
de Salazar, Juan. 210,
214–215.
de Valera, Diego. 210, 214.
Dighton, John. 177.
*Dorset. Thomas, First
Marquis of. 1451–1501;
Character of. 52; Created
Marquis. 1475. 52;
Marries Anne Holland.
53; Marries Cecily
Bonville. 63; Disputes
with Hastings. 76; In
possession of Tower.
April. 75, 97; Conspires
against Gloucester? 81;
Proclaims Edward V?
April 11. 82; Boasts of
family power. 89; Takes
Treasure from Tower.
April. 99; Attempts to
raise troops. May 1. 100;
Estates distributed by
Gloucester. May. 112;
Consorts with Mistress
Shore. 123; Richard
searches for. 132;
Supports Buckingham's
rebellion. October. 186,
189; Proclaimed rebel.
190; Escapes to Brittany.
192.
Drake, Francis.
(Antiquarian.) 245.
Dymmock, Andrew. 75.
Dymmock, Sir Robert. 170.

Edgecote. Battle of. 1469.
55.
*Edward IV. 1442–1483;
Character and appearance
of. 47–48, 147; Flees to
Calais. 1459. 43; Publishes
Calais Manifesto. 1460.
44; Victory at Mortimer's
Cross. 1461. 45;
Proclaimed King. 1461.
45–46; Victory at

Towton. 1461. 46;
Marries Elizabeth
Woodville. 1464. 46–50,
91; Announces Marriage.
1464. 52; Patronage of
Woodvilles. 52–53;
Ill-effects of Marriage. 52,
54, 75, 155; Captured by
Warwick's forces. 1469.
55; Proclaims Warwick
and Clarence traitors.
1470. 55; Flees to Low
Countries. 1470. 55;
Helped by Charles the
"Bold". 1471. 57; Lands
at Ravenspur. 1471. 57;
Defeats Warwick at
Barnet. 1471. 57; Victory
at Tewkesbury. 1471. 57,
58, 61, 189; Arbitrates
between Clarence and
Gloucester. 1472. 58;
French expedition. 1475.
60–61, 78; Objects to
Clarence's projected
Burgundian Match. 1477.
59; Trial and execution of
Clarence. 1478. 59–60;
Scottish Campaign. 1482.
61; Prepares for War with
France. 1483. 61, 114;
Alienates nobles by
predatory policy. 62–63,
233; Makes enemies for
sons. 62–63, 74–75, 219;
Increases Rivers' power in
Wales. 1483. 75; Lavish
patronage of Gloucester.
77; Final illness. April. 74,
79, 201; Deathbed
reconciliations. April.
77–78; Adds Codicils to
Will. 78; Corpse publicly
displayed. April. 79–80;
Council remains in office.
April. 80, 87; Lies in state.
April. 85; Funeral
processions. April. 85–86;
Burial at St. George's,
Windsor. April. 86–87;
Relations with Mistress
Shore. 123; Gloucester
alleges bastardy of.
142–148; Accusations of
bigamy. 150, 152,
156–157; Lechery
denounced by
Buckingham. 151;
Supposed pre-contract to
Dame Lucy. 152, 155;

Supposed pre-contract to
Lady Eleanor Butler.
155–156, 158; No
evidence of pre-contract.
157–158; Pageantry of
reign. 172.
*Edward V. 1470–1483?;
Born in Sanctuary on All
Souls' Day. 57; Character
of. 141; Becomes Knight
of the Garter. 1472. 89;
Ludlow. Household of
1473–1483. 75, 81;
Proclaimed King. April
11. 82; Control of vital.
76–77; Council debates
minority government.
April. 80; Council decides
Coronation date. April.
80, 89; Rivers instructed
to bring to London. April.
80; Letter to Mayor of
Lynn. April 16. 80; Age of
regal majority? 81;
Gloucester acknowledges
fealty to. 84; Size of escort
debated. April. 88–89;
Celebrates St. George's
Day. April 23. 82, 89; Sets
out from Ludlow to
London. April 24. 89–90;
Makes detour to meet
Gloucester. April. 90;
Stays at Stony Stratford.
April 29. 91; Seized by
Gloucester. April 30.
95–98; Defends Mother's
family. 97; Resents
seizure. 98–99, 219;
Greeted by Mayor at
Harringay. May 4. 103;
Lodges at Bishop of
London's Palace. 103;
Oaths of fealty to. May.
104; Gloucester
recognised as Protector.
May. 109; Coronation
robes begun. 110; Lodged
in Tower. May. 111;
Gloucester plans to extend
Protectorate? 113–114;
Hastings fears deposition
of. 116; Fidelity of
Hastings to. 101, 128;
Possible plot to release.
130; Need for brother to
attend Coronation.
133–134; Last document
signed as King. June 17.
141; Coronation

postponed. June.
139–140; Withdrawn into
inner quarters of Tower.
141; Rumours of Murder.
141, 186; Supporters
powerless to resist
deposition. 142;
Gloucester accuses of
bastardy. 143, 223; Shaa's
Sermon on. 142–143;
Bastardy suspect. 144,
158; Called "Lord
Bastard". 181; Mistaken ?
allegiance to. 164–165;
Innocence of. 171–172,
182, 187; Seen playing in
Tower garden. 175;
Risings on behalf of. 174,
186; Supposed Murder of.
141, 167, 174–182, 186,
190, 250; Bones
discovered ? 1674. 179,
181; Survives until 1485?
181.
★Edward of Lancaster.
Prince of Wales.
1453–1471;
Birth of. 39; Escapes after
Battle of Northampton.
1460. 44; Disinherited by
Act of Accord. 1460. 44,
46; At Mother's Court in
France. 1463. 48;
Betrothed to Anne
Neville. 1470. 55, 58;
Lands at Weymouth.
April 1471. 57; Killed at
Battle of Tewkesbury.
1471. 57, 58, 69, 244.
★Edward of York. Earl of
Salisbury. Prince of
Wales. 1473–1484; Born
at Middleham. 82;
Created Prince of Wales.
June 28. 165–166; Not at
Richard's Coronation.
170; State visit to York.
August. 183–185;
Investiture of. September
8. 184–185; Returns to
Middleham. 185;
Projected Marriage of?
200; Dies at Middleham.
82, 201; Buried at Sheriff
Hutton? 235.
★Elizabeth of York. Queen
of Henry VII. 1466–1503.
60–61, 156, 157, 176, 189,
190, 196, 200, 202.
Ellis, Sir Henry. 247.

Ely. Bishop of. See Morton,
John.
Ely Place. 117, 122.
Eton College. 45, 86, 173.
Exeter. See Courtenay,
Bishop of.
★Exeter. Anne of York.
Duchess of. 1439–1476.
62–63.
★Exeter. Henry Holland.
Duke of. d. 1475. 62–63.

Fabyan, Robert. 72, 153,
175, 230.
Fauconberg. See Neville,
Thomas.
Finsbury Fields. 166.
Fogge, Sir John. 186.
Forest, Miles. 177.
Fortescue, Sir John. 48.
Fotheringhay. 55.

Gairdner, James. 222, 248,
249, 250.
Gaunt, John of. See
Lancaster. John, Duke of.
Gibbon, Edward. 71, 229.
Gloucester. 174.
Gloucester, Duchess of. See
Neville, Anne. Queen.
★Gloucester. Humphrey,
Duke of. 1390–1477. 38,
77, 124, 160.
Gloucester, John of. 181.
Gloucester. Richard, Duke
of. See Richard III.
★Gloucester. Thomas, Duke
of. 1355–1397. 77, 93, 94,
134, 189.
Grafton. 49, 50.
Grafton, Richard. 186–187,
242.
Grantham. 190.
Great Chronicle. See "The
Great Chronicle of
London".
Green, John. 176.
Grey, Sir John. 1432–1461.
49.
★Grey, Richard.
1453?–1483. 52, 91, 97,
102, 159.
Grey, Thomas. See Dorset,
First Marquis of.
Grey, Thomas. (Son of
Dorset, Marquis of.) 63.
Grocyn, William. 172, 173.
Guildhall. 149, 204.
Guildford, Sir Richard. 186.

Hall, Edward. 54, 71–72,
200, 205, 240–241.
Halsted, Caroline. 248–249.
Harleian Manuscript 433.
72, 230, 251.
Hastings, Catherine. (Born
Neville.) 56, 129.
Hastings. William, Lord.
1430?–1483.
Character and family
history of. 56; Appointed
Lord Chamberlain. 1461.
56; Marries Catherine
Neville. 1462. 56;
Hostility to Woodvilles.
56, 76; Accompanies
Edward IV into exile.
1470. 56; Assists restore
Edward IV. 1471. 57;
Lieutenant of Calais.
1471. 76; Sent to Tower.
1477. 76; Informs
Gloucester of Edward
IV's death? April. 83;
Threatens to retire to
Calais. April. 88–89; On
bloodless coup. April 30.
101; Hastings' address.
May 1. 101; Loyal to
Edward V. 101, 128;
Confirmed as Lord
Chamberlain. May. 113;
Unrewarded by
Gloucester. 113, 116;
Fears deposition of
Edward V. 116; Sounded
by Catesby. 118; Warned
by Stanley. 117–118;
Alleged plots of. 121,
126–127, 130; Ordered to
Tower Council. June 13.
122; Trusts Gloucester's
friendship. 122; Consorts
with Mistress Shore. 123,
130; Accused by
Gloucester of treason.
124; Execution of. June
13. 125, 223–224; Debate
over execution date. 129;
Fear inspired by
execution. 126, 131, 142;
Buried at St. George's.
128; Not tried for treason.
128–129; Tributes to. 128.
Haute, Sir Richard. 98.
Haute, Sir William. 186.
Hedgeley Moor. Battle of.
1464. 48.
★Henry IV. 1367–1413. 57,
94, 162, 171, 189, 240.

*Henry V. 1387–1422. 37, 38, 48.

*Henry VI. 1421–1471; Birth of. 1421. 38; Reputation of. 37–38; Succeeds Charles VI. 1422. 38; Crowned at Westminster. 1429. 38; Marries Margaret of Anjou. 1445. 38; Misgovernment of. 38–39, 47; Breakdown. 1453. 39; Birth of son to. 1453. 39; Doubts over claim to Throne. 39–40; Defeated at St. Albans. 1455. 43; Love Day. 1458. 43, 78; Captured at Northampton. 1460. 44; Recaptured at St. Albans. 1461. 45; Flees after Towton. 1461. 46–47; Captured. 1465. 48; Restored by Warwick. 1470–1471. 56–57; Paraded through London. 1471. 57; Death of. 58, 180, 245; Loyalty to. 233, 245.

*Henry VII. 1457–1509. Birth of. 1457. 189; Nature of claim to Throne. 189; Exile in Brittany. 1471. 189; Offers of Crown. 1483. 186, 187; Projected Marriage to Elizabeth of York. 1483. 189, 190, 196; Invited to invade. 1483. 189; Sets sail. October 12. 192; Fleet scattered. 192; Anchors off Plymouth? 192; Returns to Brittany. 193; Joined by eminent exiles. 194, 203–204; Attempts to extradite. 189, 196, 203; Helped by Charles VIII. 178; Proclaimed traitor. June 23. 1485. 205–206; Sets sail from Harfleur. August 1. 1485. 206; Lands at Milford Haven. August 7. 1485. 207; Route followed. 207; Negotiations with Stanleys. 207–208; Manoeuvres at Bosworth. August 22. 1485. 211–212; Attacked by

Richard III. 213–215. Crowned by Stanley. 217; Proclaims Richard's death. 216. Murders Princes in Tower? 180–181, 251; Sends for Elizabeth of York. August 23. 1485. 202; Repeals Royal Title Act. 1485. 156; Commissions Monument for Richard. 216; Parades Warwick through London. 1487. 176; Visits Surrey in Tower. 1488. 234; Need to defame Richard's memory. 239.

Heralds, College of. 198.
Herbert. See Pembroke, Earls of.
Hexham. Battle of. 1464. 48.
"Historia Regum Angliae". See Rous, John.
Holinshed, Raphael. 242.
Holland, Anne. 53.
Holland. See Exeter, Duke of.
Homilies. 1547, 1569. 240, 241.
Howard, John. See Norfolk, Duke of.
Howard, Thomas. See Surrey, Earl of.
Hume, David. 245.
Huntingdon, Earl of. See Pembroke, Second Earl of.

Jacquetta of Luxembourg. See Bedford, Duchess of.
*James III. King of Scots. 1452–1488. 44, 61.
Jesse, John. 220.

Kendall, John. 183, 208.
Kendall, Professor Paul. 252, 253.
Kemp, Thomas. Bishop of London. 123.
King's Bench. 46, 162, 163.
Kirby Muxloe. 129.
Knole. 135.

Lancaster. Edward of. See Edward of Lancaster.
*Lancaster. John of Gaunt, Duke of. 1340–1399. 39, 42, 189.
Landois, Pierre. 203.

Langton, Thomas. Bishop of St. David's. 183, 229, 230.
Legge, Thomas. 218–219, 221, 222.
Leicester. 183, 209.
Lewis, Dr. 190.
Lincoln. 185, 190.
Lincoln. John de la Pole, Earl of. 1464?–1487. 168, 172, 199, 201, 238.
Lisle. Viscount Arthur. 152, 155.
London.
Threatened in 1461. 45, 237; Reaction to coup at Stony Stratford. April 30. 100; Feeling of disquiet. June. 118; Alarmed by news of Hastings' execution. June 13. 126; Approach of Northern army. June. 121; Overawed by Gloucester's forces. 121; Richard's military domination of. 141, 142, 237; Helpless spectator of Edward V's overthrow. 142; Curfew imposed on. July. 166–167; At centre of Usurpation. 237.
London, Bishop of. See Kemp, Thomas.
London Chronicles. 72, 82, 151. See also "The Great Chronicle of London."
London, Lord Mayor of. See Shaa, Sir Edmund.
*Louis XI of France. 1423–1483. 48, 52, 55, 60, 66, 114, 156, 176.
Love Day. 1458. 43, 78.
Lovell, Francis. Viscount. 1454–1487?
Supports Gloucester in Council. May. 108; Rewarded by Richard III. June 28. 165; Serves King at Coronation banquet. July 6. 170; Accompanies Richard on Progress. July. 172; Visited by Richard. July. 173; Given command of Southampton fleet. 1485. 205; Loyalty to Richard III. 233, 237, 238; Northern extraction of. 237' Skeleton discovered ? 173.

Lucy. Dame Elizabeth. 152, 155.

Ludford Bridge. 1459. 43, 90.

Ludlow. 43, 80, 89.

Machiavelli. 70, 180, 238, 239.

Magdalen College, Oxford. 172–173.

Mancini, Dominic. Contemporary narrative. 64; Discovery of Manuscript. 1936. 64; Defects of Narrative. 65; Merits of. 65; Unique independence of. 65; Rumours of Gloucester's regal ambition. 107; On death of Hastings. June 13. 125; Hastings' "plot" feigned. 127; Gloucester's reasons for seeking Prince Richard's release. 133; Duress employed against Queen Mother. June 16. 136; Inviolability of Sanctuary. 137; Princes withdrawn in Tower. 141; On qualities of Edward V. 141; leaves England. July. 141; Rumours of Princes' murder. 141, 175; Nobles terrorised into submission. 142; Bastardy charges false. 157–158; Usurpation unpopular. 165; Richard's use of duress. 226.

March, Edward, Earl of. See Edward IV.

*Margaret of Anjou. Queen of Henry VI. 1430–1482; Marries Henry VI. 1445. 38; Gives birth to Prince Edward. 1453. 39; Attends "Love Day". 1458. 43; Attacks Yorkist power. 43; Escapes after Battle of Northampton. 1460. 44; Refuses to recognise Act of Accord. 1460. 44; Exchanges Berwick for troops. 44; Wins Battle of Wakefield. 1460. 44; Marches on London. 1461. 44–45; Wins Battle of St. Albans. 1461. 44; Flees after Towton. 1461. 46; Sets up

Court in France. 1463. 48; Signs Treaty of Angers. 1470. 55, 57, 58; Lands at Weymouth. April. 1471. 57; Captured after Tewkesbury. 1471. 57.

Margaret of York. See Burgundy, Duchess of.

Markham, Sir Clements. 70–71, 181, 249–250.

Middleham Castle. 55, 77, 82–83, 102, 185, 201, 249.

Milford Haven. 207.

Minster Lovell. 173.

Montagu, Marquis of. See Neville, John.

More, Sir Thomas. 1478–1535. Serves in Morton's Household. 71; Leaves "The History of King Richard III" unfinished. 69; Work more a sermon than history. 70; Fondness for clowning. 70; Sources of history. 71; Conflicting views of More's history. 71–72, 243, 245; Gloucester's desire to be King. 79; Debates on Edward V's escort. 89; Arrest of Rivers. April 30. 95–96; Richard Grey arrested. 97; Hastings' address. May 1. 101; Rotherham gives Queen Great Seal. May 1. 101; Display of Woodville arms. May 4. 105–106; "King's games". 108; Incongruity of Gloucester's "Protectorship". 109; Praise of Russell. 110; Stanley warns Hastings. 117–118; Catesby fails to sound Hastings. 118; Morton's strawberries. 122; Mistress Shore. 122–124, 130; Stanley wounded. June 13. 125; Tribute to Hastings. 128; Gloucester anxious to secure Prince Richard. 132–134; Queen victim of force and fraud. 136–138; Gloucester persuades Buckingham to help him usurp. 140; Bastardy charges against Edward

IV and Edward V. 142–148; Buckingham's Guildhall speech. June 24. 149–153; Richard's "mockish" election. June 26. 162; Buckingham at Richard's Coronation. July 6. 168; Murder of Princes in the Tower. 174–179; Buckingham's reasons for rebelling. 187; Richard a hypocrite and dissembler. 227; Richard's unavailing bribery. 230.

*Mortimer, Anne. 39, 42.

Mortimer, Edmund. 1391–1425. 42.

Mortimer's Cross. Battle of. 1461. 45, 189.

Morton, John. Bishop of Ely. Later Archbishop of Canterbury. 1420–1500; Character and Career of. 117; At Court of Margaret of Anjou. 48; Loyal to Edward IV and V. 108; More serves in Household. 71; Ordered to Council Meeting at Tower. June 13; Sends for strawberries from Ely Place. 122; Sent prisoner to Brecknock Castle. 167, 174; Persuades Buckingham to rebel. 187–188; Proclaimed rebel. October. 190, 197–198; Escapes to Brittany. 192, 194; Warns Henry Tudor of plot to sieze. 203; Buck's portrait of. 243, 245; Markham's view of. 250.

Mowbray, Anne. d. 1481. 62.

Mytton, Thomas. 191.

*Neville. Anne. Queen of Richard III. 1456–1485; Betrothed to Prince Edward of Lancaster. 1470. 55, 58; Put in Isabel Clarence's safe keeping. 1471. 58; Marries Duke of Gloucester. 1472. 58; Division of Warwick's estate. 58; Joins Richard at Crosby's Place. June 5. 118; Coronation

Neville. Anne – *cont.*
ceremonies. July.
166–170; At Warwick.
August. 172; At York.
August. 184–185;
Becomes ill. Christmas
1484. 201; Dies. March
16. 1485. 201–202.
Neville, Catherine. See
Hastings, Catherine.
Neville, Catherine. See
Norfolk. Catherine,
Duchess of.
Neville, Cecily. See York.
Cecily, Duchess of.
*Neville. George.
Archbishop of York.
d. 1476. 45, 46, 57.
*Neville, Isabel. Duchess of
Clarence. 1451–1476.
54–55, 58, 59, 60.
Neville, John, Earl of
Northumberland.
Marquis of Montagu. 48.
*Neville. Ralph, Lord.
d. 1484. 62–63, 120, 237.
Neville. Ralph. See
Westmorland. Ralph, Earl
of.
Neville, Richard. See
Salisbury, Richard, Earl
of.
Neville, Richard. See
Warwick, Richard, Earl
of.
*Neville. Thomas. "Bastard
of Fauconberg". d. 1471.
57, 114.
Neville. William. 57.
Newton, John. Mayor of
York. 119–120, 183–185,
185–186, 235.
Nichols, John. 247.
*Norfolk. Catherine
Neville. Duchess of.
1397?–1484. 53.
*Norfolk. John Howard.
First Duke of.
1430?–1485; Victim of
Edward IV's predatory
family policy. 62, 63;
Fights for Edward IV at
Towton, Barnet and
Tewkesbury. 62;
Commands fleet during
Scottish Campaign. 1482.
62; Dines with Hastings.
April 11. 82; At Edward
IV's funeral. 85–86; Sees
Edward V arrive in

London. May 4. 103;
Supports Gloucester in
Council. May. 108;
Summoned to Parliament.
May 17. 111; Attends
Tower Council Meeting.
June 13. 122; Pays for
armed men. June 16. 136;
Attends ceremonies in
Westminster Hall. June
26. 163; Created Earl
Marshal and Admiral of
England. June 28. 165;
Created Duke of Norfolk
and granted extensive
estates. June 28. 165; At
Coronation banquet. July
6. 168, 169; Murders
Princes in Tower? 181;
Saves London from
attack. October. 191;
Tries Colyngbourne.
1484. 204; Commands
van at Bosworth. 211;
Attacked by Oxford. 213;
Dies fighting. 213.
Norfolk, Second Duke of.
See Surrey, Thomas, Earl
of.
Northampton. 90, 91, 93,
95, 98, 102, 103.
Northampton, Battle of.
1460. 44, 85.
Northcroft, George. 179.
Northern Army.
Gloucester appeals to
North for forces. June 10,
11. 119–121; Fear inspired
by Army's approach. 121,
237; Witnesses Rivers'
execution at Pontefract.
June 25. 160; Reaches
London. July 1. 166;
Troops sent back north.
July 7. 166.
*Northumberland. Henry
Percy, Fourth Earl of.
1446–1489. 108, 113, 159,
168, 211, 213–214, 232,
237.
Northumberland. John, Earl
of. See Neville, John.
Nottingham Castle. 183,
201, 205.

Oxford. 172–173.
*Oxford. John de Vere.
Thirteenth Earl of.
1443–1513; Confusion at
Barnet. 1471. 203, 215;

Captures St. Michael's
Mount. 1473. 115, 203;
Escapes from Hammes.
1484. 203; Joins Henry
Tudor at Montargis.
1484. 204; Sets sail with
Henry from Harfleur.
August 1. 1485. 207;
Strategy at Bosworth.
August 22. 1485. 211,
212, 213.

Parliament.
"Parliament of Devils".
1459. 43, 44, 135, 233;
Writ of Summons to.
May 13. 110–111;
Russell's draft Sermon to.
113–114; Writs rescinded.
June 17. 139, 140; Petition
of. June 25. 153, 154–156,
162, 164; Dubious
authority of Petitioners.
154, 197; Parliamentary
session. 1484. 197–198;
Royal Title Act. 1484.
154–156, 158, 197, 244;
Attainder of rebels. 1484.
187, 193, 197; Act of
Attainder. 1485. 242.
Paston, John. 191.
Paul's Cross. 46, 145, 224.
*Pembroke. Jasper Tudor.
Earl of. 1431–1495. 45,
189, 193, 205, 207.
Pembroke. William
Herbert, First Earl of. 55,
63.
Pembroke. William
Herbert, Second Earl of
Pembroke. Later Earl of
Huntingdon. 53, 63, 168,
205.
Percival, Humphrey. 85.
Percy, Henry. See
Northumberland, Fourth
Earl of.
Percy. Sir Robert. 170, 237.
Petition. June 25. See
Parliament.
Picquigny. Truce of. 1475.
60, 61.
Plymouth. 192.
Pontefract Castle. 90, 102,
120, 159, 160, 183, 185.
Pre-contract.
Betrothal regarded as
binding as marriage. 150;
Edward IV's pre-contract
to Dame Elizabeth Lucy.

152, 155; Edward IV's pre-contract to Lady Eleanor Butler. 155–156, 158; Stillington tells Gloucester of pre-contract. 156; Motives for Stillington's probable perjury. 157; No evidence of pre-contract. 157, 158; Bishops consoled by allegation. 231.
Prince of Wales. See Edward V. Edward of Lancaster. Edward, Earl of Salisbury.
"Princes in the Tower". See Edward V. See also York. Richard, Prince of.
Protector. Office of. Humphrey Duke of Gloucester's appointment as. 1422. 38, 39, 79; Richard Duke of York's appointment as. 1455. 39, 42; Gloucester appointed in 1483 by Edward IV's ordinance? 78–79; Gloucester designated Protector May 14. 79; Edward IV not entitled to make Gloucester Protector by Will. 78–79; Power lapsed on King's coronation. 80–81; Council discusses government during Edward V's minority. April. 87–88; Gloucester eager to be proclaimed Protector. May. 109; Russell's draft sermon envisages extending Protectorate. 113–114.

Raby Castle. 42.
Raine, Angelo. 237.
Ratcliffe, Sir Richard. 99, 119–120, 121, 159–160, 194, 204, 237, 238.
Ravenspur. 57.
Reading. Council of. 1464. 52.
Redmoor. 209.
Rennes. 196.
Richard. Prince. See York. Richard, Duke of. 1473–1483?
*Richard II. 1367–1400. 88, 162, 194, 241.

*Richard III. 1452–1485; *career of.*
Born at Fotheringhay Castle. 55; Early Career of. 55; In Warwick's Middleham Household. 55, 82; Created Duke of Gloucester. 1461. 55; Evil reputation of Gloucester title. 77; Proclaimed guilty of treason by Parliament. 1470. 56; Accompanies Edward IV into exile. 1470. 55; Commands at Tewkesbury. 1471. 61; Accused of murdering Edward of Lancaster. 1471. 58, 69, 244; Accused of murdering Henry VI. 1471. 58, 244; Marries Anne Neville. 1472. 58; Granted Warwick estates. 1472. 58, 77; Regards Picquigny as disgraceful. 1475. 60; Responsible for Clarence's death? 1478. 60, 244; Granted Clarence's titles and perquisites. 1478. 77; Establishes College at Middleham. 1478. 82–83; Commands expedition against Scotland. 1482. 61, 62; Warden of Western Marches. 1483. 77; Appointed Protector in Edward IV's will? 78–79; At Middleham when Edward IV dies? 82; Hears of King's death from Hastings? 83; Writes to Queen Elizabeth. April. 83; Writes about Protectorate to Council. April. 83; Protests at Edward V remaining under Woodville control. 83–84; Attends Requiem at York for Edward IV. April 20. 84; Takes Oath of fealty to Edward V. April 20. 84; Offered help by Buckingham. 85; Role debated by Council. 87–88; Alleges plot to oust from government. 88; Persuades Queen to restrict Edward V's escort. 88–89; Council

decides to proceed without. 89; Starts journey south. 90; Spends day at Pontefract. 90; Reaches Northampton. April 29. 90; Entertains Rivers. 93; Confers with Buckingham. April 29–30. 95; Arrests Rivers. April 30. 95–96; Seizes Edward V. 96–98; Picks quarrel with Grey. 97; Disperses King's escort. 98; Dismisses King's personal servants. 98; Dismisses Rotherham. May. 101; Hears London's reaction to coup. May 2. 101–102; Leaves for London. May 3. 103; Writes to Sir Edmund Shaa. May 3. 102; Escorts Edward V through London. May 4. 103; Displays Woodville arms. 105–106, 228; Stays at Crosby's Place. 104; Requires oaths of fealty to King. May. 104; Council rejects charges against Rivers. 106–107; Described as Protector. May 14. 109; Powers lapse at Coronation. 80–81; Council's concern for Woodvilles. 111–112; Illegally distributes Woodville estates. May. 112; Bounty to Buckingham. 112; Plans to extend Protectorate? May. 113–114; Orders Woodville Fleet to disband. May 14. 114–116; Ambition feared by some councillors. 116; Holds inner Council. 116–117; Decides to usurp June 5? 118; Sounds Hastings. June. 118; Attempts to gratify public. 118–119; Writes to Mayor of York. June 10. 119–120; Writes to Ralph, Lord Neville. June 11. 120; Why help sought. 121; Arranges Tower Meeting. June 13. 121; Sends for Strawberries. 122; Accusations of

Richard III – *cont.*
treachery and witchcraft. 122–124; Accuses Hastings. 124. 129–130; Orders Hasting's execution. 125; Arrests Rotherham, Morton and Stanley. 125–126; Proclaims alleged conspiracy. 126–127, 129–130; London intimidated. 121, 131; Search for Dorset. 132; Fails to persuade Queen to leave Sanctuary. 132; Discusses release of Duke of York. 132–134; Resolves on deputation to Queen. June 16. 134; Queen subjected to force and fraud. 136–138; Receives Prince Richard. 139; Prince Richard lodged in Tower. 139; Takes custody of Warwick. 139; Postpones Parliament and Coronation. 139, 140; Orders nobles to dismiss their retinues. 139–140; Persuades Buckingham to support Usurpation. 140–141; Dominates London. 141–142; Terrorises nobles into submission. 142; Consults Shaa brothers. 142; Bastardy charges. 142–143; Charges bungled. 144, 147–148, 149, 223; Charges disbelieved. 143–144, 158; Shaa's Sermon. June 22. 146–148; Edward IV's marriage challenged. 150, 152; Buckingham proclaims right to Throne. June 24. 150–151, 228; Apprentices shout for "King Richard". 153; Petitioned to become King. June 25. 153–156; Dubious legality of Petitioners. 154, 197; Learns of Edward IV's Pre-contract? 156; Fraudulently crowned? 157–158; Claims Warwick disqualified to succeed. 158–159; Orders

execution of Rivers. June 25. 159–160; Buckingham presents Petition. June 26. 160–161; Richard accepts crown. June 26. 161–163; Proclaimed Richard III. June 27. 163; Why Usurpation unopposed. 163–165; Returns Great Seal to Russell. June 27. 165; Instructions to Calais. June 28. 164–165; Rewards loyal supporters. June 28. 165; Creates son Prince of Wales. June 28. 165–166; Inspects Northern troops at Finsbury. July. 166; Procession to Tower. July 4. 166–167; Orders London curfew. 166–167; Procession to Westminster. July 5. 167; Coronation. July 6. 167–170, 230; Defective title of. 170; Royal Progress. July. 171–172; Visits Oxford. July 24. 172–173; Visits Woodstock. 173; Visits Minster Lovell. 173; Warns Russell of conspiracy. 173–174; Visits Gloucester. 174; Visits Tewkesbury. 174; Reaches Warwick. August 8. 174; Murders Princes in Tower? 174–180, 182; Odium of reputed murders. 182; Places Westminster Sanctuary under siege. 176; Fails to produce nephews. 176; Supposed lack of motive. 179–180; Probable guilt of. 181–182; State visit to York. August. 183–185; Goodwill to York. 183; Prince of Wales' investiture. September 8. 184–185; Learns of Buckingham's rebellion. October 11. 185–186; Quarrel over Bohun estates? 187–188; Writes to Russell from Lincoln. October 12. 190; Receives Seal at Grantham. October 19. 190; Offers reward for Buckingham's

capture. 190; Orders Buckingham's execution. November 2. 192; Reaches Exeter. 192; Returns to London. November 25. 193; Treats rebels leniently. 193; High price of victory. 193–194; Distributes rebel estates. 191; Plants northerners in South of England. 194, 195; Alienates landowning class. 194–196, 199; Attempts to extradite Richmond. 189, 196, 203; Reputation as legislator. 198; Establishes College of Heralds. 1484. 198; Establishes Council of North. 1484. 199; Persuades Queen Elizabeth to leave Sanctuary. March 1484. 199–200; Takes oath before Mayor. 200–201; Prince of Wales dies. May 1484. 201; Rumours of Tudor invasion. 1484. 202–203; Trial of Colyngbourne. 1484. 204–205; Death of Queen Anne. March 16. 1485. 201; Denies intention to marry his niece. March 30. 1485. 202, 229; Tudor invasion expected. 1485. 205; Headquarters at Nottingham Castle. 205; Proclaims Henry Tudor a traitor. June 23. 1485. 205; Permits Stanley to leave Court. 206; Hears of Henry Tudor's landing. August 1485. 207, 208; Summons nobles. 208; Equivocal conduct of Stanleys. 208; Moves to Leicester. 210; Camps at Sutton Cheyney. August 21. 1485. 209; Nightmares of. 209; Disposition of army at Bosworth. August 22. 209, 211; Threatens to behead Lord Strange. 212; Fears treachery. 213–214; Resolves to engage Henry personally. 213–215; Contemplates strategic withdrawal? 214; Urged to fly. 214; Dies courageously. 215; Possible heraldic confusion. 215; Memorial on Battlefield. 216; Corpse abused. 216; Burial of. 216–217. *Characteristics of.* Character and appearance. 55–56, 67–68, 242; Military prowess. 61–62; Inimacable interests to Woodvilles. 76–77, 219; Tyranny of. 199, 239; Impetuosity of. 222–223; Hypocrisy of. 183, 228–229; Censoriousness of. 155, 190, 206, 229; Enlightened legislator? 198; Motives for usurping. 218–221; Ambition of. 79, 84, 102, 107, 218, 220; Need to reward supporters. 219; Genesis of decision to usurp. 220–221; Foresight of? 221–224; Politically inept? 223–224; Exploits force and fear. 225–227, 237; Duplicity of? 227–229; Immorality of Court. 229–230; Bribery of. 230; Church supports? 230–232; Lords support? 232–234; Northerners support. 234–235; Popularity in York? 235–237; Preference for Northerners. 199, 237; Dominates London. 237–238; Supported by family and friends. 238; A creature of his age. 238.

Opinions of. Contemporary historians portray faithfully. 64; Techniques for discovering truth about Richard. 72–73; Contemporary opinions of. 64–73; Praised by Langton and Kendall. 183; Evil reputation of in Tudor England. 65, 239–243, 244, 245; Shakespeare's portrait of. 69, 221–222, 240–243; Buck's defence of. 243–245; Eighteenth

century opinions of. 245–247; Horace Walpole defends. 246–247; Changed attitudes of Nineteenth Century historians, 247–248; Sharon Turner defends, 248; Caroline Halsted admires. 248–249; Gairdner's traditional criticism. 248, 249; Markham's apology for. 249–251; Richard III Society vindicates. 251–252; Recent biographies of. 252.
Richard III Society. 251–252.
"Richardus Tertius". 218, 221, 222.
Richmond, Countess of. See Beaufort, Lady Margaret.
*Richmond. Edmund, Earl of. d. 1456. 126, 189.
Richmond. Henry, Earl of. See Henry VII.
*Rivers. Anthony Woodville. Second Earl of. 1442?–1483; Character of. 52; Marries Elizabeth Scales. 1460. 52; Accompanies Edward IV into exile. 1470. 56; Replaced by Hastings as Lieutenant of Calais. 1471. 76; President of Council of Wales. 1473. 75; Gives Edward IV his book printed by Caxton. 1477. 50; Created Knight of the Garter. 1478. 89; Transfers his interest in Tower to Dorset. 1483. 75; Instructed to bring Edward V to London. April. 80; Supposed conspiracy against Gloucester. 88, 90; Gloucester resents custody of Edward V. 83–84; Size of royal escort. April. 88–89; Celebrates St. George's Day. April 23. 89; Sets out with Edward V from Ludlow. April 24. 89–90; Makes detour to join Gloucester. 90; Lodges King at Stony Stratford. April 29. 91, 93; Returns

to greet Gloucester at Northampton. 93, 227–228; Convivial supper with Gloucester. 93; Arrested by Gloucester. April 30. 95–97; Sent prisoner to Sheriff Hutton. May. 102; Council reluctant to prosecute. May. 106–107, 111; Estates and Offices given away. 112; Execution of. June 25. 159–160.
*Rivers. Richard Woodville. First Earl of. d. 1469. 48, 49, 55.
Rochefort, Guillaume de. 175.
Ross, Professor Charles. 252, 253.
Rotherham, Thomas. Archbishop of York. 1423–1500. 85, 87, 101, 122, 126, 167, 185, 237.
Rous, John. Chaplain of Chantry Chapel near Warwick. 67; Author of "Chronicle Rolls of Earls of Warwick". 67; Author of "Historia Regum Angliae". 67; Portrays Richard as Monster. 67–68; Gloucester's feigned title to Crown. 157; Claims Rivers tried by Northumberland. 159; Alleges Richard poisoned Queen Anne. 201; On Richard's courageous death. 215; On Russell's reluctance to be Lord Chancellor. 231.
Royal Title Act. 1484. See Parliament.
Russell, John. Bishop of Lincoln. d. 1490. Career of. 66, 110; Possibly Croyland Continuator. 66–67; Says Mass at Edward IV's Funeral. April. 86; Trimmer in Council. 87, 109; Succeeds Rotherham as Lord Chancellor. May 10. 109; Drafts Sermon for opening of Parliament. 113–114; Presides over Westminster Council.

Russell, John – cont.
June 13. 121–122; Richard
returns Great Seal to. June
27. 165; Attends
Coronation banquet. July
6. 169–170; Instructed to
deal with "enterprise".
July. 173–174; Sends
Great Seal to Grantham.
October. 190; Great Seal
restored to. November
25. 193; Dismissed
August 1485? 231.
*Rutland. Edmund, Earl of.
1443–1460. 44.

Salic Law. 42.
Salisbury. 192.
Salisbury. See Woodville.
Lionel, Bishop of.
Salisbury. Edward, Earl of.
See Edward, Earl of
Salisbury.
*Salisbury. Richard Neville.
Earl of. 1400–1460. 42,
43, 44.
Sanctuary, inviolability of.
135–137.
Sandal Castle. 44, 199.
Savage, Sir John. 86, 207,
208, 212.
Scrope of Bolton. John,
Lord. 194, 237.
Shaa, Sir Edmund. Lord
Mayor of London.
Receives letter from
Goucester from
Northampton. May. 102;
Meets Edward V at
Harringay. May 4. 103;
Takes Oath of fealty to
Edward V. 104; Promises
Gloucester support of
Aldermen and City. 141;
Gloucester consults. 142;
Receives Buckingham at
Guildhall. June 24. 149;
Suggests Duke repeats
arguments. 152; At
Baynard's Castle. June 26.
160–161; At Coronation
Banquet. July 6. 170;
Buys Silver from Richard.
1484. 194; Richard's
fervent partisan. 237.
Shaa, Dr. Ralph. 142,
146–148, 149, 224.
Shakespeare, William.
Indebted to Sir T. More.
69; On origin of Richard's

ambition. 107; On
proclamation of Hasting's
treason. 127; On
Buckingham's Guildhall
speech. 152–153; On
Richard's "reluctance" to
accept Crown. 161; On
Richard's resourcefulness.
221–222; Portrays
Richard as dissembler.
227; Lessons of historical
plays. 240–242; Sources of
Richard III. 242–243; Evil
fruits of rebellion.
239–241; Hostile portrait
of Richard. 243.
Sheriff Hutton. 77, 102–103,
159, 202, 235.
Shore, Elizabeth. ("Jane").
122–124, 127, 130, 151.
Simnel, Lambert. 156–157,
176, 180.
Slaughter, Will. 179.
*Somerset. Edmund,
Second Duke of.
1406?–1455. 39, 43.
*Somerset. Edmund.
Fourth Duke of.
1438–1471. 57, 61, 137.
*Somerset. Henry, Third
Duke of. 1436–1464. 43.
*Somerset. John, First Duke
of. 1404–1444. 189.
St. Albans. 103.
St. Albans. First Battle of.
1455. 43.
St. Albans. Second Battle of.
1461. 44, 45, 49.
St. Aubyn, Sir John. 118.
St. Aubyn, Piers. 195.
St. George's Chapel.
Windsor. 86, 128.
St. Leger, Anne. 63.
St. Leger, Sir Thomas.
d.1483. 63, 186, 192.
St. Martin-le-Grand. 58.
St. Mary the Virgin.
Grafton. 50.
St. Michael in Barrois. 48.
St. Michael's Mount. 115,
203.
St. Paul's Cathedral. See also
Paul's Cross. 43, 162, 204.
St. Stephen's Chapel.
Westminster. 85.
Stallworth, Simon. 109,
121, 123, 136.
Stanley, Sir William. d.
1495. 195, 205, 207, 208,
211–215.

Stanley, Thomas, Lord.
1435?–1504.
Career of. 125–126;
Marries Lady Margaret
Beaufort. 1482? 126;
Successfully besieges
Berwick. 1482. 61; Loyal
to Edward IV and V. 108;
Warns Hastings of
danger. 117–118; Ordered
to Council Meeting at
Tower. June 13. 122;
Wounded during scuffle.
125; Soon restored to
favour. 125; Released
from Tower. Appointed
Lord Steward. July. 167;
Accompanies Richard on
Progress. July. 172; Given
charge of Lady Margaret.
1484. 193; Requests
permission to leave
Court. June 1485. 206;
Equivocal attitude
towards Henry Tudor.
206, 208; Pleads
"sweating sickness". 208;
On field of Bosworth.
1485. 212; Disobeys
Richard's orders. 212;
Crowns Henry Tudor.
217.
Star Chamber. Westminster.
133, 138, 193.
Stillington, Robert. Bishop
of Bath and Wells.
156–157, 168, 237, 238.
Stonor, Sir William. 85, 109,
121, 123, 186.
Stony Stratford. 50, 91, 93,
95, 96, 98–101.
Stow, John. 130, 242.
Strange. George Stanley,
Lord. 125, 206, 208, 212.
Stubbs, William. Bishop,
221, 249.
Supersedeas. Writs of. 139,
140.
Surrey. Thomas Howard,
Earl of. Second Duke of
Norfolk. 1443–1524. 122,
165, 234.
Sutton Cheyney. 209.
Sweating sickness. 208.
Swynford, Catherine. 189.
Syon Abbey. 86.

Talbot, Sir Gilbert. 207,
212.
Tewkesbury. 57, 60, 61,

137, 174.
Tewkesbury. Battle of 1471.
57, 58, 61, 189.
Tey, Josephine. 251
"The Great Chronicle of
London". 72, 98, 125,
128, 138, 153, 163, 201,
228.
"The Ricardian". 251.
Thomas, Rhys ap. 207.
Tower of London.
Henry VI prisoner in.
1465. 48; Henry VI found
dead in. 1471. 58;
Clarence executed in.
1478. 59–60; Dorset's
control of. April. 75;
Edward V lodged in.
May. 110, 111.
Council meets at. 116;
Council Meeting at. June
13. 121–125; Richard III
resides at. July 4. 166–167;
Supposed murder of
Princes in. 1483. 141, 167,
174–182; Remains
discovered at. 1674. 179,
181; Colyngbourne's
execution at. 1484. 205.
Towton. Battle of. 1461. 46,
212.
Tudor. See Henry VII.
Pembroke, Jasper Tudor.
Richmond, Edmund
Tudor.
★Tudor, Owen. 1400–1461.
45, 189.
Turner, Sharon. 248.
Tyrrel, Sir James. 126, 175,
177, 178, 194, 195, 237.

Vaughan, Sir Thomas.
Edward V's Chamberlain.
97, 102, 112.
Vaughan, Sir Thomas.
Cousin of Edward V's
Chamberlain. 191.
Vergil, Polydore.
1470?–1555.
Career of. 68; Publishes
"Anglica Historia". 1534.
68; Writes in critical
renaissance spirit. 68, 69;
Consults Richard III's
contemporaries. 68; No
Tudor hack. 68–69; Treats
cherished myths
sceptically. 69; Lists
armed men in Tower.
June 13. 122; On release of

Prince Richard. June 16.
226; Richard III permits
rumours of nephews'
deaths. 180; On Richard's
counterfeit virtue. 183;
Disparages women's wit.
193; Describes Battle of
Bosworth. 209; On
Richard's nervous trait.
223; On fear Richard
inspired. 226; On
Richard's craft and
cunning. 228; On
Richard's bribes. 230;
Makes no use of Tyrell's
confession. 178.

Wakefield. Battle of. 1460.
44, 222.
Wales. Council of. 75.
Walpole, Horace. 131, 227,
238, 246–247.
Wars of the Roses.
1455–1485; First Battle of
St. Albans. 1455. 43;
Battle of Northampton.
1460. 44, 85; Battle of
Wakefield. 1460. 44;
Second Battle of St.
Albans. 1461. 44, 45, 49;
Battle of Mortimer's
Cross. 1461. 45, 189;
Battle of Towton. 1461.
46, 212; Battle of
Hedgeley Moor. 1464. 48;
Battle of Hexham. 1464.
48; Battle of Edgecote.
1469. 55; Treaty of
Angers. 1470. 55, 57, 58;
Battle of Barnet. 1471. 57,
215; Battle of
Tewkesbury. 1471. 57,
58, 61, 189; Battle of
Bosworth. 1485. 210–216;
Methods of fighting.
212–213.
Warwick Castle. 172, 174.
★Warwick. Edward, Earl of.
1475–1499. 59, 139, 150,
158–159, 172, 176, 181,
201.
★Warwick, Richard Neville,
Earl of. "The
King-maker". 1428–1471;
Supports Yorkists. 42;
Stronghold at
Middleham. 55; Flees to
Calais. 1459. 43; Publishes
"Calais Manifesto". 1460.
44; Defeated at St. Albans.

1461. 44–45; Joins
Edward at Chipping
Norton. 1461. 45;
Supports proclamation of
Edward IV. 1461. 45–46;
Negotiates Edward IV's
marriage to Princess
Bona. 1463. 52, 150, 156;
Resents Edward IV's
Woodville marriage.
1464. 52, 75; Denounces
Woodvilles. 53, 54;
Accuses Edward IV of
bastardy. 1469. 144;
Opposes Burgundian
alliance. 54; Rebels against
Edward IV. 1469. 54, 88;
Joined by Clarence. 1469.
54–55; Wins Battle of
Edgecote. 1469. 55;
Denounced as traitor.
1470. 55; Signs Treaty of
Angers. 1470. 55; Lands at
Dartmouth. 1470. 55;
Summons Parliament.
1470. 56; Acts as Henry
VI's Regent. 1470–1471.
56; Declares War on
Burgundy. 1470. 57;
Defeated and killed at
Barnet. 1471. 57.
Waynflete, William. Bishop
of Winchester. 172–173.
Westminster Abbey. 57, 85,
100, 163, 165–169, 176,
179, 217.
Westminster Hall. 46, 138,
149, 162, 167–170.
★Westmorland. Ralph
Neville, Earl of.
1365–1425. 42, 47.
Weymouth. 57.
Windsor. 85, 86, 128.
Witchcraft. 122, 123, 124.
Woodville, Anne. 134.
Woodville, Anthony. See
Rivers. Anthony, Second
Earl of.
★Woodville. Catherine.
Duchess of Buckingham.
Duchess of Bedford.
1442?–1512? 53, 94, 95,
193.
Woodville, Sir Edward. 52,
97, 99, 114–116, 189, 192,
205.
★Woodville, Elizabeth.
Queen of Edward IV.
1437?–1492; Family
origins of. 48–49; Beauty

of. 49; Character of
49–50; Refuses to be
King's Mistress. 49;
Marries Edward IV. 1464.
48, 50, 91; Arranges
marriages for family. 53;
Maligns King's kindred.
54; Unpopularity of
Woodvilles. 54, 75;
Hostility to Lord
Hastings. 56, 76;
Withdraws to Sanctuary.
1470. 57; Gives birth to
Prince Edward. 1470. 57;
Needs to retain possession
of son. 1483. 76–77;
Supposed conspiracy
against Gloucester. April.
81–82, 88, 105; Persuaded
to restrict Edward V's
escort. April. 88–89;
Queen's prospects
shattered. April 30.
99–100; Withdraws to
Sanctuary. May 1.
100–101; Council's
concern for. 111–112;
Accused of witchcraft.
June 13. 122–124;
Attempts to persuade to
leave Sanctuary. 132;
Begged to release Prince
Richard. 132–134;
Bourchier's deputation to.
June 16. 134–139;
Bourchier's promises to.
137; Force and fraud used
on. 138, 182; Yields
Prince Richard under
duress. 136–137; Edward
IV's marriage to declared
bigamous. 150, 155;
Reaction to news of death
of Princes. 1483. 182;
Supports Buckingham's
rebellion. October.
189–190; Negotiates
Elizabeth's betrothal to
Henry Tudor. 190; Agrees
to leave Sanctuary. March
1. 1484. 199–200.
★Woodville. John.
1445?–1469. 53, 55.

Woodville, Lionel. Bishop
of Salisbury. 1453–1484.
52, 186, 194, 197–198.
Woodville, Sir Richard. See
Rivers, First Earl of.
Woodstock. 173.
Wren, Sir Christopher. 179.
Wright, Professor William.
179.

York. Mayor of. See
Newton, John.
York.
Duke of York's head sent
to. 1460. 44; Relieved of
taxes. 1483. 236;
Gloucester at York. April.
84–85; Gloucester appeals
for aid from. June 10, 119;
Receives writ of
Supersedeas. June 21. 140;
Richard's state visit to.
August. 183–185; Creed
Play at. September. 184;
Meetings of Council of
North at. 199; Regard for
Richard. 235; Richard's
popularity with
exaggerated? 236; Slow to
send troops to Bosworth?
1485. 236–237.
★York. Cecily Neville.
Duchess of. 1415–1495;
Character of. 42; Marries
Richard, Duke of York.
1438. 42; Reputed to have
opposed Edward IV's
marriage. 50, 53; Arrives
in London. June. 143:
Gloucester implies an
adulteress. 142–143, 144,
146–148; Previous charges
of adultery. 144; Shaa's
sermon on. 146–148;
Complains of accusations.
147; Resides at Baynard's
Castle. 160–161; Employs
Colyngbourne as
Steward. 204; Ambition
of children of. 218;
Supports Richard III. 238.
★York. Edmund. Duke of.

1341–1402. 42, 47, 222.
★York. Edward. Duke of.
d. 1415. 42.
York. Elizabeth. Princess of
See Elizabeth, Princess of
York.
★York. Richard. Duke of.
1411–1460; Claim to
Throne of. 39, 40, 42;
Irresolute character of.
222; Succeeds to
Dukedom. 1415. 42;
Marries Cecily Neville.
1438. 42; Excluded from
Henry VI's Council. 1452.
43; Appointed Henry VI's
Protector. 1455. 39, 42;
Wins Battle of St. Albans.
1455. 43; Attends Love
Day. 1458. 43; Routed at
Ludford Bridge. 1459. 43;
Proscribed by Parliament
of Devils. 1459. 43;
Acknowledged as Henry
VI's heir; 1460. 44, 46,
163; Killed at Wakefield.
1460. 44, 222; Masses said
for at Middleham. 83.
★York. Richard. Prince of.
1473–1483?; Marries
Anne Mowbray. 1478. 62;
Wife dies. 1481. 62;
Parliament settles Anne's
inheritance on Prince
Richard. 1483. 62;
Gloucester anxious to
release from Santuary.
June. 132–134; Threat of
forceful seizure. 135;
Bourchier's delegation to
Queen Mother. June 16.
134–138; Takes Farewell
of Queen. 138; Lodged in
Tower. 139; Withdrawn
into inner quarters of
Tower. 141; Seen playing
in garden of Tower. 175;
Supposed murder of. 141,
174–182, 186, 250; Bones
discovered? 1674. 179,
181; Lambert Simnel
impersonates. 1487. 180;
Survived until 1485? 250.